P9-DGE-487

fP

Valparaiso Public Library
103 Jefferson Street
Valparaiso, IN 46383

Also by Richard Grant

American Nomads
Travels with Lost Conquistadors, Mountain Men,
Cowboys, Indians, Hoboes, Truckers, and Bullriders

God's Middle Finger
Into the Lawless Heart of the Sierra Madre

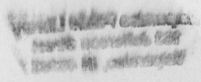

CRAZY RIVER

Exploration and Folly
in East Africa

RICHARD GRANT

PORTER COUNTY PUBLIC LIBRARY

Valparaiso Public Library
103 Jefferson Street
Valparaiso, IN 46383

Free Press

New York   London   Toronto   Sydney   New Delhi

NF   916.7029 GRA   VAL
Grant, Richard, 1963-
Crazy river : exploration and
33410011332659

OCT 2 1 2010

*f*P
Free Press
A Division of Simon & Schuster, Inc.
1230 Avenue of the Americas
New York, NY 10020

Copyright © 2011 by Richard Grant

All rights reserved, including the right to reproduce this book or
portions thereof in any form whatsoever. For information address
Free Press Subsidiary Rights Department, 1230 Avenue of
the Americas, New York, NY 10020

First Free Press trade paperback edition October 2011

FREE PRESS and colophon are trademarks of Simon & Schuster, Inc.

For information about special discounts for bulk purchases, please
contact Simon & Schuster Special Sales at 1-866-506-1949 or
business@simonandschuster.com

The Simon & Schuster Speakers Bureau can bring authors to your
live event. For more information or to book an event contact the
Simon & Schuster Speakers Bureau at 1-866-248-3049 or
visit our website at www.simonspeakers.com.

Manufactured in the United States of America

1   3   5   7   9   10   8   6   4   2

Library of Congress Cataloging-in-Publication Data
Grant, Richard.
Crazy river : exploration and folly in East Africa
/ by Richard Grant.
p. cm.
1. Grant, Richard—Travel—Africa, East.   2. Malagarasi River (Burundi
and Tanzania)—Discovery and exploration.   3. Tanzania—
Description and travel.   4. Africa, East—Description and travel.
5. Tanzania—Social conditions.   6. Africa, East—Social conditions.
7. Africa, East—Discovery and exploration.   8. Burton, Richard
Francis, Sir, 1821–1890—Travel—Africa, East.   I. Title.
DT427.G72 2011
916.78'280442—dc22   2011012168

ISBN 978-1-4391-5414-4
ISBN 978-1-4391-5764-0 (ebook)

The names and identifying characteristics of
some individuals depicted have been changed.

Contents

Introduction

IN THE EARLY YEARS of the twenty-first century, when it seemed like all the exploring had been done so long ago, and every conceivable piece of information was now available on a pocket phone, I heard about a river in Africa that no one had ever gone down in a boat before, or "explored" in the old-fashioned sense of the word. It had been mapped, and presumably the local people knew what was there, but no one had published a written description of the river's course and character, and the Internet had barely heard of it.

The Malagarasi is the second longest river in Tanzania. One renowned encyclopedia informed me that it flowed for 250 miles through the far west of the country. Another said 310 miles and identified its headwaters in the neighboring country of Burundi, which satellite maps appeared to confirm, although it was hard to tell the main stem from the tributaries. A few European explorers had crossed the river in the nineteenth century and mentioned it briefly in their journals. More recently, a fish study had been completed in one area, a hunting area established, and a wetlands protected because of a rare bird, the whale-headed stork. That was all the world's preeminent search engine could tell me, because that was all that had been written about the river.

Were there impassable cataracts or giant whirlpools? Was it roiling with hippos and crocodiles? Who were the people living alongside the river? What languages did they speak? How were they making a living? If I could get there in a boat, would they be friendly or hostile? Would they have food to sell? How did they regard their neighbors? What were their customs? I felt a strange compulsion to hurl myself into the unknown and bring back answers to these questions, and a hundred more like them.

For twenty years I have collected the biographies and journals of explorers, especially the ones who "discovered" Africa and the Americas. The native people, of course, always know where they live, and exploration is usually a matter of entering this local knowledge into bigger information systems. I started reading about explorers out of historical curiosity. I wanted to know what these continents were like before the colonists and imperialists arrived and changed things forever. I was fascinated by that moment of first contact between such utterly different cultures. Then I grew curious about the explorers themselves, their personalities and motivations, their willingness to court danger in far-flung places, their chronic inability to stay at home and be good husbands and fathers, and I wondered if my own tendencies in these directions were part of the same psychological syndrome. But it had never occurred to me that there might be some actual exploring left to do, some holes in our information systems that needed filling.

I was already looking for an excuse to get back into the African wilds, and preferably on a river. In 2005, I had been invited as a journalist on an expedition to re-create and commemorate Dr. Livingstone's historic journey down the Zambezi River to Victoria Falls. That was my first experience of Africa: eight days in dugout canoes among the hippos and crocodiles, camping on the riverbanks, following in the traces of a dead British explorer. I arrived full of trepidation, but nothing bad happened on the river, there were no close calls, I saw wild elephants for the first time, and I had seldom felt so free and happy and full of life. That was the feeling I was looking to recapture.

The man who told me about the Malagarasi was a white Zimbabwean safari guide and kayaking legend called Paul Connolly, a friend of someone I had met on the Zambezi. He had set out by himself to make the first descent of the Malagarasi in 2007, and abandoned his attempt because of all the refugees and mayhem spilling across the border into Tanzania from Congo and Burundi. In 2009, with the political situation calmer, he wanted to try again, and in return for a hefty fee plus all the expenses, he agreed to take me with him in a two-man kayak. I had no kayaking experience but he said that wouldn't be a problem. He didn't envisage a lot of technical white water on the river. The important thing was to arrive in the best physical condition of my life and understand the dangers involved, as far as we could guess them in the great void of information.

The local people, he e-mailed, said it was a river of bad spirits. He didn't know about that, but there would certainly be plenty of hippos and crocodiles and other dangerous animals on the riverbanks where we would be camping—lions, hyenas, probably elephant and buffalo, snakes, disease-carrying insects. But the main danger, he kept stressing, was remoteness. If something went wrong, there was no way for help to get in and out.

We would be traveling fast and light with a minimum of food and gear, and if all went well, we would emerge from the river into Lake Tanganyika. From there, he wanted to go overland through Burundi to the mountains of southern Rwanda, where the furthest source of the White Nile, after some four thousand years of speculation, had finally been located by a British and Kiwi expedition in 2006. That sounded like a suitable destination to me. Finding the source of the Nile was the grand fixation of the nineteenth-century British explorers, most notably Richard Burton, John Hanning Speke, James Grant, and Dr. David Livingstone, and our willingness to risk life and limb to explore the Malagarasi placed us in the same deranged tradition. In the spirit of homage, I decided to begin my journey in Zanzibar, the old spice island off the coast of Tanzania, because that was where the explorers had begun their obsessive, fever-ravaged journeys in search of the "coy fountains" rumored to be the wellspring of the White Nile. My plan was to follow Burton and Speke's route across Tanzania, meet up with Connolly to make the first descent of the Malagarasi, and conclude my journey at the source of the Nile in the geographical heart of Africa.

I took basic Swahili lessons from a Tanzanian medical student in Tucson, Arizona. I read a lot of books about East and Central Africa, trying to get a grounding in the history, the politics, the ecology and animal behavior, the sociology and anthropology, the civil war in Burundi, the genocide in Rwanda, witchcraft and tribalism, the problems of aid, poverty, disease, and development. I carved out three months of time, secured a magazine assignment and a book advance to pay the expenses and Paul Connolly's fee. I got my vaccinations, antimalaria pills, and expedition medical kit. I bought plane tickets, visas, and safari shirts, and then, at the eleventh hour, Connolly e-mailed to say he was backing out of the expedition. The global recession had wrecked his safari business. He had reopened his law practice in Zimbabwe and could no longer spare the time because of contractual obligations to his clients, and sorry for any inconvenience.

After discharging a foul storm of oaths, I started scrabbling around desperately for a replacement river guide. I had enough experience on African rivers to know how dangerous they could be, and how much vital knowledge I lacked. I made contact with a guide called Ryan Shallom in Dar es Salaam, the big city on the Tanzanian coast. He was a professional hunter with some river-rafting experience, and he came well recommended by river runners I knew in Arizona. He sounded enthusiastic about running the Malagarasi, and then his e-mail went dead, his phone kept ringing unanswered, and it was time for me to get on the plane or call the whole thing off.

I couldn't stand the idea of the river slipping away from me, or giving back all the money I'd hustled. I said good-bye to my girlfriend and my dog, and went to the airport with a backpack heavily laden with camping gear and books. The die was cast. One way or another, I would make my way from Zanzibar to the source of the Nile and go down the Malagarasi with local fishermen if that's what it took. I tried to maintain a cavalier attitude, but already doubt, stress, and panic were gnawing away at me. My Swahili was so bad, and my experience of Africa so limited: three outdoorsy magazine assignments that had all taken place inside the safari bubble, with experienced professionals meeting me at the airport, whisking me away in air-conditioned vehicles, smoothing away all the difficulties and dangers to ensure I had a fantastic time. Coming back from those trips, I had told everyone who would listen how much I loved Africa, but I had never walked down an African street by myself or bought myself a drink in an African bar, and I had certainly never negotiated an African bus station at midnight.

This book is the story of what happened next, the journey that emerged from the collision of my ill-laid plans with African reality in all its messy, complicated, unpredictable glory. It began with a broken promise and dashed hopes, and proceeded by improvisation, accident, mistake, interventions of luck, acts of kindness, innumerable delays, frustrations, detours, and distractions. It was punishing to mind and body. In three months I was never at ease, always wary and uncertain, often sick and feverish. The purpose and meaning of the journey were never quite clear to me, because I kept clinging to the broken wreckage of my plans, even as I grew more and more absorbed by what was happening around me in contemporary Africa.

I had trained and prepared for a physical adventure in the wilderness, but the biggest challenges were intellectual, simply trying to understand where I was, how it had come to be this way, what it was like to live here, and what was likely to happen next. My Western mind-set often seemed uniquely ill-suited to the task of understanding this maddening, mesmerizing, impossible continent, and it seemed no coincidence that the plans of the so-called international community kept failing here in unexpected ways.

The questions I ask about Africa are very different now, but I have no solutions. All I can offer are the experiences and impressions of a traveler who fell backward out of the safari bubble, struggled to keep his balance, tried to keep his eyes open, fell short of most of his objectives, and blundered his way in a spellbound daze toward a hole in the ground.

CRAZY RIVER

1

Stone Town

**Into the labyrinth—Golf pro on the skids—Bat demon—
Doors—Jaws Corner—Hope for the river—Burton's trace—
Fish stew for junkies—Prostitutes**

ON MY FIRST evening in Zanzibar, looking for echoes and
traces of dead explorers, I made my way through the teeming
labyrinth of Stone Town to the old British consulate on the
waterfront. Most of the building was now grimy, crumbling,
and shuttered, but a small blue plaque on the wall confirmed
that Burton and the others had been here, and one large room
downstairs had been renovated into the Livingstone bar and
restaurant.

I went inside and sat down with a beer and scribbled down
my first impressions of the labyrinth. Turbans and prayer caps,
souk-like alleys, collapsed buildings and amplified minarets,
touts, and hustlers of extraordinary persistence, "Hey tall man,
how are you my friend? Yes I come with you." Africa blends and
swirls with Arabia, India, the old Shirazi culture from Persia.
Red-robed Masais from the mainland with knives and clubs on
their belts, elongated earlobes, white plastic sunglasses. Arab
women in long black robes and veils, talking on cell phones.
Swahili women wrapped in bright patterned cloth, butterflies
against the dirty old buildings. European tourists shopping

for souvenirs. A muezzin calls from a minaret—no, it's a muez-zin ring tone on someone's phone. The air smells of cloves, bad drains, old fish, charcoal smoke, freshly peeled oranges, African bodies.

I paused at my labors to order another beer and noticed two men sitting further along the bar. One was dark-skinned, non-chalant, casually elegant. The other was thin, light brown, very alert, and slightly shifty. They looked like the only locals in this high-ceilinged bar slowly filling with tourists, so I went over and introduced myself as a writer and journalist just arrived in Zanzibar. The darker man was the owner of the bar. He spoke perfect English and seemed sophisticated, highly intelligent, and well educated. His name was Abeid, he was thirty-seven years old; later that night someone whispered in my ear that his surname was Karume and his father was the president of Zanzibar.

The light brown man was also thirty-seven and he made a great deal of this fact, presenting it as evidence that he and Abeid were soul mates and brother men. His name was Milan and he had a sharp, jumpy, fast-talking, ingratiating quality that reminded me of Tony Curtis in *Sweet Smell of Success*. His short wavy hair was brushed back and until quite recently his face must have looked unusually boyish and innocent. Now there was some dark damage around the eyes, cheeks pinching in, a discolored tooth in front. He was wearing an ironed pro-motional T-shirt from the bar, ironed gray slacks, and a pair of brown-and-white golf shoes. "I don't know what you're doing here," he said with a self-deprecating grin, "but I'm a profes-sional golfer."

He wanted me to know that he was PGA-qualified from The Belfry in England, "certified in teaching, playing tournaments, the rules of golf, club repair, merchandising, tournament administration, and first aid. It's a four-year course and I graduated in 1997. I've got three course records in Holland. I won the Tanzanian Open as an amateur. I won the Swiss Air Open. I got second place in the Belgian Red Cross Open and won twelve thousand euros. I was the pro at a public course just outside Rotterdam and I won two Monday tour events, two Highlander events."

And what he was doing in Zanzibar, an island without a golf course? "I'm just living, bro, taking each day as it comes. I've been here two years and I love it. This island is so mysterious. It's a magical place, bro, a crazy place, and the chicks! *Augh!* You are not going to *believe* the chicks, bro."

He was half-Dutch and half-Indian South African. He spoke English with a very slight South African accent, short clipped phrases, and a tense, insistent, hyped-up delivery, with plenty of knuckle-bumps and low-fives thrown in for emphasis. He showed me the Zanzibar handshake, a three-part maneuver that ends with a thumb swivel and a finger snap. "Everyone knows me on the streets," he said. "They accept me for who I am. We all help each other out, and it's a good life, man."

After another round of drinks, he told me about the weeks he had been homeless in Zanzibar, sleeping on the beach with the junkies. The worst thing about it, he said, apart from the lack of food, was trying to keep his clothes ironed. "As a professional golfer, you're expected to keep up certain codes of appearance, yes? Haircut short and neat. Clean shave. No jeans or trainers. We're ambassadors for the sport and the code of conduct and behavior that goes along with the sport. We wear golf clothes on and off the course, and we're expected to keep them properly ironed."

He grew up in Durban, South Africa, and then Dar es Salaam, Tanzania, where he and Abeid went to school together, and he learned fluent Swahili and the basics of East African street knowledge. Then, after winning the Tanzanian Open and playing the East African golf tour as an amateur, he went to Europe, turned professional, learned fluent Dutch, and almost succeeded in turning himself into a stable, bourgeois, suburban Dutchman. "The truth is I'm African and European," he said. "I come from both worlds. I feel at home in both worlds. I need both worlds." He was drinking liter bottles of Kilimanjaro beer on Abeid's tab, and there was something fierce and remorseless about the way he smoked his cigarettes.

The two of them had a system for women. The golf pro, who had extraordinary visual acuity, was able to carry on an animated conversation at the bar and simultaneously spot attractive women in the dark street outside as they approached the front door. If Abeid gave the nod, he would dart over to greet the women as they came into the room and escort them to the bar for their complimentary drinks, courtesy of the management. For the next two hours or so, there was a changing cast of slightly awkward, self-conscious young European women around us. Then all of them were gone, suddenly and mysteriously, and we were sitting there half drunk.

Milan felt like he'd let me down. He belonged to that masculine school of hospitality that insists on trying to get your buddy laid, and he had been so sure that a certain young Irishwoman was mine for the night. I kept telling him it was fine, that I had a girlfriend at home and wasn't looking for another woman, but this didn't seem to register with him. Then he noticed one of the local prostitutes walking in the door, and he leaned in to my ear.

"Look at the way she carries herself, bro. Five feet one, no hips, no tits to speak of, and she walks in the room like a queen. Don't you love it? Ah, Hindu's a good girl, a good friend of mine. Come on, I'll introduce you, but hey, I wouldn't go there if I was you. Know what I mean? And definitely not without a condom, bro."

Hindu was wearing a long, sequined purple dress and a gold-threaded headscarf with frosted black curls spilling out of the front. She was beautiful, her face more Indian than African as her name suggested, and she did carry herself with a certain regal haughtiness. She asked me to light her cigarette and sit down next to her. When I said I had a girlfriend, she laughed a husky, sarcastic chuckle. "Oh, you're one of the *loyal* ones, are you? I've heard about men like you. Well, I'm sure she's a wonderful, fantastic girl, and that's why she's over there, and you're over here. How long did you say you're going to be in Africa? Three months?"

She let that hang there a moment, and then elbowed me in the ribs. "Hey, relax. You and me? We're cool, we're friends, no problem. So you can buy me a drink."

I bought the drink. She thumbed through her phone, and then held it up to show me a text she had sent to a client earlier: "Darling, I have missed you so much. It makes me so happy when I am with you. Pls call me soon! XXXX."

She lit the next cigarette without my assistance and told me about him. "He's German, much older. He took me to the beach for six days. We stay at a nice resort. He has a *fantastic* time, we go shopping, he buys me this and that. Now this is the third text I send him, and he doesn't reply." She was a seasoned professional, under no illusions, but to get the cold shoulder from a man she'd been so intimate with for six days still seemed to rankle her slightly.

She thanked me for the drink, said she would see me around, and click-clacked out of the door. The golf pro swooped in next to me. He wanted me to understand the difference between Zanzibar prostitutes and their counterparts in Europe or America. "Here, they want you to be like a boyfriend," he said. "They want you to take them shopping, buy them dinner, take them to the beach, take them to Europe. Basically they want to take you for as much as they can get, and they're smart enough to know that's not going to happen in one night. Hindu's a good girl, but some of these whores around here are evil bitches, man, and you need to be careful around them, you know what I mean?"

I didn't know. What did he mean? "*Augh!* They'll be on your case all night, my friend. They won't leave you alone, and they won't take no for an answer, but if you tell them to piss off, they'll start screaming to everyone that you just copped a feel and didn't pay for it. Or you spent last night with them and didn't pay."

"And then what do you do?"

"Bro, you don't let it get to that point. If you get angry, it's all over. People lose respect for you. They come in and take advantage. It's the same thing on the mainland."

Milan and I came to an agreement that night. I would sing the praises of the Livingstone bar and restaurant in a travel piece I was writing for an in-flight magazine. In return, and for no charge, he would show me around Zanzibar, translate for me, teach me some Swahili, and try to get me a little more streetwise. I was so green I couldn't even buy a round of drinks properly.

I pulled out my wallet and started thumbing through the unfamiliar currency, squinting at the numbers in the dim light, and it agonized him to see it. "Bro, bro, bro," he said, screwing up his face. "In here, you can get away with it, but don't ever flash your cash like that in a local bar. Here, I'll show you how I do it."

He went into the front pocket of his golf slacks, rummaged a moment, and produced a single banknote folded into sixteenths, with just the tip of it extruding from his fingers. He called over the bartender, slid the bill into his hand, and said, "Cigarettes."

Zanzibar was a place where people looked out for each other, he said, but it was also a place with plenty of snatch and grab, diversion ploys, con games, and swindling. "I've had so many phones stolen I've lost count. Half the time someone will tell me they know who's got it, and they can get it back for me if I give them half the price of a new phone. So what happens? You give them the money and they disappear. You see them a week later and they don't know what you're talking about. It happens all the time, bro, but what are you going to do? Call the police? Break their legs? Come on, man, it's just a phone and people have got to live."

Violent crime was rare in Zanzibar, but lone tourists on foot did sometimes get mugged on the streets of Stone Town at night, so Abeid, who had sobered up, and Milan, who had gone in the other direction, delivered me back to my hotel in Abeid's glossy SUV. "Tomorrow," intoned the golf pro with outstretched forefinger, "I'll meet you in the lobby at eight a.m. and I mean eight sharp. I'm a punctual man, and when someone tells me eight sharp, I make sure I'm there at ten to eight. Bring your notebook, bring your camera. I'll show you some shit, my friend, the real Zanzibar that the tourists don't see."

"Fantastic," I said. "I want to see it all. I want to know everything."

"OK, you saw how I gave that two thousand to the barman for cigarettes, yes? Well that was my last one, bro. So give me ten grand now and I'll pay you back tomorrow."

I was going to give him the money—ten thousand shillings was about ten dollars—but Abeid exploded at him. "What the hell is wrong with you? You're hitting him up for money already?"

"Hey, no, I'm cool, it's nothing," said Milan. "All right, eight sharp and don't be late."

MY BRAIN WAS RACING too fast for sleep and unaccountably sober. I sat at the heavy Arab desk in my hotel room and wrote down everything I could remember about the evening and what it might signify. After a series of disappointments and setbacks, it seemed like a fantastic thunderbolt of good fortune to meet the golf pro and the president's son on the first night. What if I had been rigorous and efficient, lined up all my contacts in advance, and mapped out an itinerary? I would have missed them entirely. No, the best things always happened unexpectedly when traveling. The trick was to keep planning to a minimum and allow plenty of time and opportunity for random encounters, happenstance, and the pursuing of sudden whims.

The best thing of all was to be lucky when you were traveling, but I didn't believe that luck could be influenced, although it clearly ran in patterns sometimes, and favored some people more than others. The golf pro kept saying it was "meant to be" that I had run into him, but I didn't believe in fate or destiny either. My universe was vast, cold, mechanistic, lacking gods or spirits, and as indifferent to human desires as the desires of eels or hamsters. But this was very much a minority viewpoint in America, and from what I had read, it was absolutely unimaginable to most Africans.

Almost everything on this continent, from sporting events to the catching of diseases, and the outcomes of wars and elections, is amenable to prayers, curses, spells, and other forms of magical influence. On the East African golf tour, apparently, the players were constantly inserting feathered hex fetishes into each other's golf bags, because once discovered, all the confidence would drain out of the victim's game.

Milan poked a little gentle fun at this practice, but he believed strongly in an African-style magical universe. When he arrived in Zanzibar he visited a witch doctor to divine the future of his golf career. "Your star once shone bright but now it has faded," he was told. "It will shine brightly again, but this will take time and you must be patient." Milan took this as certain fact, and seemed to derive great comfort from it. Nor was he willing to discount the existence of Popo Bawa, who I had just read about in the newspaper, under an irresistible headline: "Sex Attacks Blamed on Bat Demon."

Like the incubus in the European supernatural tradition, Popo Bawa is a male sexual predator who appears in the night and ravishes his victims without leaving any physical traces or DNA samples. But while the incubus is shaped like a man and heterosexual, Popo Bawa takes the form of a giant bat and he rapes both men and women, with a preference for men. According to the newspaper, he operates mainly in Zanzibar and the neighboring island of Pemba, where he had been on an appalling rampage. Villagers in some areas were now too afraid to sleep in their huts at night. Instead they were staying awake, or smearing themselves in protective pig oil and sleeping in communal circles around big bonfires.

"I'm not saying Popo Bawa exists, or that he doesn't exist, because there's a lot of shit going on in this world we don't understand," said the golf pro. "When you get around these witch doctors, bro, you see things that make your head spin. I mean scary shit, man."

To understand anything at all about Africa, I was going to have to come to terms with African magical thinking, or spiritual thinking if you prefer, the two terms being interchangeable to me. The golf pro said the best way to understand Africa was to go hungry. He had experienced real hunger for the first time when he was homeless, and even now he sometimes ate only one meal a day, which he didn't count as going hungry. Most people in East Africa ate only once a day, and if you were getting that meal, you weren't considered to be really suffering. In local parlance, poverty was strictly a measure of hunger, and one meal a day didn't count as poor.

"When you go without food for two or three days, everything changes," he said. "There's a mentality in Africa of give it to me now, I must have it now, tomorrow no matter and next week doesn't exist. And if I don't get it now, my best friend will become my enemy. That's how you think when you're hungry, and there's been so much hunger in Africa that the mentality has got into the culture. What blows my mind is that people here will be hungry-hungry and they'll still share what food they have."

It was two-fifteen in the morning when I finally pulled down the long, draping mosquito nets on my traditional Zanzibari bed, a four-poster with an elaborately carved frame and fretted panels, and clambered inside. At five in the morning, there was an amplified call to prayer from a minaret. They were talking about this particular muezzin in the bar last night, saying he was particularly insistent and hectoring. "Wake up! Prayer is more beautiful than sleep. Wake up, stop sleeping, come to the mosque now."

I dozed off again, and then at ten past seven, there was a soft knocking at the door. It was a member of the hotel staff, saying there was a gentleman downstairs to see me.

MILAN WAS WEARING the same clothes as the night before, with bloodshot eyeballs and a chagrined smile. "Hey brother man, not too early I hope," he croaked. "*Augh,* it was crazy last night, man. Complete and utter madness. Abeid went home and I ended up in this fucked-up nightclub. It was deepest, darkest Africa in there, bro, whores screaming, fights breaking out all over the place. You should have been there, man. I got two hours' shut-eye on a friend's couch and then I came over here. Because I'm a man of my word and a gentleman is always punctual. I need one cup of coffee and then we bounce. Oh, and give me two grand for some smokes. I'll pay you back later."

"Listen, man," I said. "You're doing me a service by showing me around. Why not let me pay you for it?"

"Oh, no. No, no, no. You and me? We're gentlemen of honor, my friend, and not like some around here. I just need two grand for some cigarettes and I'll pay you back this afternoon. There's a guy who owes me sixty thousand for a favor I did him, and he's coming over from the mainland on the lunchtime ferry."

"OK," I said, giving him a five-thousand-shilling note. "Do you want to get some coffee here?"

"Sure. Wait. No. I've got a better idea. We'll go to Jaws Corner, a local place. Follow me."

He marched out of the hotel with the soles flapping loose on his golf shoes. He bought cigarettes from a street vendor, handed me back the change, and then spotted one of his Masai friends coming around the corner with a spear in his hand and the usual knob-headed club and dagger on his belt. He was wearing the usual red tartan blanket like a toga with a pair of black lace-up shoes, a lion's claw necklace, and a white Las Vegas baseball cap, and he stood about six foot four on long, thin, stork legs. They hailed each other with exuberant grins, did the three-part handshake, and went into the exchange of Swahili greetings.

"Good morning. Problems?"

"No problems. And you?"

"I'm well. What news?"

"The news is all good. What's up?"

"It's cool. What's up with you?"

"It's all smooth. How has it been?"

"It's been very good. How are they at home?"

"They are fine."

This, Milan said afterward, was a slangy, truncated version of the longer traditional greetings, without the usual inquiries after each other's cattle, goats, parents, and relatives. And I should understand that even if you were lying on your death-bed with your last starving goat outside your hut and all your children trembling with malaria, the answer would always be, "I am well, the news is all good, everything is fine."

These elaborate, lengthy greetings were a vital part of social etiquette all over East Africa, and it was a rudeness to forgo them or rush them. "In Europe, you've got clocks and watches, yes?" said Milan. "Well, here in Africa we've got time, and one of the ways we use it is to greet each other with the proper respect. The trouble comes on the bloody phone. Look around you. Nearly everyone has a mobile now. It's all pay-as-you-go, and the credit isn't cheap, my friend. It's a lot more expensive than it is in Europe, and all that hello-how-are-you-I-am-fine really eats it up."

In our technology-worshipping societies, the fact that one in three Africans now had access to a cell phone was being taken as a wonderful sign of progress. I had a file of glowing reports about this phenomenon, collected from the British and American media, and not one of them had asked the obvious question: how are so many of the world's poorest people able to pay for a handset, air-time, and the fees to charge their phones at the local electricity shacks? Now, finally, some studies had been completed. Cell phone users in the slums of Nairobi and Dar es Salaam were, on average, spending a third of their income on this vital new tool and status symbol, and to pay the bills, they were cutting back on food for themselves and their children.

The golf pro led me through a curving street no more than eight yards wide, with two- and three-story buildings on either side. The walls of this narrow canyon were grimy and peeling, with latticed balconies up high and huge wooden doors. The doors were old and weathered and cracked, carved around the frames with patterns, symbols, and verses from the Koran in Arabic, and sometimes studded with brass knobs or sharp spikes. Chain carvings around a door were there to bind up evil spirits and prevent them from entering the house, fish scales brought fertility, and the doors in their entirety were status displays. Traditional Arabic architecture values modesty and simplicity in a building's exterior but in Zanzibar, where transplanted Arabs from Oman made fantastic fortunes in the nineteenth century from trading in slaves, ivory, and spices, the need to flaunt their wealth was too strong and became manifested in their doors. The brass spikes were a stylistic innovation borrowed from India, where they were originally designed to defend buildings against war elephants.

Another twist, another turn. A group of chickens came down a flight of stairs and out through an open doorway into the street, much to the golf pro's delight. "Don't you love it, man? The chickens here all belong to someone, and they go home at night! I tell you, bro, I've been here two years and I never get tired of this place. And I still get lost sometimes in these crazy streets."

I was completely disoriented and we were only just entering the real maze. If you look at a map of old Stone Town, with all its curves, folds, dead ends, and tiny alleys crammed in so tightly together, it resembles a diagram of the human brain. Why build such narrow curving streets? What did these people have against straight lines? The urban geography seemed secretive, defensive, a way of keeping outsiders lost and confused. Then we came to a pile of rubble where a building had collapsed, and we were suddenly squinting in the glare of the fierce equatorial sun, sweating in the sudden heat, and I understood. The twisting, turning, high-walled labyrinth was first and foremost a way of maximizing shade.

It also encouraged fellowship. Neighbors talked to each other window-to-window across the narrow streets. There were stone benches everywhere for further conversation, and pedestrians acknowledged each other's presence with a nod or a greeting. Living in such close quarters also generated tensions and conflicts, and Milan told me about a Zanzibari custom that had evolved to diffuse them. At the turn of the New Year, men go out in the streets and whack each other with sticks, raising welts, bruises, and bloody contusions on their most annoying neighbors and clearing away the tensions so the New Year can start fresh and clean.

We turned down an even more claustrophobic alleyway, lined with hole-in-the-wall shops that were barely large enough to contain their reclining proprietors, and then emerged at a small grubby crossroads deep in the maze. "Here we are," said the golf pro. "The best cup of coffee in Zanzibar and probably the cheapest, too." On one wall, written in English in red paint, were the words JAWS CORNER. Facing those words was an old man with a kind half-smile and a white *kofia* prayer cap, sitting on a stone step making coffee on a charcoal brazier and clacking together his tiny round cups to attract business.

We sat down next to him on the step and sipped the strong, black, excellent coffee. It left a thick slurry in the bottom of the cups, which the vendor rinsed out in a pail of dubious-looking water before pouring us refills from his big, dented coffee kettle. The morning streets were coming to life now and the crossroads soon turned into a wild carnival of activity and chaos. The streets were too narrow for cars, but clogging traffic jams formed out of handcarts, donkey carts, motorbikes, scooters, and bicycles. Men pushed and pulled, tugged and yelled, honked their horns. The air filled with angry shouting, accusations, denials, counteraccusations, until the jam unclogged and everyone smiled and went on their way.

An orange vendor peeled his fruit to release the aroma. The grimy stone steps and nearby benches filled up with coffee-drinkers—a Rasta on a red, gold, and green scooter, a young man in T-shirt reading NEW HOUND, a mumbling drooler in a Phat Farm T-shirt, an old man in a long, dirty white robe with a dark mark in the center of his forehead from decades of touching it to the prayer mat. Women didn't stop for coffee but swayed elegantly past in robes, saris, and *kangas*.

The *kanga* struck me as a brilliant invention. It's a rectangle of patterned cloth printed on the border with a proverb or declaration such as "The eyes have no curtains," or "Sweetness is subject to be tested," or "A ripe mango should be peeled and eaten slowly," or "Hate me but I won't stop telling the truth." One *kanga* is worn as a skirt, another as a top, a third as a shawl or headscarf, perhaps a fourth as a baby sling. They also serve as curtains, towels, shopping bags, and something to sit on when women gather. It weighs nothing, costs a few dollars, is cool in the heat, and female tourists in Zanzibar don't last long without winding one around their hips.

A boy in rags cycled past at top speed with a huge fish strapped to his bicycle, looking absolutely gleeful. What was his story? Did he catch that fish or steal it? Where did he live? Would it feed his siblings, or would he sell it? I was abuzz with curiosity and caffeine, reveling in the energy and the sensory input of the streets, and it occurred to me that most of this would be illegal where I live—the motorbikes with two and sometimes three young children on the back, the unlicensed food vendors with their sloppy hygiene, the counterfeit watches and pirated DVDs for sale. The Zanzibar government had passed a helmet law for riders of motorbikes, but helmets were expensive, and some people did their best to comply by wearing plastic buckets and bowls on their heads, tied under the chin with string.

There was a big television set mounted high on one of the walls and in the evenings people gathered here to watch English Premier League soccer, an absolute obsession all over East Africa. It was often the first question out of people's mouths after the greetings: which team do you support? Manchester United? Chelsea? Liverpool? The markets were full of team shirts, knocked off on the cheap in a Chinese factory, like almost everything in an African market these days except the fresh food. In the newspapers, a vigorous debate was underway about the Premier League obsession, sparked by the suicide of an Arsenal fan in Nairobi, who hung himself from a bridge after his team lost 3-1 to Liverpool. Professors argued that it was a legacy of imperialism, proof that Kenyans and Tanzanians were still looking up to their former colonial masters. Sports columnists said this was nonsense. It was a plain, bald, universally acknowledged fact that the English Premier League produced the most exciting football in the world.

I sipped four cups of coffee in purest traveler's delight. I bought a fifth, sixth, and seventh for the golf pro, who was now chain-smoking cigarettes, passing them out to anyone who approached him, and keeping up a running commentary on the events in the street. "Wait, bro, look at this one. He's got three kids on the back of his bike and ohhhh! Nearly hit Phat Farm. . . . Bro! Hot tourist chick at my nine o'clock. Swedish not German, check the shoes. I could baboon-lash that one against a fence right now. OK, bye honey! Have a nice life without me. . . . Look at this. Kid whacking a donkey, donkey's not moving, and here comes a handcart full of mangrove poles. Traffic jam! OK, here we go. Everyone start yelling. Complete chaos. Fucking Zanzibar, man, don't you love it?"

Tourism was the economic lifeblood of the island now, and

the best business that had happened along since the British muscled in and banned the slave trade. Tourism was busily turning Zanzibar into a modern, sanitized version of itself, but here in the crumbling labyrinth of old Stone Town the process still had a long way to go. There were tourists in the mix but they felt off balance, wary about bringing out their cameras in a place where mothers were still putting kohl around the eyes of their baby daughters to ward off the evil eye.

Milan was fully in favor of tourism, because it brought young, gullible European women into his field of orbit and because finally it was bringing a golf course. Completion was still two years away, and if he could survive until then, he felt sure he could get the job of course professional, run the pro's shop and give lessons, and maybe start playing tournaments again and validate the witch doctor's prophecy. I asked him what had gone wrong in Holland. A look of sour, brooding darkness passed across his face and he said, "It's a long fucked-up story, my friend, and today is not the day for it. Today we're going to have a good time. Can you feel it, bro? The energy? There's a flow to these streets and it's going our way. One more cigarette here and it's time to bounce. We'll go to Livingstone's and I'll show you upstairs where the explorers used to hang out."

IN THE THREE QUARTERS of a mile between Jaws Corner and the old British consulate, he stopped to exchange greetings and cigarettes with eleven different friends and acquaintances, and went on to discuss some sort of tense business arrangement with one of them. I ducked into a greasy little Internet café, where I settled in between two dark young Muslim men watching shaven blonde porn. I felt bad for the women on the island, sorry for the intrusion of my culture. When these men married, the sight of their wives, finally unveiled and naked on their wedding night, would no longer have the same impact. Comparisons would now be inevitable, disappointments and hurts that didn't exist in previous generations.

Opening my in-box, I found such unexpectedly good news that I thumped the table and startled my lust-glazed neighbors. A magazine editor in London had agreed to my proposed interview and profile of President Paul Kagame of Rwanda, a hardline authoritarian who had turned his country from a genocidal ground zero into the safest, cleanest country in Africa, with the highest sustained rate of economic growth. And Kagame's press secretary was sounding guardedly optimistic that the president would agree to the interview.

Even better was a message from Ryan Shallom in Dar es Salaam. He had been away on a hunt, and then at a hunting conference, but now he was back at his desk and confident that our expedition down the Malagarasi would happen, although he still hadn't responded to my queries about his fee and the expenses, and there were a few other potential problems. It would be the end of the dry season and there might not be enough water in the river to float his inflatable raft, especially in the upper sections. A kayak could operate in shallower water but he thought it was "suicidally adventurous" to kayak through hippos and crocs on a dwindling, dry season river.

Furthermore, the headwaters of the river lay on the borderline with Burundi, where a U.S. State Department travel advisory warned of lawlessness, banditry, rampant crime, and political instability. I thought the State Department was exaggerating the threat as usual, because I had read several blogs by aid workers saying things were precariously calm, although you could buy a hand grenade for three dollars and people were using them to settle land disputes and domestic quarrels. Ryan wanted to launch his raft further downstream in Tanzania, where there was less danger and hopefully more water.

That would mean no first descent of the river, no reason for my name to appear in the annals of exploration, the crushing of my original hopes, the loss of a once-in-a-lifetime opportunity, and the Malagarasi still ripe for the picking by someone else. If I was a real explorer, this would have been violently unacceptable to me, instead of just woefully disappointing. Reaching that paragraph of Ryan's e-mail was a moment of self-discovery. I was willing to take risks, but I wasn't crazed and obsessive and vainglorious enough to make a real explorer. I was too willing to compromise in the face of reality, rather than make it bend to my indomitable will, and I was always more interested in what happened along the way than achieving goals or reaching destinations.

It still sounded entirely possible to have a grueling and terrifying ordeal on the Malagarasi, according to Ryan's sources and guesswork. He thought the swamp in the river's midsection was probably impenetrable. His hunting contacts had confirmed that there were plenty of hippos and crocodiles, lions that used the swamp as a stronghold, biting, disease-carrying insects in terrible abundance, and extreme remoteness—"all the lovely ingredients for a great adventure," as he summed it up. He said we should meet and talk it over when I got to Dar es Salaam.

That sounded good to me, and maybe I could inspire, browbeat, or offer him enough money to consider the whole river from source to mouth. To the golf pro, it sounded like a complete bloody nightmare. The insects alone would be hell on earth, he insisted, and where were the girls, the nightclubs, the party action? Following his profession, he liked nature best when it was tamed and trammeled, mown and manicured, carefully treated with pesticides and fertilizers, and artfully strewn with bunkers. I liked wild, primordial places. They seemed like the only honest places left in the world, but the Malagarasi was sounding wilder than anywhere I had been before.

When we reached the old consulate, Milan secured a key from the bar manager, unpadlocked a wooden door, and led me up some raw concrete stairs to a big, open, torn-out room. The glass and frames were gone from the windows, and there were empty gin bottles and old human turds on the floor. "Locals have been up here partying," he surmised. "Drink gin till you pass out, wake up in the morning, and take a crap. But can you picture it, bro? Back in the day? They probably had club chairs up here, a full bar, a billiards table. It blows my mind to think of Livingstone standing right here. Then Stanley came through here on his way to find him."

The explorer I found most interesting was the first Englishman into East Africa, the brilliant, sardonic, scholar-adventurer Richard Burton, and not just because I would be following his footsteps across Tanzania. Milan had seen his name on the plaque outside but knew nothing about him, so I started trying to explain. "You speak English, Dutch, Swahili, and some Afrikaans, right? You know what it takes to learn a language. Burton could master a language in three months. By the end of his career, he spoke twenty-nine languages, forty including dialects, and he could speak and understand sixty different sounds made by monkeys. He could play four games of chess at once, blindfolded, and never lose. He was an expert swordsman and a master of disguise. He went into Mecca disguised as an Arab merchant, got himself circumcised, dyed his skin with walnut juice, wore the robes, and of course he spoke flawless Arabic and got away with it. He wrote more than forty books, including two volumes on Zanzibar that every historian still depends on."

"The only Richard Burton I know is the actor," said Milan.

"This one was also a drinker and a womanizer."

Burton was intensely curious about all facets of human behavior, but sex in particular, which made no end of trouble for him in Victorian Britain, although he enjoyed the notoriety.

During his travels in India, Egypt, and Arabia, he had sought out all the secrets of brothel and harem, and he liked to do his research firsthand. I told Milan what Burton had discovered in Somalia, where unmarried adolescent girls were fully circumcised, with the labia sewn up and the clitoris cut off, as most of them are today. Burton found out that they knew how to unsew themselves, that they liked having sex with strangers, that they could have orgasms, and then sew themselves back up afterward.

"Whoah freaky man," said the golf pro. "A lot of girls here have their clits cut off. It's all over East Africa, man, and it's not for me. Sorry, girls, but I won't go there."

The old derelict club room had a commanding view over the beautiful turquoise and sapphire sea stretching away to the African mainland, and traditional dhows with lateen sails, virtually unchanged in their design for nineteen centuries, were ferrying goods to and fro, and bringing in the day's catch of fish. There was a big, steel tourist ferry out there too, but it was easy to smooth it out of the picture, and imagine Burton with his brandy glass and cigar looking out over this same view a hundred and fifty years earlier, contemplating his upcoming expedition into the interior where no white man had been before. There were rumors of lakes the size of oceans, snow-capped mountain ranges on the very equator, and surely somewhere in that big blank space on the maps was the source of the Nile River, the great mystery of African geography since the time of Herodotus.

Burton was an extremely imposing figure. He stood just under six feet, with a bullish chest and massive shoulders. He had close-cropped black hair, a long handlebar mustache, a complexion usually described as "swarthy," and dark, fierce, blazing eyes that unnerved most of his contemporaries, especially at the first meeting. Bram Stoker wrote of his "iron countenance" and his extraordinary intellect and learning, "as he talked . . . the whole world of thought seemed to flame with gorgeous colour." The poet Arthur Symons saw "a tremendous animalism, an air of repressed ferocity, a devilish fascination." Others likened Burton to a pirate, a bandit chief, and a panther, and the impression he made on people was heightened by a dramatic scar on his left cheek, where a Somali javelin had pierced it in 1855.

Then as now, Somalia was one of the most dangerous, unstable places in Africa. Burton was on the way back from the holy Muslim city of Harar, which no European had seen before him, when his expedition was attacked by plundering coastal tribesmen. The barbed head of the javelin passed through his left cheek, tore out some back teeth, fixed the upper jaw to the lower, and pierced an exit through his right cheek. With the javelin still impaled in his face, he managed to fight his way out of the melee and escape to a waiting ship.

Burton's chief assistant on that expedition was John Hanning Speke, a young, aristocratic army officer with a fanatical lust for shooting birds and animals, a peculiar attitude toward women, and a well-concealed envy that bordered on loathing for Richard Burton. Lacking suitable alternatives and not yet understanding what festered in his protégé's heart, Burton had invited him again as his second-in-command. Arriving in Zanzibar, the two Englishmen came straight from the ship to this big, solid building, which Burton compared to a claret chest lying on its side.

Speke was disgusted by the stench and squalor of Zanzibar, bored with nothing to kill, and impatient to leave. Burton, as always, plunged into the local culture, hired tutors to perfect his Swahili, conducted dozens of interviews with knowledgeable locals, and filled up notebooks with his microscopic handwriting. In six months, as they waited for the rainy season to end so their expedition could begin, he collected enough material for his two-volume book on the geography, ethnography, economy, and history of Zanzibar and, despite a severe attack of malaria that lasted three weeks, and a two-month survey of the mainland coast, he somehow found the time to write the thousand-page manuscript as well.

My interest in Burton was historical—he is indispensable if you want to know what East Africa was like before Europeans arrived and colonized it—and also personal. I possess only a sliver of his talents and energy, but a greater portion of his restlessness and curiosity. Like him, I'm an Englishman who grew up abroad, moving frequently, and never managing to feel at home in England. I too find it difficult and depressing to stay in one place for too long, and like Burton, who described himself as "migratory," I have organized my life and career around this personality trait. Before leaving for Mecca, he described "a paroxysm of ennui coming on by slow degrees . . . ," which exactly describes what happens to me between journeys.

"Travellers, like poets, are mostly an angry race," he wrote elsewhere, and the cure for the anger is the same as the cure for the ennui. Both disappear when you set out on a long journey. "Shaking off with one mighty effort the fetters of Habit, the leaden weight of Routine, the cloak of many Cares and the slavery of Home, man feels once more happy. The blood flows with the fast circulation of childhood . . ."

One day in Zanzibar, and I too felt like my better, brighter, younger self again. A persistent dreary fatigue that I had attributed to the onset of middle age was gone, and I was full of energy and enthusiasm, hungry for experience, thirsty for knowledge, pacing after the golf pro with a spring in my stride.

THE MAN ON the mainland failed to materialize on the afternoon ferry, and Milan needed money. Again I offered to pay him and again he refused. "No, no. I just need something for cigarettes and some superglue. I've got to fix these shoes, man. Lend me ten grand and I can get a haircut too."

With his soles of his golf shoes reattached to his uppers, a newly ironed golf shirt, a hole darned in his golf slacks, and a fresh shave and haircut, he walked me along the beach to meet his junkie friends. They stood in a cluster around a trash fire and hailed him enthusiastically as Kombi, the Bushbaby, a nickname referring to the sweet cherubic look that was still in his face. He finger-snapped and knuckle-bumped and handed out cigarettes. The junkies offered us fish stew from a blackened cauldron, which we declined. There were a dozen of them, and most were halfway to rags, and some had a white circle of dried spittle around their mouths. A tall man with short dreadlocks assured me in good English that he and I were friends now, that I would have no problems in Zanzibar, and I was welcome like a brother here at this place anytime. He asked if I could help him out and I gave him two dollars.

Although the hellos are interminable in this part of the world, one can leave suddenly with barely a word of good-bye, and we were soon picking our way up an alley that doubled as a sewer to Milan's local bar.

"How do they survive?" I asked. "Where do they get the money to buy the heroin and eat?"

"They live one day at a time," he said. "Some of them take tourists out to the reef in fishing boats. Some of them scam the tourists, or tout themselves as guides. They do a bit of dealing, hustling, maybe an odd job here and there. They smoke raw, unrefined heroin and they always find a way to get it, but not food. I saw how hungry they were and decided to feed these guys."

For twenty dollars, which he usually got from Abeid, Milan could buy enough cornmeal, rice, and fish to feed twenty-five junkies. In return, they agreed not to beg, steal, or hassle people at Livingstone's. Milan fed them somewhat erratically, but often enough to keep this arrangement in place and make himself a lot of friends who were well disposed to do him favors, keep him clued into the streets, and help him track down stolen goods, and he always had a safe place to sleep here on the beach.

"That's Zanzibar, man. We help each other out. It breaks my heart that I can't help everybody, but I do what I can, and everyone here knows that about me."

We went in the front door of a souvenir shop and emerged from the back door into an open-air pitted-concrete courtyard with a bar in the corner, a few potted plants, and some grimy white plastic tables and chairs. There was a red pool table under an overhang, where men glanced at us over their pool cues and prostitutes lounged around in sunglasses. Dub reggae was bubbling and backfiring through big, half-blown speakers and people were rolling and smoking joints openly.

"This is a place for locals to relax and take it easy," said Milan. "You can do anything you want in here. Drink too much, smoke till you're silly, fall over, get in a fight. No one cares. No one is going to call the police. They all know me here. We won't have any problems. If people hassle you for money, just say you don't have it."

The bartender, alcohol, and cash register were locked in behind heavy steel bars. I slipped Milan a banknote for beers, and he folded it up and slid it through the bars to a fantastically bored and slouchy female bartender. She asked if we wanted the beers *moto* or *baridi*, hot or cold. Everyone else was drinking them "hot," the same temperature as the muggy tropical air, and this is the norm in East Africa, where most people live without electricity or refrigeration and prefer to drink bottled beer at the same temperature as their home-brewed banana and sorghum beers.

We sat down at a table with two cold liter bottles and a beautiful young prostitute in big white sunglasses sat down with us. Her hair was straightened and pulled back and she wore a miniskirt and a tank top. She pointed her thumb sideways at me and said something in Swahili to Milan.

"She wants to be your girlfriend," he said.

"A kind offer, but I already have a girlfriend."

"Oh, she knows all about you, my friend. She's heard about you from Hindu. You're the loyal one. Except she doesn't believe it."

"Don't you like me?" she challenged in English.

"No, it's not . . ."

"You don't like black women."

"I think black women are absolutely fantastic, but please, me and my friend have some business we need to discuss here."

Ignoring my cue, the golf pro jumped out of his seat and started dancing next to her, bumping her hip, smiling and gesturing for her to dance with him. She gave him a few desultory shimmies, shot me an evil look, and then stalked back to her coterie at the pool table, doubtless telling everyone that I hated black women.

Milan leaned in conspiratorially, eyes darting off to the side. "You see that guy at my three o'clock with the dreads and the *kofia*, smoking a joint? Watch out for that one. He's a professional thief. He's stolen from me many times. It's unbelievable how quick he is. He has a network of boys, and you'll have one here, one distracting you over here, and the next thing you know, but quick, man."

"These people who keep stealing from you," I said. "If this was America, you'd use violence, or at least threaten them with violence. Otherwise they'll just keep doing it. But you say that doesn't happen here."

"No man, we don't have that thug mentality here. But if you

see a guy stealing from you, and you shout out 'Thief!,' everyone on the street will go after the guy and beat him to death. Same thing on the mainland. I've seen it happen and it is quick and brutal. The word for thief is *mwizi* and it's a death sentence. Don't ever say that word unless you mean it."

"But it doesn't work as a deterrent? The threat of getting beaten to death doesn't stop people from stealing?"

"People are poor and hungry. And they have what we call *fitina*. It's like a mixture of greed and envy, and it's a powerful thing in Africa, man. People start thinking that no one is going to see them, and they're going to get away with stealing. You can't leave anything on the table here—phone, camera, videocamera. Gone. Straight to the Indian guys on the street with all the jewelry shops. They pay cash for anything digital, no questions asked."

Now approaching our table with loose, slack limbs and eyes stoned out to Venus came a junkie with a smear of dried mucus on his upper lip. He spoke some English and we went through the greetings, then Milan told him firmly and quietly that he needed to get a napkin, clean the shit off his face, and do it now. He nodded appreciatively and went off to the bar, and then up sidled the professional thief. His eyes were puffy and drooped down to reddened slits, and they checked the sunglasses and reading glasses in my left shirt pocket, the pen and notebook in the right pocket, and traveled down toward my trouser pockets, where the money and phone must be. I put on my reading glasses and gave his face a close-up inspection, which he didn't like. He wagged his forefinger at me, said nothing, turned, and walked off.

We sat and drank there for several hours, fending off the pests, beggars, thieves, and prostitutes, and gradually acquiring a table full of Milan's friends. There was Louie, a quiet, dignified Zanzibari with a gallows sense of humor, an expatriate French teacher who looked like Gerard Depardieu and was nicknamed accordingly, two Rastas who kept rolling and circulating joints, and Rashid, a wild-looking, mixed-blood with short dreadlocks who had grown up in Zanzibar and London. His father was a Zanzibar Muslim, and his mother was Irish Catholic. His religion was a blend of Islam and Rastafarianism, and it led him on strange flights of rhetoric in a Cockney Rasta accent. "California gets its name from Califa, right, because Muslims were over there before Americans. You need to read the Koran, read the Maccabee Bible, which is the blackman Bible. The devil is a living man and there's an angel who harvest the souls of the dead, and he do it nice and easy. But if you an evil man like Idi Amin or Hitler, he rip it out like this. Fierce, man. But if you a pious man, he just take out your soul like this and put it on a cushion."

Rashid was fifty years old, and despite a life of hard boozing, nightclubs, shaky hands in the morning, an unfathomable number of spliffs and cigarettes, he could have passed for a fit, athletic, forty-year-old. He had worked in London and the Arabian gulf, and then moved to Stone Town with his wife and daughter. His wife had caught him with a prostitute and left him, and now he was screwing as many of the local prostitutes as he could afford.

"You use condoms, right," I said.

"Never," he said.

"Why not?"

"Rastaman have a saying: you can't drown if you're meant to hang."

"You don't think you'll catch it?"

"If you meant to hang, you can't drown, and I love the prozzers, man."

I had a long conversation with Rashid that night, and he seemed to be one of those rare promiscuous men who genuinely loved women. He never said an unkind word about his ex-wife and plainly adored his daughter. He had put his half-sister through school in Zanzibar and would take her to the president's office—Abeid's father's office —point to the window he sat behind, and tell her she was going to be sitting there one day. The company of men bored him, he said, and to mitigate it, he was always inviting prostitutes over to the table, buying them drinks, talking and flirting with them in Swahili.

"These ones here, they're not even really prostitutes. They don't swipe your bank card with a handheld like they do in Europe now. They ask for taxi fare in the morning, and you both know you'll give her more than that, yeah."

The best prostitutes, he said, are in Cairo, followed by Bombay. White Cockney women made the best girlfriends, if you could find the right one with a good heart. African women were queens, Jamaican women were firecrackers, Arab women knew all the secrets about men. He might think about marrying a good Muslim Zanzibari girl one day, but for right now, he was happy with his prostitutes.

"Mind you," he added, "I was with one the other day, one of these with her clit cut off, and she's just lying there, right. So I say, 'How about making some noises?' And she says, 'Noises are extra. Five hundred shillings.' Hah!" Rashid shook his hand so that the fingers snapped together.

"And what did you say?"

"What do you think, man? I said, 'OK, five hundred. I pay you afterwards.' You gotta love it, man. Everything has its price here. Everything!"

IN SWAHILI, the common language of East Africa, the word for a white person is *muzungu*. The first white people in this part of the world were explorers and missionaries, and *muzungu* originally meant "those who wander around lost in an annoying way." When the cattle-herding Masai encountered these pale men who wore trousers, they came up with the term *iloridaa enjeka,* "those who confine their farts." But that term is slipping out of the Masai language now, and they are using the Swahili *muzungu* instead.

It is not a kind word, but less derogatory than it used to be, and in the weeks and months to come, like every pale-faced, pink-eared foreigner in East Africa, I would hear it shouted at me hundreds of times, and usually accompanied by demands and requests for money delivered with an extraordinary sense of entitlement. Rashid was half-Zanzibari, with coffee-colored skin, fluent Swahili, and dreadlocks. He was considered black in Jamaica, black in London, but he had finally and reluctantly accepted that in Africa he would always be a *muzungu.* "It doesn't matter how long you're here. You will always be a *muzungu* and they will always try to fleece you. They look at you, and they look at me, and they see the same thing: money."

Louie smiled and said this was true, but we should also take into account that Zanzibaris were constantly fleecing each other. "You're right," said Rashid. "And it didn't used to be that way. When I was growing up here, it was all peace, Islam, everybody taking care of everybody, stop at my house and get some food. That's gone now, man. Tourism done it in."

That local bar was always edgy, always educational, and it was a rare day in Stone Town that we didn't stop in there, or one of its equivalents. I visited a local historian, and other buildings and historical sites related to Burton, Speke, Stanley, and Livingstone, but there was a lot more to learn in the streets and dives and nightclubs, and I justified this work under the rubric of exploring unknown territory. The drinks were always on me, two cold beers and warm ones for everyone else at the table, and there was always a joint circulating, thieves and hustlers hovering, whores angling for position, Hindu barging through them to sit on my lap, people falling over and getting in fights, and the whole thing was to not get flustered, not get snooty, keep your friends close, keep the golf pro close, not let anyone see how much money you had, not get too wasted, and be ready for a swift exit when it all boiled over into madness.

2

Ramadan Saloon

Gucci di Zanzibar—Sex tourism—Kendwa—The dollar and the blood feud—Slave caravans—A barbarous conveyance—Golfing with child soldiers—Taarab nightclub—Trials of Ramadan—Witch doctor

"THE SAND IS like cocaine, and the water is clear as Malawi gin," said Louie. "Chicks in bikinis," said the golf pro. Everyone kept insisting I go to Zanzibar's famous beaches, so I contacted a hotel and resort on the east coast, promised to write nice things about them, and secured myself a free room and a van ride out there. Milan stayed in Stone Town. After a few nights of trying to keep up with him and his friends, I felt more than ready for a languid, relaxing sojourn in tropical paradise.

I can show you a photograph of the beach in front of my hotel. I took it myself and every cliché is in place: the dazzling white sand, the turquoise ocean with patches of emerald green and ultramarine, two leaning coconut palms, a local fisherman in a broad conical hat poling himself through the middle distance in a dugout canoe. But the photograph, with its suggestion of timeless pristine tranquility, gives a thoroughly dishonest impression of what it was like to be there.

When I turned around and faced inland, there was a parade of big resort hotels marching up the coast into infinity, a front

apron of souvenir shacks, massage cubicles, Jet Ski rental out-
lets, and beach volleyball courts, and in the foreground, thirty
Italian women in bikinis doing the downward-facing dog,
hands pressed down into their yoga mats and buttocks raised
at local Islamic sensibilities. The yoga instructor had a cordless
microphone clipped to her black bikini top, and her commands
were broadcast through a big, nightclub-quality sound system
over swirling, tripped-out dance beats.

Most of the resorts were built by Italian developers for Italian tourists, with Italian food and wine on the menu, a kind of
espresso temple by the swimming pool where everybody congregated, and Italian DJs playing Euro-housey dance music that
throbbed and pulsed until dawn, slowed down and chilled out
for a few hours in the morning, and then picked up its beats-
per-minute through the afternoon.

The souvenir shacks, nailed together from raw lumber and
driftwood, selling T-shirts, knickknacks, and jewelry, had
hand-painted signs announcing themselves as Cerruti, Empo-
rio Armani, Rolex Zanzibar, Gucci di Zanzibar, and the touts
and hustlers and begging children approached with an automatic "*Ciao, benvenuto*," followed by streams of Italian. They
were even more numerous, persistent, and pestilential than
their counterparts in Stone Town, and clung to me in groups
as I tried to walk along the beach. In the local Swahili, they are
known as *mupapasi*, meaning ticks: parasites that are hard to
shake off once they attach.

These beaches on Zanzibar's east coast were first "discovered"
by backpackers who came across the Indian Ocean on cargo
dhows from Goa in the 1960s and 1970s. Before that, they were
sandy areas that glared harshly in the eyes and separated the
fertile land from the fish-producing sea. Local farmers and fishermen observed that pale-skinned foreigners liked to lie down
on this heat-reflecting sand in the full sun with their clothes off,

which is strange behavior indeed when viewed by Africans sitting sensibly in the shade. A few huts, lodges, and beach shack restaurants were built to accommodate the sun-worshippers, while a slogan-chanting Afro-socialist regime drove the economy into ruins and left the country hopelessly dependent on aid from foreign powers.

In the 1990s, Tanzania finally admitted to itself that the long experiment with socialism had been an economic disaster, and a more pro-business administration came to power in Zanzibar. Seeing the potential for tourism, political leaders invited in the Italian development consortiums that were already building beach resorts for their countrymen and women on the coast of Kenya.

Most foreign tourists come to East Africa to go on safari in the national parks, but not the Italians. Seeing and photographing big wild animals just doesn't seem to interest them in the same way. Italians come to East Africa for the beaches, and most of them never leave their all-inclusive package resorts. Carcinoma holds no fear for them, and they put in long hours working up fantastic suntans. They can eat Italian food, take photographs of each other posing like fashion models on the beautiful beaches, do yoga, roar around on Jet Skis, and maybe have an exotic fling with an African sex worker.

The tourism development has now utterly transformed the east coast of Zanzibar and the northern tip of the island, with more than three hundred hotels built in fifteen years. It has produced a generation of nine-year-old boys fluent in Italian. Farmers, traders, and fishermen have turned themselves into snorkeling guides, nightwatchmen, maids, waiters, souvenir vendors, pedalo rental men, massage ladies, prostitutes, hustlers, thieves, and beggars, and these new economic opportunities have also drawn in eager hopefuls from other parts of the island and a wide swath of the mainland.

Most Zanzibaris disapprove of the way the tourists behave—wearing bikinis and Speedos while photographing the mosque is a particular gripe—but they want more and bigger tourism development because they hunger after jobs and money with fierce desperation. The obstacle to more development is an environmental reality. The island has a finite supply of fresh water. It lies in shallow aquifers replenished by the rains, and all those hotel showerheads and flushing toilets have already led to shortages.

The sex tourism in Zanzibar was still low key compared to Jamaica (where an estimated 80,000 white women show up every year with one thing in mind), the Kenyan beach resorts, Greece, or Thailand, but there was no shortage of prostitutes in either gender, and plenty of European women had paired up with the dreadlocked gigolos known in Zanzibar as beach boys. During my time on the island, inspired by Richard Burton and his endless curiosity about the human mating dance, I collected some of the beach boys' wisdom on the subject of white women. Burton, being an Englishman of his time, saw nothing wrong with using ethnic stereotypes as a way to categorize the differences between human races and cultures, and the beach boys of Zanzibar feel a similar freedom when they talk about Europeans.

Italian women, they say, can't get enough of that exotic, primitive African mystique, so leave your best shirt at home, put on your tribal jewelry (any tribe will do), and carry a spear if you've got one. The growing legions of Masai beach boys are particularly successful with the Italians. Abeid told me about a Masai who has twelve Italian women all sending him money and asking when they're going to move in together.

German women need to feel like they're in charge, so play it dumb, and pretend you just want to take her snorkeling and show her around the island. Danish women tend to be too dominant for the African male ego, and this often leads to clashes, although there have been several romances leading to marriage between the more docile Danish men and Zanzibari women.

British women? The question hardly needs asking. You get them drunk. American women are recent, infrequent visitors to the island and the beach boys don't have a handle on them yet. Instead they have questions: Are they really as naive as they appear? Or is it an act they put on?

IN A DILAPIDATED TAXI smelling strongly of marijuana smoke, with an amiable driver who spoke only a few words of English, I went up to Kendwa on the northwest coast in search of a quieter beach. A big, new, impregnable Italian disco resort had gone in at the northern point of the breathtakingly beautiful bay. Further south, there were small lodges, thatched huts, and hotels catering to backpackers and NGO* people taking a break from their humanitarian and development projects on the mainland.

I arrived on the eve of the full moon party, and rooms were hard to come by. The best I could find was a concrete cell with no hot water, a dribble of cold, and holes in the all-important mosquito netting over the bed. When I asked the price, the owner assumed a bored, long-suffering expression and pointed to a piece of paper encased in wrinkled plastic on the desk, indicating that single rooms were US$120 a night. I listed the room's faults and said it was worth no more than $20. After twenty minutes of bargaining, I grudgingly agreed to pay $60.

East Africa has never been cheap for a foreign traveler, as Burton discovered in 1857. The "twin banes" of African travel,

---

*Nongovernmental Organization. There are more than 130 foreign NGOs operating in Tanzania, and aid from the self-styled "international community" makes up 40 percent of the government's annual budget.

he wrote, were "the dollar and the blood feud." He spent thousands of dollars hiring guides and porters (most of whom pilfered and deserted), buying overpriced food supplies, and vast quantities of beads, wire, and cloth to pay the *hongo,* or tribute, to the tribal chiefs along the way, in return for permission to pass through their territories unharmed. A similar toll is extracted on African travelers today by border officials, corrupt policemen, and drunken soldiers at roadblocks.

I was carrying $12,000 in cash in two different money belts, one around my waist, the other around my right leg below the knee. In Burundi and Rwanda, where the blood feud between Hutu and Tutsi had turned into ethnic civil war and genocide, there were no ATMs that accepted foreign cards, and no banks that would cash a traveler's check. You could apparently get a cash advance on a credit card in Bujumbura and Kigali, the capital cities, unless the computers were down, or the electricity was out, and in Bujumbura the blackouts sometimes lasted for days. I was extremely uneasy about carrying so much cash, but the idea of getting stranded in the middle of Africa with no money, no access to money, no way to bribe myself out of trouble, was a deeper anxiety.

I changed into swimming trunks, put the money belts in a small daypack that detached from my backpack, and walked down the concrete steps to the Kendwa beach. Fifty yards of fine white sand brought me to a palm-thatched beach bar and restaurant, and there at two in the afternoon, well into their beers, chain-smoking cigarettes, talking in slightly drawling middle-class London accents with one foot hooked automatically through the straps of their backpacks, I came face-to-face with my younger self, and half-forgotten memories came flooding back with an awful clarity.

In my early and mid-twenties, I whiled away a lot of time in palm-shack bars on the beaches of southern Mexico, drinking with other backpackers because I couldn't speak the local language, eking out my money because I wanted to keep traveling and living in the moment for as long as possible. I had no other plans or ambitions but very strong ideas about what to avoid. So much of normal adult life looked like deluded striving, a battle that wasn't worth winning.

Now I was one of those middle-aged guys on the backpacker scene, the ones who had never stopped traveling. Some of them I had found inspiring, others weird and off-kilter, and all too many of them hopelessly lost and addled. I had always wanted to know how they managed to support themselves and keep traveling. They made jewelry, traded native handicrafts, gave massages, sold drugs, played the stock markets, or lived on their trust funds or early retirement money. They worked a season on the Alaskan fishing boats and spent the rest of the year in cheap Third World countries. On a beach in the Yucatán, I met a stoned inventor, a wonderful Italian hippie who had invented the perfect spoon to fit a small, plastic yogurt pot. Instead of being oval or round, it was squared off at the bottom and angled up one side. He dreamed up one or two product ideas like this every year, went back to Italy to sell them, and traveled the rest of the year on the proceeds.

I started traveling as a hedonistic escapee. I looked back to Kerouac and the beats and held similar ideas about the importance of getting my kicks, raising a finger to the whole idea of bosses, mortgages, responsibilities, rules, and regulations, and living as free and unencumbered as possible. Along the way I fell into the habit of keeping notes and writing letters, and from there it was a short step to freelance journalism and travel writing, which have supported and justified my wanderings ever since. Now I was forty-six. Wary of becoming addled, I kept my hedonistic tendencies in check. I no longer permitted myself an alcoholic drink before six in the evening, except on special occasions, and I had replaced cigarettes with regular exercise. I still took a snort and a puff from time to time, but no more psychedelics.

As the sun went down over the sea, gilding the slim youthful European figures taking photographs of it, I met a young French couple in their twenties at a campfire on the beach. They thought it was absolutely too cool that I could make a living by traveling and writing, and she at least had always dreamed of doing the same thing. He was an aspiring investment banker and dreamed of money.

"But what about children?" she asked. "What about family?"

"That's the big trade-off," I said, sounding and suddenly feeling just like one of those middle-aged guys I remembered. "But it's not too late for me."

I had already secured myself a life with a minimum of responsibility and a great deal of personal freedom, so there was nothing to escape now except the walls of home, the daily routine, and the feeling of grimness that crept over me when I stayed in the same place for too long, the sense that I was losing touch with myself. Like Burton, I needed the stimulation of travel in order to be stable. This was the key to his personality, according to Mary Lovell, one of his best biographers. Without that stimulation, despite his vast circle of interesting friends, his deep love for his wife, and his many intellectual passions, he became depressed and bitter. That was the thing to be warded off at all costs, and I still hadn't worked out a way to do it without packing a bag.

AS BEFITTING MY AGE, I spent the full moon party in my room swatting insects, failing to sleep, and reading Burton on Zanzibar. I was interested to learn that begging, thieving, prostitution, hustling, and swindling were all rife on the island in

1857, long before the arrival of the first Italian tourist. Young boys were already in the habit of yelling out *"Muzungu!"* when they spotted a white person. AIDS hadn't invented itself yet, but Burton reports a "remarkable prevalence" of other sexually transmitted diseases, affecting some 75 percent of the adult population. Syphilis was known as "the black lion," and gonorrhea so common that it was hardly considered a disease.

The biggest difference between Zanzibar then and Zanzibar now was the presence of slaves and slave markets. There is a modern tendency, especially in America, to think of slavery as something that white people devised for their plantations in the New World, but human bondage is as ancient as prostitution and has been practiced all over the world. African tribes were slaving on each other long before the first Europeans arrived, and 90 percent of the slaves who were shipped to the Americas were originally gathered by African slavers and often purchased from African chiefs who were selling their own people.

In East Africa, Arabs had been taking and buying slaves from the coastal tribes for two thousand years, and in the eighteenth and nineteenth centuries the trade was taken over and expanded by Omani Arabs headquartered in Zanzibar. The slaves were shipped to date palm plantations in Oman, spice plantations in Zanzibar, and households all over the Middle East. The Zanzibari slavers kept the most nubile captives for their harems, and the children of these unions were free and had full rights, and often went on to become slavers themselves.

In the filthy, reeking, disease-infested streets of Stone Town, Burton saw household domestic slaves running errands and buying food, and hungry packs of unemployed "wild" slaves, who had been kicked out of households and now lived by thieving and armed robbery. At night it was considered madness to leave one's house without a well-armed escort. In the slave markets Burton saw the new arrivals from deep in the interior, some with their teeth filed into points and elaborate scarification, nearly all half-starved and sunk in wretchedness, as Afro-Arab dealers and buyers in long white robes prodded and inspected them like livestock. "All were horribly thin, with ribs protruding like the circles of a cask, and not a few squatted sick on the ground," he wrote, and then added his usual irreverent detail, "The most interesting were the small boys, who grinned as if somewhat pleased by the degrading and hardly decent inspection to which both sexes and all ages were subjected."

No white man had ever gone where Burton and Speke intended to go, but Zanzibar slavers went there every year, returning with long, valuable caravans of human chattel, chained together at the neck and carrying ivory tusks. Over the generations these slave and ivory caravans had worn a trail that went inland more than a thousand miles, and the slavers had built a handful of settlements and stations along the way where the caravans rested and resupplied. This was the route taken by Burton and Speke on their fever-ravaged nightmare of a journey, and I was intending to go the same way, although not on foot with a hundred thieving porters and a library of Shakespeare, and not on a medicinal regimen of brandy and opium.

THE MORNING AFTER the full moon party, with a few comatose bodies still strewn on the sand where they had fallen, I spied a familiar but unexpected figure walking along the beach toward me. His thin brown legs were exposed by a pair of blue nylon shorts. His career as a professional golfer had skidded off the rails, following some dark turn of events in Holland that he didn't want to talk about, but his spirit was lively and unbowed, his mind sharp and funny, he was an incomparable guide to Zanzibar low life, and it was a welcome surprise to see him again.

Milan had come to Kendwa on the trail of a certain Dutch nurse who had been at Livingstone's, only to discover that she and her friend were already packing to leave for the mainland. Bumping into me was further proof that our partnership was meant to be, although he found it baffling and wrong that I had stayed in my room during the full moon party. Last month, he was here with a hundred golf balls and golf clubs, encouraging the revelers to whack them into the sea, and at some late point in the evening he and many others had ended up naked.

At sundown he led me past the snoozing security guards and out through the metal security gates that separated the backpacker compound from the local village. We walked along a deeply eroded street of dried terra-cotta mud, past huts and shacks, a barbershop with two chairs and a solar panel for the electric clippers, past a woman selling tomatoes stacked in little pyramids on a spread-out *kanga,* a group of jumping, pointing children yelling out *"Muzungu! Muzungu!"* and many pairs of watchful adult eyes. We sat down in a restaurant with a palm-thatched roof and no walls. It had two tables, a mud floor, and four planks of wood for chairs. "Ah, this is more like it," said Milan. "Some local flavor, bro."

The waiter was young, dreadlocked, and dreamily stoned. We ordered chicken masala and watched him saunter back to the kitchen to tell the cook, who sent out a boy for onions, called him back, gave him some money, and told him to pick up a chicken as well. Twenty minutes later, with no sign of the boy, Milan was twitching and vibrating with impatience. He stalked into the kitchen, pointed his forefinger, and gave the waiter and the cook an angry blast of Swahili. They sent out another boy to find the first.

Swahili is a mixture of Arabic and African Bantu languages. It contains several words for "hurry" and "rush." They all come from Arabic, not Bantu, and they carry a negative connotation, implying that hurrying will botch the job.

Milan sat down and fumed. Fifteen minutes later the boys returned with two onions and a freshly killed and mostly plucked chicken. The cook started cutting it up, then answered his phone and wandered off for ten minutes. He came back, finished cutting up the chicken, and started on the onions. He was in no hurry, and it turned out that he had no reason to be in a hurry. The restaurant only had six plates, and they had all just gone into service on the other table. By the time the other diners had finished their meal, and the cook had washed up and dried the plates, the masala would be done perfectly.

As a recent arrival, I found it entertaining and fascinating to watch this process unfold with such amazing slowness, but it drove Milan crazy. Here was everything that bedeviled Africa's progress and exasperated him about the motherland. "Where's the system? Why is it so hard to plan ahead? I mean, put away a few shillings and buy some fucking onions, you know. If you want to make a living selling chicken masala, make sure you have a fucking chicken, man. And do some prep work, cut the fucker up ahead of time. Look at this. We've been sitting here for an hour and forty minutes now."

The same thing had happened to us in Stone Town and would happen several times again. Milan would want to save money, get away from the tourists, show me the real Zanzibar, and so take me to some funky little local restaurant. Invariably, the food would take at least an hour and twenty minutes to reach the table, by which time Milan would be incandescent with rage. He was too African to live comfortably in Europe. It felt too controlled and antiseptic for him. But he was punctual as a Dutch policeman, and in this and other ways, too European for Africa.

The chicken masala arrived just shy of the two-hour mark. It tasted good, and I would remember it fondly in the culinary wastelands of western Tanzania. When we finished eating, the waiter made a clumsy attempt to cheat us on the bill, and Milan exploded again. The waiter backed down. Milan asked me for a banknote, which he threw down on the table in disgust. Then he stormed off into the darkness with me in pursuit.

We crossed back through the gates and went to the bar at Kendwa Rocks, the main backpacker resort. With the application of beer and marijuana, his mood improved, as did mine, and we started working out an itinerary for the next stage of my journey. First we would go back to Stone Town and find a reputable witch doctor. If the omens were good, Milan would start talking to the dhow captains on the wharves, looking for one who was willing to take us across the straits to Bagamoyo on the mainland, where Burton and Speke had set off on the old slave and ivory route into the interior. It was illegal for foreigners to ride on cargo dhows, because sometimes they sank in bad weather and one had gone down a few years ago with some European backpackers aboard, but it was a rare law in Africa that couldn't be circumvented with a few banknotes.

We would look around Bagamoyo for a day or two, then take the bus down the coast to Dar es Salaam, where he would hand me over to Ryan Shallom. "The mainland is a different vibe, bro," he cautioned. "It's harsher, it's hungrier. You really have to watch your back. Dar used to be cool, but now it's a total fucking mess, and the crime is through the roof, man. But we'll be fine. I grew up there, I speak the language, I know what I'm doing, don't you worry."

MILAN SLEPT ON the floor in my room that night, slapping at mosquitoes from time to time. The next morning we hitched a ride out to the paved road on the back of a construction truck in a sudden rain. Taxis were a waste of money, Milan insisted, and it was high time I learned how to travel by *daladala*.

Picture a vehicle like a minivan with a low roof and plank seating along the sides, all painted up with pink roses and sky blue bubbles. It was built to seat a maximum of thirteen people, but there were nineteen people squeezed inside it when it stopped. I was already looking down the road for the next one, but Milan beckoned me forward, and somehow this crush of humanity managed to wriggle, shuffle, bend, and squeeze in order to absorb the two of us and my enormous backpack. Then two more people came running up with bags and we absorbed them too.

The driver roared off down the potholed road at a ridiculous speed, a terrifying and idiotic speed. Dust poured in through the ventilation gap between the top of the walls and the roof. The driver gunned it around every curve, and we teetered and shimmied on the brink of adding one more digit to Tanzania's status as a world leader in traffic fatalities.

After ten minutes, my right foot was numb and throbbing, and I wanted desperately to shift its position, just by an inch or two, but an inch or two was impossible in the squeeze of other feet and bags, and there were people sitting on the bags, and others standing hunched over at right angles under the roof. My knees, which were squeezed together and folded up, were soon begging for release from their position, and a worse pain was starting in my crushed testicles. The driver sped over a big pothole and my skull smashed into the metal roof.

For the driver and his assistant, who rode crouched on the rear bumper holding on to the back door frame, the more people they crammed inside the *daladala* and the faster they drove, the more money they made. Doubtless they needed every last shilling and more to feed all the extended family members who show up wanting food, money, medicine, a place to sleep, whenever an African gets himself an income stream. The danger and discomfort endured by the passengers was of absolutely no concern to the driver and the assistant, and the passengers endured it with a calm, patient, well-mannered grace. This was normal, everyday life, and the only kind of bus journey they knew. There was an hour to go. I tried to will myself into a blank, passive, indifferent, fatalistic state of mind, which I had come to understand as a basic survival mechanism for the poorest people in this world, although not necessarily helpful for their future.

We arrived at the Stone Town bus station in a welter of noise, heat, confusion, belches of diesel exhaust, trash-strewn mud and potholes, men yelling in Swahili and broken English, swarming around the *daladala* and offering their services as bag carriers, guides, taxi drivers. Vendors walked around hawking oranges, boiled sweets, calendars, peanuts, children's toys. Unemployed young men hung around looking for something to steal, something to pass comment on, a pretty girl to walk by.

I felt particularly tall, white, and foreign as I waited for the golf pro to come out of the reeking bathroom, sweating under the weight of my backpack with its cargo of twelve books, two pairs of shoes, a liter bottle of whiskey, medicinal supplies, sleeping bag, camping gear, and clothes. Somewhere in there was my hat. I hadn't put it on because the sky was overcast with rain clouds when we had set out. Now the sun was pounding down on my head with astounding force, but it didn't feel like the right time or place to open my backpack and start hunting through my possessions. My face and neck were pink from the heat and sunburn, and not for the first time in Africa, my skin felt like a poorly designed thing, wholly inadequate to the task at hand. Like everyone else on this planet, I had ancestors who evolved under this sun, but they had left so long ago.

Milan led me though the pungent, flyblown meat market and the famous spice market —less fragrant than it used to be, because so many of the spices are now sealed in plastic—and soon afterward I bought him a reconditioned Nokia phone from a tiny street stall that also sold hand and body lotions.

I checked into a room, dumped my bag, and we went to a small local bar called Bottoms Up. Milan said things could get a little sketchy here at night, but the afternoon crowd was calm and friendly, and all were drinking warm Konyagi, the self-described "spirit of Tanzania." Distilled from sugarcane with added flavors, it smelled like gin, was usually referred to as gin, but technically was closer to rum. Two prostitutes at the bar made a cursory attempt to join us but gave up easily and shuffled back to their barstools. Kenyan music videos were playing on a television mounted to the wall. An enormously fat singer in a red suit was executing astonishing dance moves, with four booty-shaking prodigies dancing alongside him, somewhere out in the green hills of Kenya with a black SUV parked on the grass among grazing cattle and goats.

We stationed ourselves in the corner with cold beers and talked English soccer to the men sitting next to us, with Milan translating. An old man drinking alone leaned over from his table and said "Better a thief than a sorcerer" for no reason that we could determine. Five minutes later he did it again, nodding gravely at his own wisdom.

Milan started reminiscing about his days on the East African golf tour and told a story about playing the Ugandan Open in the middle of a civil war. Apolo Milton Obote, the dictator who both preceded and followed Idi Amin, was fighting a rebel army led by the current president, Yoweri Museveni. The fighting had reached the edge of Kampala, where the golf course was, and on the night before the first round, the golfers heard artillery and antiaircraft fire way too close for comfort.

"I was fucking nervous, bro. We all were. We could hear the war coming closer, but they weren't fighting during the day, so the tournament directors said it was safe to play. So we go out there, first round, and here come Obote's soldiers trooping down the bloody fairways, and sprawled out in the rough under the trees. They had child soldiers with them, too, and they were pointing at us, laughing, calling us names. It was nuts, man. Trying to concentrate? Forget it, bro. I played like shit."

He ordered another round of beer, and automatically now, I dug out a banknote to pay for it. "Every night, the fighting got closer. Now we've got mortars going off, machine guns, artillery, bloody antiaircraft going *ack-ack-ack*. Forget about sleeping. We go out for the third round and there's an unexploded mortar shell stuck in the ground by the eighteenth tee with its bloody tailfins sticking up. The tournament directors just painted a white line around it and put up a sign saying 'Ground Under Repair.' Funny, right, but if you topped your tee shot and hit that thing, you were a goner. I couldn't wait to get on a plane and fly out of there."

When he first arrived in Zanzibar, Milan had some clubs and a supply of golf balls, and he took it upon himself to teach the noble sport to the local children and youth. He would line them up, give them lessons one by one, and then they would hit balls across the weedy goat pasture that had once been the British cricket ground. The kids enjoyed whacking golf balls and some of them showed real talent and promise. With introductions from Abeid, Milan met with various government officials, and petitioned and pleaded with them to build a golf course in Zanzibar. It would make the island more attractive to wealthy tourists, establish Zanzibar as a truly world-class destination, and be fantastic for the children he was teaching.

"The thing about golf is that it teaches you a whole way of conducting yourself," he said. "It's about honesty, decency, good manners, a gentleman's code of honor, your word is your bond, taking care of your appearance. I tried to explain, but they just didn't get it. It's fucking Africa, bro. Some things just don't get through."

The officials did nothing to further the cause of golf in Zanzibar, but now private investors had hired golf course architects who were surveying a location north of Kendwa. Milan was the only PGA-certified professional living on the island and an old friend of the president's son. But the course was still at least two years away from completion, and his challenge was surviving until then.

MIDNIGHT FOUND US at a nightclub on the roof of a half-derelict hotel. Bats were zigzagging overhead, hunting mosquitoes, and Rashid was yelling taunts and abuse at Popo Bawa. "I'd like to see that batty-boy come around my arse. I clench up and rip him dick off, man. Hah! Popo Bawa, you ain't shit, man."

The whores were in a particularly aggressive mood, thieves were circling for an unguarded phone or wallet, and the lurching, weaving drunks were in grave danger of falling into the kidney-shaped swimming pool, which was about fifteen feet deep and visible through portholes from the floor below. The hotel was built by the government in the early 1970s and intended to show that African socialists could do the modern luxury style just as well as Western capitalists. The extra-deep swimming pool was its centerpiece, but now it contained only an inch or two of evil-looking slime and a few hundred empty bottles and beer cans.

There was a peculiar concrete structure, shaped like a giant mushroom or spaceship, that overspread the poolside bar, and I sat underneath it drinking with Milan and Louie, who fended away the whores that came swarming after my white skin and the money it implied. In the far corner of the rooftop, a hunchbacked *taarab* singer with a withered leg sat at a three-tiered synthesizer, making a peculiar, haunting, fake-orchestral music, and singing a song about a romance that foundered for lack of money.

Taarab, which gets its name from the Arabic word *tariba*, meaning "to be moved or agitated," is a musical form that evolved here in the nineteenth century and draws on Arabic, Indian, and African influences. Traditionally, it's played by orchestras of thirty or forty musicians, all dressed in formal attire, but it's easier for a *taarab* singer these days to make a living with a synthesizer.

Milan and Louie took turns translating the lyrics for me, which Louie dismissed as "blah-blah-blah, oh my heart, blah-blah-blah." Noticing my blue shirt and white arms, he said in his grave, dignified baritone, "You look like Barclays Bank tonight. That's where I've got my money invested, all twenty dollars of it. Zanzibar is hard come, easy go. Do you know what I mean?"

"Not really," I said.

"It's hard to get money, and it goes away easily." Louie, who worked from time to time as a DJ, didn't like *taarab*. Nor did he like the *bongo flava* hip-hop coming out of Dar es Salaam and taking over East Africa. "I like that old-time rock and roll," he said. "And give me some of that funky old soul. Also music from Congo, some from Nigeria and other places in West Africa. *Bongo flava* is stupid, and *taarab* is too much blah-blah-blah."

I shared his dislike of *bongo flava*, which was too sappy and commercial for my tastes, but the *taarab* was working a spell on me. It sounded a little like an old Indian movie sound track, tinny, wailing, and mournful, and as the night developed, women dressed in sparkling *kangas* and magnificent evening gowns appeared on the rooftop and assembled in front of the singer. They danced and swayed to the music and held up banknotes between their fingers. I watched a woman of about forty, wearing a spectacular red dress with sparkling earrings and a flower behind her ear, dance her way up to the singer. She held up her banknote, made sure that all eyes in the room were on her, and then handed it over slowly when she heard a line of the song that she particularly liked. Then the next woman came up and did the same.

Meanwhile the men were getting drunk by themselves, and the first scuffles and fisticuffs were breaking out. At the bar where we sat, there was a steady traffic of people asking for cigarettes and money, and three prostitutes who would not give up. Then they started sneering and taunting us, saying we weren't real men. Breaking his own rule, Milan snapped at them, and this provoked a fury of snarling and screeching, false accusations, and demands for money, much to Louie's amusement.

That was the night that Milan finally told me what had happened to his comfortable bourgeois life as the resident professional at a public golf course in Rotterdam. "I had a nice house, two cars, three horses, and a trailer—my fiancée was crazy about horses—and two dogs. Huskies. Fantastic dogs. I had built up the pro's shop to the point where I had to hire three other pros to help out with the teaching, and they were all selling for me in the shop. Plus I was winning money on the Monday tour. I was clearing fifty thousand euros a year, no problem. The first thing that happened was basically a case of *fitina*: that envy and greed that gets into people and makes them do bad things. You see it in Africa, you see it in Europe."

The manager of the Dutch golf club and the three assistant pros saw how much money he was making and initiated a long and ruinously expensive legal battle to get rid of him. Then his father died of lung cancer. His fiancée said that she was leaving, to which he responded by drinking a bottle of vodka and smashing the house up in a rage. They split up, sold everything, and he went back to South Africa to be with his mother.

He walked straight into a good job as a course pro in Durban, started making money again, then his mother died. Another funeral. Then her best friend died. Meanwhile the crime in South Africa was soaring out of control. In one week, there was a shooting, a rape, and a beating on his block. He sold his mother's house and went back to Dar es Salaam. The city was almost unrecognizable. It had tripled in size and was choking on dust, fumes, traffic jams, exploding slums. He found a job teaching golf, but he couldn't handle the urban stress, so he came to Zanzibar, where he knew he would find a soft landing.

"Abeid is my brother man. We go back. He found me some work organizing things at a construction site. Another guy paid me to arrange his wedding. Finally I started to relax. I remembered how to breathe and laugh again, after all this heaviness just piling up and crushing me. Aw man! It was a long fucking ordeal, bro, and Zanzibar saved me. I love it here. It's a good life, but I miss my golf. I really miss it, bro."

There is a small driving range in Zanzibar, and when he goes there and hits off thirty balls, he can feel that he's out of practice, that he's lost weight, strength, and power off the tee. But the skill is still there, the body remembers, and the ball nearly always flies straight and true. I asked him what it would take to get back into tournament form.

"Fuck," he said. "So much of it is mental, you know. You need a calm, clear mind. You need to be in good physical condition, and have a quiet, stable home life. You can't be hanging out in bars and nightclubs all the time, drinking and smoking and chasing chicks. But I could do it. I could give up my bad habits. And you know why? Because I love the game, bro. The sport of golf. The feeling in your hands when you hold the club, and you know for an absolute certainty that you're going to make a perfect shot."

He dismounted from his barstool, amid the whores and thieves and marijuana smoke, with the bats darting overhead and the *taarab* singer wailing. He bent slightly at the knees and addressed an imaginary golf ball with an imaginary golf club. Then he showed me, himself, and anyone else who cared to watch that his golf swing was still a smooth, oiled, precision instrument and remarkably well balanced under the circumstances.

I WAS EAGER to get to a witch doctor and catch a dhow to the mainland. Milan kept promising to make the arrangements, telling me about African time, and spending less and less time sober. Then Ramadan started. It was forbidden for Muslims to eat, drink, or smoke between dawn and seven in the evening, and anyone who did so in public risked being physically attacked. For the believers, the worst of it was not being allowed to drink water, especially for people doing hard physical labor. From my hotel window I could see men working on a roof across the street, lifting, carrying, hammering, climbing ladders made from mangrove poles, exposed all day to the full force of the sun. Just wandering the half-deserted, newly sullen streets and taking notes, I was getting through two liters of water a day, and careful to drink it only in my hotel.

People were on edge. They were hungry, thirsty, tired from waking up in the middle of the night to eat the big meal of the day. Tempers frayed and religious intolerance increased. Someone threw a rock through the window of the liquor store, even though it kept itself shuttered between dawn and dusk, and someone buying alcohol there had acid thrown in his face. The main tactic for getting through Ramadan was to conserve energy and do as little as possible, and this meant that less money was circulating through the local economy, adding a further layer of stress.

The local bars and nightclubs closed down for the month, with the lone exception of Milan's local dive, which turned into a kind of last chance saloon for the sporting life in Stone Town. In deference to Ramadan, the owners turned the sound system off for a month, so the patrons listened instead to music on their phones, which they propped up on the white plastic tables among the beer bottles and ashtrays.

Ali the professional thief was in there every day. He was allowing himself joints and cigarettes before sundown, but no food, and he was denying himself beer for the whole month. "Ramadan is very hard," he said to me one night. "A month is too long to go without beer."

"I agree."

"The prophet says you should never drink alcohol. But I cannot do this."

"Neither can I."

"But you are not a Muslim."

"True."

"So give me money. This is Muslim place. Give me five thousand."

"No, I will not insult you that way. For me, a thief is better than a beggar."

"But you are white man. You have big plenty money, and I am poor. Why won't you share with me?"

"Maybe later. I have important business to discuss now with my friend."

Aside from the tourist places, there was only one restaurant open for lunch, and that was at the Anglican church erected on the site of the old slave market. A dark, cramped, underground slave chamber had been preserved there with the original chains, and it seldom failed to creep out a visitor. The golf pro and I would eat lunch in the adjoining cafeteria, alongside Christian converts in slacks and button-up shirts and Masais in red tartan robes.

FINALLY MILAN FOUND a taxi driver named Omar who knew a reputable witch doctor, and after protracted haggling, he agreed to take us there in his limping, groaning, sputtering, clattering taxi. Emerging from the labyrinth, we went down a broad avenue lined with big shady trees and bustling market stalls, and turned off onto a humped and pitted dirt road that ran out to the ragged, rural fringes of Stone Town. There were half-built, one-room, concrete-block houses by the side of the road, and it was hard to tell if they were more likely to achieve completion or fall into ruin. Small boys with stern faces kept the cows and goats away from the maize and cassava patches.

The road ended at an insurmountable pothole surrounded by weedy hummocks of concrete rubble. The three of us got out of the taxi and went on by foot, flanked by small children and toddlers sucking their fingers, and following an old man in a wide-lapeled suit jacket fraying at the seams who had appointed himself as our guide and was expecting a fee for his services. It was late morning. The air was still and heavy, with a metallic whine of insects, a bleating goat in the distance. Sweat ran down between my shoulder blades.

The witch doctor was a woman in her mid-thirties, barefoot and wrapped in *kangas*. She was beautiful, quizzical, and slightly unnerved to have three strange men at her doorstep, especially with one of them so tall and white. She had perfect teeth. Her eyes were a deep luscious chestnut color, and they had a hazy, faraway look. Her two young daughters scampered past her, and she smiled with unrestrained delight. Her husband was at a funeral, she said. Her name, if I wrote it down with the correct spelling, was Kame Musa.

She invited us into her one-room house. There was a thin mattress on the floor, a mosquito net attached with ropes to the walls, and plastic bead necklaces hanging from the ropes. Small glass and plastic medicine bottles were loosely arranged in groupings on the floor. A short, three-legged stool was covered with a white cloth and draped with strings of beads.

We sat down cross-legged on flattened-out cardboard boxes and leaned our backs against the roughness of the concrete-block wall. After the greetings, Milan said in Swahili that I was going on a long journey. First there would be an ocean crossing by dhow to the mainland. Later I would go down a long river in the far west, then up through Burundi and Rwanda, where I hoped to meet a very important man. We would like to know if the omens were favorable for this journey, and anything else the spirits could tell her.

She replied by saying it was Ramadan, and we should understand this. She said it to Omar, who repeated it in Swahili to Milan, who gave the translation to me in a low voice. Normally, she explained, she would sit on the stool, cover her head with the white cloth, and the spirits would enter her and talk through her mouth. This was not possible during Ramadan, because the spirits were too busy. Nor would she be able to see as deeply inside me.

I took it for a polite refusal and suggested we leave. Milan persisted. What could she tell us about the journey? He told her I suffered from insomnia, which was true, and was there anything she could do about that?

"The spirits can come close to me," she said. "They can give me signs and tell me things, but they cannot enter me." We said this would be fine. She sent off one of her daughters to fetch a root for insomnia, and she took some dried saffron from her stores and made up a protective liquid in a tiny medicine bottle. Then she let out a long deep breath and looked me in the eyes for the first time. She closed her eyes for a minute, then opened them slowly and began talking to Omar.

She said the journey would go very well. Men who might do me harm would be afraid of me, and know that I am protected. Normally she saw both black and white in a person's future, but for me she saw only white, and this was very good. The journey would be very long, and I would succeed in my aims.

"What are my aims?" I asked.

"To set your mind at rest," she replied. "It is too busy. This is why you are always traveling. This is why you don't sleep well. Someone in your family has too many worries. Do you have a younger brother?"

"No."

"Then it is you. You must stop worrying. The river will be fine. Everything is good."

I asked how she became a *mganga*, a witch doctor. She said the spirits first arrived when she was fifteen. They sat down around her, and she wasn't frightened because they were in charge. A sick man came to her soon afterward. The spirits told her what to do, and he was healed. Then she married a witch doctor and learned more.

I asked her about the difference between sorcerers and witch doctors. Sorcerers made bad things happen to people, she said, and the job of witch doctors was to counteract their influence, and make good things happen.

All in all, it was a soothing, flattering, extremely pleasant experience. Here was this lovely woman telling me that everything would be fine. She went on to say that my financial situation would improve, and I would marry my girlfriend. Would there be a child? She said I was fertile, but she would have to meet the woman to say.

"Anything else?" I asked.

"Yes," she said. "There will be many more journeys in your future."

We said our thanks, and Milan asked how much it cost. She said that was up to us, whatever we thought it was worth, and I gave her the equivalent of fifteen dollars. Nothing she said astonished me, and I had the feeling that she didn't want to say anything bad or discouraging to the big, strange, white man in her house. But she had read me well, interpreted wisely from the questions asked and the fact that I had come to see her in the first place. She seemed honest and genuine, and I wondered if basic human intuition could manifest itself in a person's mind as messages from the spirits. I thought it probably could, especially in Africa, where the universe is so magical and spirit haunted.

Walking back to Omar's taxi, I felt very calm and satisfied. I had my root for insomnia and my protective saffron water to keep me safe. Intellectually, I thought it was nonsense, but emotionally I couldn't help feeling reassured. Luck exists, and so does the urge to influence it. Science can't explain everything, and as children we all believed in a magical universe. It made sense to us, and we drew comfort from it, and this is one reason why religion/spirituality/magical thinking will never go away. Would I dab on the saffron water? It couldn't do any harm. What if something went wrong and I hadn't dabbed it on? But the moment I had that thought, I had set my foot on the road that leads to Popo Bawa. So I decided to throw the saffron water away and keep my faith in rationality instead. And I would lie to Milan about this, assure him that I complied with the witch doctor's instructions. Otherwise there was no way he would get on a dhow with me. For him, that would be running a crazy risk.

Milan said he would go to the docks in the morning and find us a dhow captain. He was satisfied with the omens, but he thought it was a shame about Ramadan. I would have got a better show without it, with the full trance and the weird voices coming out of her mouth. The last witch doctor he went to see, in Tanga on the mainland coast, pulled out a razor blade and slashed a chicken with it, to see if it died on its back, which was bad, or on its side, which was good.

"And how did the chicken die?" I asked.

"On its side, bro. It was all good, but there was something I had to be careful of. Indulgence, self-indulgence, something like that."

3

Lay Down Your Heart

**The crossing—Burton's hubris—The perfidy of Speke—
Bagamoyo—Money—A Texan—Shitting in the Fridge—
Dar es Salaam—Slum economics—Gin party—Farewell**

THREE DAYS WENT BY with no progress. I was losing faith in
my trusty golf pro and his ability to get me onto a dhow. The
problem, perversely, was money. The man from the mainland
had finally appeared and Milan now had some of his own. The
first thing he bought was a new iron for his clothes, then a big
bag of *halwa*, a sweet, brown, gelatinous treat much favored for
breaking the daily Ramadan fast, which he gave out to every
member of the staff at Livingstone's.

He bought me a secondhand golf shirt, an elephant-charm
necklace, and a new phone to replace the one that drowned in
my trouser pocket during a torrential rainstorm. He loaded up
his own phone with credit, passed it around to his Masai and
junkie friends, and encouraged them to call their mothers. He
bought them food. Then he went on a bender for forty-eight
hours, slipping over into the dark, shadow self that waited for
him at the bottom of the twelfth or thirteenth beer and kept
him drinking after that.

He turned up at my hotel on the morning of the fourth day,
looking terrible, penniless, and carrying a small blue shoulder

bag. "I need five grand for a quick beer and some smokes," he croaked. "Then we go. The captain says it's six to eight hours to Bagamoyo, so bring water and something to bite on."

Wending our way through the labyrinth to the docks, I was excited to be going, nervous about capsizing in a storm, and bittersweet about leaving Stone Town. I had found it constantly stimulating, and part of me wanted to rent a room in a crumbling old Arab mansion, learn Swahili, read the Koran, make and deepen friendships, and peel back the layers of mystery that enshroud this complex, wary, concealing place. Some other time perhaps, if my curiosity ever divorced itself from my restlessness.

At the entrance to the docks, two uniformed officials stood by an open gate, with crowds of people streaming in and out and a chaotic traffic jam of handcarts, donkey carts, and trucks. We tried to blend ourselves into the inflowing stream, and the officials pounced on us immediately. They called us into a small office with scratched plastic windows and an old typewriter on a battered table. Milan, despite the dire ravages of his hangover, instantly transformed himself into a model of supplicating charm and deferential good humor. He was calm, confident, and respectful, and he spoke in soft and soothing tones. At one point in his patter, he asked me casually in English for five thousand shillings, took the banknote, and passed it into the hand of one of the officials, with a smooth and unfurtive motion, and we were waved on our way with good wishes.

"Five dollars," I said. "That's actually a good deal."

"That's right, bro. A five-dollar bribe will get you a long way in Africa, and don't give it to the man like you're buying weed or something. He's doing you a service. You're giving him a tip. I don't like it though. I get sick of the bloody corruption, but what can you do? It's the system, bro. Learn to live with it."

Our dhow was moored behind two others at a stone dock that smelled of old fish and was stacked up with coils of rope, barrels of diesel, fishing nets, rusty refrigerators, all manner of boxes and crates, and seven big nightclub speakers wrapped in plastic. We sat down with a few other passengers, all Zanzibaris, on a long mangrove pole that served as a bench, and the captain came over to take our money. He was a big, hearty, bearded man wearing a faded red T-shirt and threadbare basketball shorts, and he said it would be twenty dollars each to take us to Bagamoyo. I paid him the money and Milan asked how much he charged the local passengers.

"For them, it is four dollars," he said with a laugh. "You are very welcome on our dhow."

Then he busied himself yelling at the crew and the dock hands, who were carrying the nightclub speakers along a series of greasy, wobbly gangplanks that joined the dock to the first swaying dhow, the dhow behind it, and our dhow with open water behind it. I was studying this operation and trying to fend off a sense of dread about walking those planks under the weight of my backpack, when Milan nudged me. A Tanzanian police officer in a crisp tan uniform was walking confidently toward us, twirling his swagger stick.

He asked in Swahili what we were doing here, and the golf pro, again with that wonderful calm confidence, explained that we were catching the dhow to Bagamoyo with these other passengers, that we had paid the captain and paid the necessary fee to the port officials.

"So where is your permit?" asked the officer.

"They didn't give us a permit."

"You cannot go without a permit."

Milan went off to get the permits from the officials we had bribed. I slipped him another twenty thousand. The police officer gave me a threatening smile, and I sat hunkered low on the mangrove pole with my backpack between my legs, thinking, "Here it comes."

He started asking me questions in broken English about laws and permits and what I was doing here. In a calm friendly manner, I told him about the in-flight magazine, the friendship of the president's son, the fact that I was promoting tourism on the island, and that nowhere else in the world had I found such fine people. He sat down next to me on the mangrove pole. To my great surprise, he said I was most welcome and please come back soon. There would be no problem so long as my friend came back with the permits correctly stamped.

Milan came back with the permits. They were correctly stamped, and there was no change from the twenty thousand. I shook hands with the police officer and he wished us a safe voyage. The crew took my backpack, and I followed them across the wobbly planks to the dhow, where the captain pointed at my feet. "Must take off *bootsi*," he said. Was it a question of Islamic etiquette? Was the dhow like his home?

"No, no," he said. He made a slipping motion with his hands, and immediately afterward, as I took a half step forward, my rubber-soled boots shot out from under me, and I sat down with a hard thud. I took off my boots and, sure enough, bare feet were able to get a good purchase on the wet greasy wooden deck.

The dhow smelled of diesel and bilge and cigarettes. The high-spirited six-man crew yelled and laughed with a hoarse bellowing exuberance. Everything was uttered at top volume, presumably because they were so accustomed to shouting over the noise of the wind.

They untied the ropes and detached the gangplanks. The captain started up the engine to chug us away from the docks, and then he turned it off because diesel is expensive, and the wind is free. The crew leapt around athletically, unfurling the big, patched, lateen sail, warning us when the boom swung over our heads, then gathering back on the helm to smoke and laugh and yell. A steady breeze filled the sail and took us out past white sand spits and tiny islands, through patches of turquoise, ultramarine, jade, emerald, and out with a gentle rocking and swaying into the sapphire waters of the deep ocean.

I slathered on the sunblock, pulled my hat down low, leaned back against the curved wooden sides of the dhow, and experienced another moment of traveler's bliss. Then writerly curiosity started nagging at me. What were the sailors bellowing to each other that made them laugh so loudly? For the thousandth time, I yearned for a tenth of Burton's linguistic abilities. I had picked up a little Swahili. I knew the basic phrasebook stuff, and also that a bank was a *benki* and a roundabout was a *keepilefti*. Most Swahili nouns ended in "i" and borrowed English words were given the same treatment, hence the captain's *bootsi*. When an item on a restaurant menu was unavailable, it was often *sold-outi*. And the wealthy elite and corrupt politicians were known as the *benzi*, because they all seemed to drive Mercedes-Benz cars.

Milan was lying down with his eyes closed, but I pestered him to translate. What were they yelling and laughing about? "It's nothing, man, just blah-blah-blah. This guy is saying he had a wet dream last night. This guy is saying he doesn't want to share any of the money from the trip with the dhow's owner. This guy is saying he is broke and wants a woman. Just bullshit, bro. Now it's time for me to get some shut-eye."

I lay down too, dozing and daydreaming there under the fraying edge of the lateen sail, broiled by the sun and cooled by the fine salt spray rising off the bow, thinking about Burton and Speke crossing these waters in an old navy frigate with their servants, gun carriers, Baluchi mercenaries, and an immense quantity of supplies and equipment. Burton spent most of the voyage writing, finishing up his thousand-page report on Zanzibar and a magazine piece on the same subject.

"THE GREATEST MIND of his generation," as some called Burton, was a fiercely ambitious man who craved the acclaim and honors his extraordinary talents merited, but he was also a natural-born rebel and iconoclast, a sarcastic and cynical wit who loved to skewer Victorian sensibilities, and he was absolutely incapable of deferring to his superiors, or toning down his opinions, when he thought they were wrong. And of course the fact that Burton was nearly always right only made things worse for him. All his life he worked for the British government, as a soldier, explorer, and later as a consul, but surprise, surprise, he never got the promotions he was expecting. He was dogged instead by smear campaigns, backstabbed by enemies in high places, and followed by a persistent rumor that he was a homosexual at a time when this was considered gross moral turpitude.

Burton was certainly interested in homosexuality, and may have tried it out. In India, his commanding officer sent him in native disguise into a local brothel where teenage boys and eunuchs were for hire, to make sure no British soldiers had disgraced themselves in there. Once inside, Burton clicked into his observer anthropologist mode and wrote a far longer and more detailed report than his officer was expecting. Boys were twice the price of eunuchs, he wrote, because "the scrotum of the unmutilated boy could be used as a kind of bridle for directing [his] movements . . ." This report, which was supposed to be secret but subsequently leaked, provided fuel for Burton's enemies for the rest of his life.

For all his shrewdness and love of provocation, Burton was often taken aback by his ability to make enemies and the strength of their hatred for him. A case in point was John Hanning Speke, his tall, fair-haired protégé and second-in-command. Burton had no idea that Speke had already been whispering and scheming against him in Zanzibar, and denouncing him viciously in his letters back home, casting doubt on his journeys to Mecca and Harar, and describing him as a "rotten person." It's strange to think that we know this now, but Burton didn't realize it at the time.

On the outside, Speke was all smooth charm and youthful deference. There was an air of innocence and openness about him that was entirely deceiving. Underneath it lay arrogance and a prickly sense of entitlement, "an overweening vanity and pettiness," in Mary Lovell's words, that was bottling up every little grievance, resentment, and perceived insult and distilling them into poison.

Speke's grudges began accumulating in Somalia, when he felt that Burton hadn't shown him enough respect, or given him enough responsibility, and he particularly resented the fact that Burton had rewritten his journal and included it as an appendix to his own book about the expedition. There was also jealousy at work and inflamed morality. The prurient, priggish Speke was disgusted by Burton's open sexual interest in the native women. Speke wrote of "blackguard conduct," but Burton's own writing leaves it fairly clear what he was up to. Here he is among the Galla people, investigating vaginal muscles: "a woman can exert them so as to cause pain to a man, and, when sitting on his thighs, she can induce the orgasm without moving any other part of her person."

Now Burton was engaged to a very proper Englishwoman called Isabel Arundel, the daughter of an old, aristocratic family of English Catholics. Much to her mother's disgust, she had been swept up in a great romantic passion for the dashing, disreputable, agnostic, and almost penniless Burton, and it had begun the moment she first laid eyes on him as a schoolgirl. Six years later he proposed marriage, she accepted swooningly, and they kissed for the first time. A few weeks later, he set sail for Zanzibar, wearing her good luck charm on a silver chain around his neck. Isabel had wanted the talisman on a gold chain, but Burton said no. "They will cut my throat for it out there."

He hadn't said good-bye to her before leaving, because he had a morbid horror of saying good-bye to people he loved or cared about. His hands would tremble and he would break down weeping. Good-byes unmanned him completely, so he made a lifelong habit of slipping away without saying a word. He left Isabel a note explaining how painful it was and estimating that they would be together again in two or three years. She folded up the note, put it in a small pouch, and wore it around her neck until his return. Earlier he had given her an Arabic motto in Arabic script, which she kept next to her heart. Years later she had it translated and discovered what it said: "Consult women, and do the contrary." This was typical Burton, sarcastic and irreverent, and she saw it for what it was: a joke, not an insult.

THE WINDS PICKED UP, the sea roughened, and the dhow began a heavy, creaking pitch and roll. To counteract seasickness, I stood up and kept my gaze fixed on the far horizon, where a pale suggestion of land was just becoming discernible. The golf pro stood up too, for the same reason, but the other passengers continued to lie down and soon all of them were vomiting, some of them over the side, others down into the bilge. One woman stayed lying down, vomited into the *kanga* covering her head, bundled it up, wrapped another *kanga* around her head, and vomited into that one too, curling into a smaller ball of misery, while the ragtag crew laughed and mocked their seasick passengers and bellowed to each other with wide grins.

A humpback whale breached a hundred yards to starboard, and for the next twenty minutes we sailed parallel to the great beast as it breached and dove, breached and dove. Then flying fish appeared. The swells grew and the troughs deepened, and great slabs of water crashed and broke over the leaky old dhow. The crew busied themselves with bailing buckets, and slowly slowly slowly, as I fought back the fear and nausea, the pale strip of land became more distinct, until one could make out the difference between the white beach and the low green hills of mainland Africa.

The harbor at Bagamoyo is so shallow that we dropped anchor two hundred yards from shore. Men in their underwear waded out to meet us, pulling little skiffs behind them. One by one, with lots of shouting and jockeying for position, the passengers were lifted down into the skiffs with their bags, and the men towed them into shore. The seasick woman went first, and we went last with the captain and two of his sailors, who were panicky and alarmed that the flimsy little skiff was going to overturn and dump us in four feet of water. "Phones," explained the golf pro. "They're worried about their phones."

Bagamoyo had a harsh, sullen, dusty feel. Some NGO had got funding for an art project, and there were big, strange sculptures of heads by the side of the road from the trash-strewn harbor into the town. The young men hanging around with nothing to do looked markedly more aggressive and predatory than their counterparts in Zanzibar. "It's the mainland, bro," said the golf pro. "In Zanzibar they'll steal what you have. Here, they'll stab you for it."

One of the sailors became concerned for us. His name was Ali. He was in his early twenties, with a missing front tooth, and he turned quietly soft-spoken in the company of strangers. He said he would take us to a nice guesthouse he knew and show us around the town tomorrow. It was understood without saying that I would pay him some money for this service. "You must be careful here as a *muzungu,*" he said. "There are bad people. You must not walk at night. You must be careful on the beach. Tourists have been robbed and killed."

We walked into town along a dusty street lined with market stalls. Synthesized *taarab* and *bongo flava* came out of blown, fuzzed-out speakers, big crows hopped through the trash piles, and every human eye followed our progress solemnly. The vendors were selling brightly colored household items, toys, trinkets, flip-flops, all made out of the cheapest, flimsiest, crappiest Chinese plastic imaginable, surely designed to break soon after purchase. "If it's cheap and brightly colored, people will buy it," said Milan. "They own it for a week and it falls apart. Oh well, it didn't cost much. When they get money again, they buy another one."

Ali rapped his knuckles on the steel gates of a small guesthouse, or *gesti.* (A *hoteli,* confusingly, is a restaurant.) "They are good people in this place," said Ali. "No one will rob you here." The *askari,* or security guard/nightwatchman, came forward and let us into the front courtyard.

We stepped inside the building and stood by the check-in desk. Two large women shuffled toward us in flip-flops along a dark, narrow, low-ceilinged corridor. They smiled and told us we were welcome. The rooms were six dollars apiece. They were small and hot with grimy, pitted floors and clean lumpy beds. The mosquito nets were more or less intact. In the bathroom, I found no toilet, showerhead, tub, sink, or mirror. So what qualified it as a bathroom? A hole in the tiled floor and a plastic bucket of water. You could piss and shit in the hole, and pour cold water over yourself while standing above it. I was feeling beat down from the sun and the wind and the voyage, and the golf pro was shattered with exhaustion. We collapsed into our beds, and Ali went on to another guesthouse that he said was cheaper but not so nice, and not as safe as he would like.

WE MET HIM in the morning for a proper Tanzanian breakfast: chai tea with milk and spices, a greasy chapati, and a bowl of beef soup that requires strong jaw muscles and firmly rooted teeth. The traditional recipe calls for large chunks of beef containing plenty of gristle, fat, sinew, and bone, and they are boiled in plain water for half an hour or so, keeping the meat as tough as it can possibly be. Milan and I ate ours with scorching nibbles of fresh habanero peppers, known here as goat chillies, while Ali explained the cruel economics of the seafaring life.

The dhows were still built by hand, and they cost about $6,000 new. The owners of the dhows, the men with capital, made the rules of the business, and the sailors had no choice but to accept their terms—there is almost never a labor shortage in Africa. The captain and the crew had to pay 50 percent of their earnings to the owner and share the rest among the seven of them, with a slightly larger share going to the captain. It was possible to hit a real bonanza if you could catch a tuna—a large one brought $20,000—but the tuna were disappearing rapidly, and someone had stolen their fishing line some months ago, and they couldn't afford to buy another one.

So they were reduced to ferrying goods and passengers, and here the problem was a shortage of business and too much competition from other dhows and their crews. On this last voyage, the only cargo they could find was the seven nightclub speakers, for which they earned fourteen dollars, plus four dollars each from the six Zanzibari passengers. It was my forty dollars that had made their trip worthwhile. Ali's share of the take was four dollars, enough to eat for two days. "Today and tomorrow we look for cargo to take back to Zanzibar," he said. "I hope we will find some. If not, we go back empty, because we have no money to stay longer."

It felt good to give ten dollars, rather than the agreed six, to this kind, helpful young man for taking us to the *gesti* and telling us about the dhow trade. But during my time in East Africa, I gave nothing to the many hundreds of people who asked me for money and offered nothing in return. Often it came as a shouted demand for something I owed them, "Eh, *muzungu*, give me my money!"

"No," I would say. "It's my money."

"Give me money. You are *muzungu*."

Small boys shout the same words in higher-pitched voices, and when you ask them why, they point to their mouths with bunched fingers, indicating that they're hungry. I would give people money if they gave me directions, or gave me their time, or showed me where they lived, or told me about their lives, but not to the outstretched hands or the shouted demands. I thought Africa was doomed if its children learned that white people would always give them money.

Another thing you hear from small boys is "*Muzungu! Muzungu!* Give me my plastic!" This is not a request for your credit card. They know that white people always have plastic water bottles, and they want your empties. These I would give happily, in the spirit of recycling a useful tool.

If you think America is obsessed with money, as I used to, try Africa. I've never been anywhere like it for money-hunger, money-fixation, grasping haggling fervent desire for money, money, money, and this extraordinary sense of entitlement to the money I had. For a *muzungu*, not only is it possible to buy genuine, meaningful friendship in Africa, but if the African is poor, real friendship is virtually impossible without a transfer of money. If you who have so much will not give some to your friend who has so little, how can you call yourself his friend? Communal sharing is a deeply ingrained concept here, as fundamental and unquestioned as individualism in the West. If an African has money, he is supposed to share it out to his friends and extended family, and there are social penalties if he doesn't.

Is all this simply because Africa is poorer than anywhere else in the world? I don't think so. In other parts of what we used to call the Third World, I have met desperately poor people who have refused my money out of a sense of pride and hospitality. It's almost impossible to imagine a poor African refusing to take your money, or accepting it grudgingly, and then slipping it back into your bag, or your jacket pocket, while you're sleeping on the dirt floor of his shack, as happened to me several times in rural Mexico.

No doubt the experience of colonialism has also left Africans with a sense of entitlement to the white man's money, and forty years of aid has surely solidified it. But the handout culture goes deeper than that. In many African tribal societies, people were ruled by paternalistic kings and chiefs who hoarded the wealth and kept the social bonds in place by giving out gifts. White colonialists operated a similar system, and in several African countries after independence, politicians used to walk down the streets handing out banknotes, not simply to buy votes, but to show that they understood their chiefly obligations to provide. One way and another, those who've got are expected to give.

THE WORD *BAGAMOYO* means "lay down your heart." To the slaves who trudged across the endless plains of present-day Tanzania toward the ocean, often chained at the neck and car-

rying elephant tusks, or yoked across the shoulders with heavy
wooden "slave-tamers," the sight of Bagamoyo meant slave
dhows and the end of their last hopes of ever returning to their
home villages. They laid down their hearts in sorrow.

For the slave-drivers, who walked alongside their captives
all day and chewed the bitter cola nut to stay awake at night, to
make sure their chattel didn't escape, and for the professional
porters who carried the caravan's trade goods and supplies on
their heads, the word *Bagamoyo* had an entirely different meaning. Finally, they could lay down the burdens of their hearts
and rest, relax, throw off their cares. As they smelled the sea air
and approached the town, the porters would sing a joyful song:

> *There the women wear their hair parted*
> *You can drink palm wine all year round in the garden of love*
> *Bagamoyo!*
> *The dhows arrive with streaming sails*
> *And take aboard the treasures in the harbor in Bagamoyo*
> *Oh, what a delight to see the drums*
> *Where the lovely girls are swaying in dance at night in*
>   *Bagamoyo*
> *Be quiet, my heart, all worries are gone*
> *The drum beats and with rejoicing*
> *We are reaching Bagamoyo*

The three museums of Bagamoyo were cool, quiet, and agree-
ably ramshackle. Each came equipped with a proud young guide
who would deliver a short, well-informed lecture about each
and every exhibit in passable English. At the old caravanse-
rai, where slavers and porters would stay before and after their
journeys, the guide explained how slaves were first obtained.
The slave traders very seldom went to the trouble of capturing people, because there was no need. The local chiefs had

monopolized that end of the business, raiding other tribes for captives to sell and in many instances, selling their own people.

"The chief sell them for metal objects, yes. Trays and plates and teapotsi. Also guns and powder. Yes. And many beads and cloth. When they collecti slaves from different areas, they bring them all to Bagamoyo, and then Zanzibar, yes. From Ujiji and Lake Tanganyika region, it was sixi month to pass through here by the legsi."

Around Bagamoyo and the coastal areas, it was common for people to sell their nephews, cousins, and even their brothers and sisters into slavery. "Oh, sir, it was terrible. Your relative ask you for your childi to help with cattle or fieldi work, and the childi never come back. Your very good friends invite you into their house, and you are capturedi."

Even cynical, unshockable Burton was taken aback by the greedy eagerness of the coastal chiefs to sell their own people. Near the Usumbura Hills, just north of Bagamoyo, he met a chief called Sultan Mamba. "He stated that his people had but three wants—powder, ball and brandy, and that they could supply in return three things—men, women, and children." King Kimwere, an Islamic convert who called himself "Lion of the Land," had three hundred wives, each with her own retinue of slaves, and he had achieved his prosperity entirely by selling his subjects. When human beings are the most valuable commodities around, and demand for them is high, market forces would appear to trump social bonds, family bonds, and just about everything else.

What were the after-effects of the slave trade in East Africa? For many years it was very difficult for boys to marry if they were descended from slaves, although no problem for girls. Agriculture and manual labor are still despised and avoided on the coast because of the association with slavery, and this has not been helpful in reducing poverty or hunger. Are there lingering psychological effects? Perhaps a shortage of compassion and kindness for one's fellow human beings? There was certainly less of these qualities in evidence than I was used to. Reading about Africa in books and newspapers, I was consistently shocked and appalled by the levels of callousness and cruelty. But factoring in colonialism, poverty, disease, climate, and everything else that has contributed to the harshness of African lives, trying to measure the ripples of the slave trade seems like a dubious exercise, and Africans certainly don't like to look back in that direction.

At the Holy Ghost Catholic Mission museum, there were photographs of slave caravans. Gaunt bewildered African faces and proud, strutting, bearded slavers in long white robes. Another photograph showed an elephant tusk so huge it required four men to carry it. You don't see tusks like that on elephants anymore. The biggest bulls were hunted out first, because their tusks were most valuable, and this allowed the smaller bulls to breed and pass on their genes into the rapidly dwindling herds. The great ivory boom of the mid-nineteenth century was driven by the demand in industrializing Europe for combs, piano keys, and billiard balls. It ended because there were so few elephants left within a thousand miles of Bagamoyo.

Next to the ivory display was a small exhibit on wizards. In a glass-fronted case, there was a whistle-horn for summoning genies, a handheld whisk for thrashing genies or Satan, and a mirror of highly polished wood in which a "doctor" can make the image of his enemy wizard appear. A placard gave a basic introduction to wizard behavior:

> Wizards like acting by night: they go around on a winnowing tray. They like very much places where is a misfortune, especially a dead person. They go there, calling each other with various signals eg. the very distressing cries of a cat.

Also by imitating the sound of a mortar and pestle. They harass sleeping people so these people awake very tired. Wizards disgrace corpses laid in houses, or also corpses already buried, unearthing them with their tricks.

The golf pro read this with keen interest. He had often wondered why people became so distressed when they heard cats yowling at night and covered their ears against the sound. Now he knew. For me it was further proof that human beings can make themselves believe anything at all, but I kept my atheism to myself, like a dirty little secret.

WALKING BACK through the town, Milan's European side came to the fore. He was appalled by the collapsing colonial buildings, erected by the Germans and the British during their turns at ruling Tanzania, and the general air of decay, disrepair, and listlessness. He took particular exception to the marauding gangs of crows. "Horrible bloody birds," he said. "They wipe out all the chicken eggs, the songbirds, even eagles. There used to be a bounty on crows. All these buildings were kept up, man. Now look. Crows are the only birds here now."

I found it amazing that he could know Africa as well as he did and fail to accept that things were slow and inefficient here, that people didn't care about punctuality, that problems were mounting faster than they were getting solved. Maybe it was easier for me to accept these things because I didn't love Africa, or feel African like he did. I didn't have any hope invested here, or remember it when things were better. At this stage of my journey, I was fully occupied just trying to observe and understand. Annoyance, exasperation, rage, and despair would come later, along with love, terror, and a strange kind of hope, but all that was still a long way down the road.

We walked down to the harbor past phone shacks and market stalls, crumbling stone buildings and graffitied walls, a group of men getting barbered under a big spreading shade tree. A Norwegian NGO had got funding to come here and teach dance of all things, and we passed several lissom young Norwegians strolling with their dreadlocked boyfriends.

I was hungry but depressed by the prospect of *ugali*, the plasticene-like corn paste upon which most Tanzanians subsist, and the ubiquitous soggy fries known as *chipsi*. I was the perfect mark for a sign in English reading Smoke House Store, Best Hamburger in Bagamoyo. The staff wore matching yellow T-shirts and the owner was a retired oil man from deep south Texas called Walton Davies. He had been all over the world and met his seventh wife in Dar es Salaam. She was about half his age, with multicolored dreadlocks twisted up together into a sprouting ball, and seemed like a very confident and capable woman. They had two daughters, and the older one, who was eight, would help out Walton when something needed translating. In three years in Tanzania, he had learned almost no Swahili.

He had a solid, unflappable country charm and one of those accents that makes oil business into "awl bidness" and barbed wire into "bob whorr." When he bought his land three years ago, it was in the bush outside Bagamoyo with plenty of peace and quiet. The electricity company brought a line out there. Then people started showing up and chopping down the trees, and now he lives in the middle of a fast-expanding African village. He built walls around his compound because he was getting "stole blind," but it hadn't really worked. His own employees and workmen would steal his tools and building supplies, and when he let in the local children to play with his daughters, they would stuff DVDs and other items into their shorts before leaving.

"Thangs are a li'l different here," he said. "I got rid of my watch because nothing runs on time. Work ethic is different. The kids are a bunch of li'l outlaws. They got no morals. Ain't raised up to have them. But I like it. I've done trial and error on my wives, and I think I've got a good one this time. My daughters are just great. Got me a li'l ole pineapple farm, and the Smoke House here. It's the best burger in Bagamoyo and we like to think maybe East Africa."

It was a little greasy for me, but I would remember it fondly in western Tanzania. While I was talking to Walton, Milan met a German traveler called Frank who was staying in our guest house and had been in Bagamoyo for months. He was in his early forties, ex–music business, big, blond, and extrovert, and full of enthusiasm about Africa. That night we went out bar-hopping with him.

There's a simple technique for getting around places like Bagamoyo at night, where it's unsafe for a *muzungu* to be on foot after dark. In daylight, you approach the driver of a *bajaj*, a little three-wheel tuk-tuk taxi, and you get his phone number. You call him later and if he gets you to your first destination at a fair price, you call him again every time you want to change location. Then, when he starts showing up late and haggling for more money, you ditch him and find a new driver.

We started out at Hill Side, a nice outdoor place with a lawn and an attentive manager called William in a spotless white shirt and tie. English Premier League was playing on a big screen, and the well-dressed elite of Bagamoyo were eating grilled beef and goat meat and washing it down with beers and cocktails. The kitchen must have been running low on goat meat, because a waiter went off and came back a few minutes later with a recalcitrant goat on a rope and dragged it screaming across the lawn to the kitchen door.

Frank was drinking Konyagi, the gin-like rum, which came in small plastic bags that the waiter cut open with scissors. "Are you spiritual?" he asked me. "Do you have a religion?"

"Not really," I told him.

He nodded. "I'm very spiritual," he said. "I believe that shit. But let me ask you this: do you have a moral code?"

"Yes."

"I can see this. I know Englishmen. And maybe this comes from education or your upbringing or whatever. But if you tell Africans you have no religion, they will be disturbed, because they will think you have no moral code. You must lie about this if they ask you."

Frank described himself as "obsessed" with Africa. He had spent years traveling the continent. He had learned African languages, made deep friendships with Africans, and had many relationships with African women. He wanted to marry an African wife, partly because he hated the rules and schedules that European mothers impose on their children. When he first started traveling in Africa, he assumed that Africans were more or less the same as him, with a few minor cultural differences, but sharing the same universal values.

"In Europe, it is more or less racist not to believe this. But the more I traveled, and the more Africans I got to know well, especially in their languages, the more I understood that the way they think and look at the world is *completely* different. Now I am at the point where I think I will never work out exactly what Africa is. And I cannot accept this. The basics I know. Sure, all human types are here. This is obvious. And of course you cannot generalize about such a big, diverse continent, but I'm going to generalize anyway. Because there is something you find everywhere, an attitude toward change, toward responsibility, toward community and family. I can't quite put my finger on it, and it's driving me crazy! I mean, look at us. Three men our age without families, being irresponsible. It is common in our culture, but here it is unthinkable."

Frank was collecting material for a book he wanted to write. "I have the title," he said. "The book is called *Shitting in the Fridge*. It's a good one, right? Anyway, it comes from this crazy European I met who lost his mind here with drink, and drugs, and girls, and he would shit in the fridge. Unbelievable! It was a revelation to me! Africa is no longer this hippie travel scene or this exotic Bruce Chatwin Africa. Do you understand? It's shitting in the fridge. European travelers come here now because they are dark and crazy, and they want drugs and prostitutes, no responsibilities of any kind, and they lose their minds here. I see this all over. Even in Yemen, which by the way is my favorite country in Africa. The Islamic culture there is so beautiful, and the prostitutes are incredible. When she takes off the veil, and you realize this is just what her *eyes* are doing to you. Unbelievable!"

He punched me hard on the shoulder and collapsed back in absolute glee. Then he seized my arm and continued. "There are no individualists in Africa. And they don't want change in the same way that Europeans do. Maybe this is to do with the ancestor worship. I don't know. But I go crazy looking at the same menu every night, and they will happily eat *ugali* every day."

I wanted to know Frank's thoughts about aid and NGOs in Africa. I had met an ex-UN worker in Stone Town, a Dutch woman with twenty years' experience in the field, who had delivered the most damning critique of the whole enterprise I had ever heard. She had been in Darfur and was convinced that aid was prolonging the war; it was being sold to buy weapons and ammunition, as it nearly always was in African war zones. She thought aid impeded development and trapped people in poverty by making them dependent on handouts. She was even opposed to medical aid, because overpopulation was such a huge problem, and medical aid enabled people to have more children that they couldn't feed without more aid.

Emergency aid was the only part of it she believed in anymore. But she detested the aid organizations so much that she wouldn't deliver emergency aid on their behalf. Instead she was going to drive a water truck by herself into drought-stricken northern Kenya, where the cattle tribes were raiding and counterraiding each other with AK-47s.

I was still agnostic on the question of aid, but Frank was amazed that I even gave it the benefit of the doubt. "Ultimately it is stupid, to keep pouring money into an idea that obviously doesn't work. It is a failure of intelligence. I understand that people want to help, that is their Christian duty, but they are not helping. We have fucking Norwegians here teaching Africans how to dance! Maybe you can find an aid project that doesn't fall apart when the aid workers leave. I have never seen one. In Ethiopia they have had so much aid that farmers don't want to farm anymore. Why should they work all day in the hot sun when white people will bring them food?"

Milan was bored by this conversation. It had been too long since he had a woman, and he couldn't see any prospects here. He missed his beloved Zanzibar, and he was not looking forward to the battle with dust, smog, traffic, crime, and chaos in Dar es Salaam tomorrow. Frank offered to buy him a whore, but he declined, saying he liked them sweet and innocent.

Our next stop was a raucous dive with pool tables called the Corner Bar, where the new, digital *taarab* was pounding and wailing out of the jukebox. The golf pro had switched from beer to gin in an unsuccessful ploy to boost his mood, and then he lost at pool, which hardly ever happens. Meanwhile I was happily drunk, knuckle-bumping the locals and lighting my first cigarette in seven years. I had been puffing on the occasional joint in Zanzibar, where they mixed the weed with tobacco, and it had reignited my old nicotine addiction. The golf pro, like a true friend, was disgusted and angry to see me smoking. "Give me that," he snapped, and took it away half-smoked.

In the *bajaj* back to the guesthouse, we all swapped phone numbers and made a plan to meet up in Dar in a few days. Frank knew some women there, and he wanted to throw a party.

THE NEXT MORNING—had I really smoked half a cigarette?—one thing was certain: I was not going to Dar es Salaam squeezed into a goddamn *daladala*. We would be taking the most expensive bus available. I assembled my backpack and emerged from my room to find the golf pro paring his toenails with a razor blade in the front courtyard, looking fully alert and focused. "Now when you get to the bus station in Dar, you must really watch it," he said. He raised his eyes and held up the razor blade. "I will walk behind you. Otherwise they will slash your backpack open with one of these, and take what they can before you even know it's happening."

At the Bagamoyo bus station, we bought tickets for a twenty-eight-seater that was battered but perfectly adequate. In the usual African fashion, it left when all its seats were full, not according to any departure time, but the aisles were left free and clear. The driver played concert videos of Congolese music on a DVD player strapped to his sun visor, and not for the first time I marveled at how exuberant the music was coming out of a country where 3, or 5, or 7 million people had died in the last fifteen years because of war. Eastern Congo was so ruined, violent, and chaotic that counting the victims accurately was beyond the capability of the UN or the human rights groups there, which appeared to be manipulating the numbers as hard as they could to attract more funding and attention. But hearing the music, you knew for a solid fact that hope and pride had not died in Congo, or the capacity for joy and happiness.

We were barely out of Bagamoyo before we entered the outlying sprawl of Dar es Salaam, a city whose center was still forty miles away. "None of this was here eight years ago," said Milan. "This was all bush." The population of Tanzania had doubled in the last twenty years, the population of Dar had tripled, and both these numbers were growing faster than ever. Looking out of the bus window, we saw men burning off scrub and hacking down trees with axes, roadside carpenters turning the trees into bed frames, one construction supply yard after another selling breeze blocks, rebar, and concrete, and every half mile or so, another group of forty or fifty women breaking up coral stone with hammers, the bright colors of their *kangas* shining through the pale dust they were raising, while groups of young men sat in the shade doing nothing. Mixing smashed coral with concrete was a cheap way to build a solid house, but it still required some capital. This wasn't going to be a slum or shantytown, but a suburb for people fleeing the increasingly unmanageable urban core.

Dar es Salaam was the biggest city in East Africa, having overtaken Nairobi, which was also growing faster than ever. There were more than 4 million people in Dar now, and 5.2 million were expected by 2020. The economy was booming, but the population had far outrun the infrastructure, and 80 percent of the city's inhabitants were living without electricity, running water, or sanitation. They shat on patches of waste ground, or into plastic bags, which they threw on the hundreds of trash fires that burned around the clock, and the wind whipped the acrid smoke together with the choking clouds of dust and the exhaust fumes from Dar's ever-worsening traffic jams.

Further into the city, we got caught in one. It took the bus an hour to cover a mile and a half. Then we sat there stationary for thirty minutes, watching a murder of thirty crows splashing and enjoying themselves in a filthy puddle from a burst water main.

"They've got to do something," said the golf pro. "Build infrastructure. City planning. Something. This can't go on. This is impossible."

Fifteen years ago, when the world's population was 5 billion and chaotic urban slums were smaller, I used to look at them and wonder when they were going to get fixed, when these people would catch up with the rest of us. For people to be living without running water and electricity in that day and age seemed like an oversight, a glitch in the engine of progress. Now I look at a place like Dar es Salaam and see the future gathering strength. I see a crucible where the skills for the future are being forged and honed.

It won't be like this in the rich, successful countries, but the poor are rapidly outnumbering the rich in this world. With the global population set to increase from 7 billion to 8 billion in the next fifteen years, with resources diminishing inexorably, the climate getting harsher in the parts of the world where most of the poor live, does anyone still seriously believe that slums are a problem that will get fixed? It's true that modern India has been successful in getting people out of its slums, but they fill right back up again with refugees from the overcrowded, desiccating countryside. Africa has been singularly unsuccessful in providing a path out of its slums, mainly because its governing elites have been so single-mindedly focused on enriching themselves, and the fastest growing slums in the world are all in African cities. Populations are growing faster in sub-Saharan Africa than anywhere else in the world, and this is despite the ravages of AIDS, malaria, and other diseases, despite the wars and ethnic slaughters, and the world's highest rates of infant mortality and lowest life expectancies. The population of black Africa, currently 1 billion, is expected to double by 2050, and most of these new Africans will be urban slum-dwellers pioneering new ways of surviving.

THE GOLF PRO had old friends to see and errands to run. He found us some rooms in a friend's house behind steel gates. I dumped my backpack there, agonized about my money belts, and decided to keep them under my clothing. I found a knowledgeable driver with good English to take me through the slums and explain what I was seeing.

The streets and alleys were black with charcoal dust. Charcoal was the cooking fuel of the poor, not helpful for the air quality or the deforestation around the city, but who cares about these abstractions when they're hungry? The charcoal was prepared outside the city, driven in by truck, and distributed through the slums by men with handcarts hammered together from scrap wood and metal.

We passed women sitting on the ground with their wares set out in front of them. One was selling three tomatoes and an orange. Another was selling beef soup from a cooking pot. Another was selling five eggs in a plastic bowl. Why were men hacking at old car radiators with machetes? My driver explained that they were getting out the copper. Recycling copper was a big business here, stripping it out of wires and appliances that richer people had thrown away. Yes, there were prostitutes. Yes, there were thieves and bad men wearing big sneakers, and no, *bwana*, it was not a good idea to get out of the car in this place.

Young men pulled handcarts laden with grimy, yellow plastic containers full of water. We stopped and talked to one out of the car window and offered him money to tell us about his business. He was suspicious. He had deliveries to make. He was out of breath and pouring sweat. Why did this *muzungu* want his name? The driver talked to him for a few minutes in Swahili and translated afterward.

There is a boss with a water tank that he fills from the city water system. The tank is on the edge of the slum, twenty minutes away on foot. The cart man goes there and fills ten containers, because this is all he can pull. On each cart load that he sells, he makes four hundred shillings profit, a little less than fifty cents. He brings in four or five loads a day, so earns about two dollars a day.

I thought about that for a moment. Why only four or five loads a day? Surely it wouldn't take more than an hour to collect and deliver a load. Was it too exhausting to make more than four or five journeys with the heavy cart in the oppressive heat? The driver explained it to me. It was a problem of competition, of surplus labor. There were so many other strong young men with water carts, competing for a finite amount of business. He could easily haul more water, but he couldn't sell it. The market was saturated. The slum was already getting all the water it could afford.

In Burton's day, the unknown regions on this continent were its great interior savannahs, mountain ranges, lakes, and rivers. I had felt called to Africa by a nostalgic impulse to engage with this physical geography and fill a small gap in our understanding of it. But it was becoming increasingly clear to me that the real terra incognita in Africa today was urban and modern, and to explore the human geography of these sprawling, rapidly expanding and evolving slum cities was to make discoveries about the future. If Burton was here today, he would be taking notes in slum brothels and nightclubs, interviewing rappers and bartenders, scrap metal kings, crooked cops and crime bosses.

MY LAST NIGHT with the golf pro was the night of Frank's party. It took place in the small, stuffy, seafood-smelling house of a Zimbabwean woman called Maddy. A cheap plastic fan pushed the warm stale air around, and everyone had a light sheen of sweat on their face. Maddy was about forty, with a broad-hipped sensual grace and heavy-lidded eyes that regarded the world with a weary amusement. She and Frank were spending their last night together before her married American boyfriend arrived in the morning. She had owned a ghetto bar in Dar es Salaam, fallen to the bottle, and seen it all on the way down. Now she was a recovered alcoholic, bored but tolerant of the drunken foreigners making fools of themselves in her living room.

Her younger sister Lisa was there, a born-again Christian who had married the only man she had ever slept with. She was rapping and singing along to her *bongo flava* CDs, which Frank parodied as "I love you so much/No, I love you more . . ." before commandeering the CD player and putting on Isaac Hayes.

Milan had been drinking plastic bags of Konyagi all day and he hadn't eaten. Somehow he had persuaded a young German woman staying at the house to come with him to the party. Her name was Melanie and she worked for the local branch of the Goethe Institute, in the service of some worthy cause or other. She was blonde and prim, wore concealing clothes, no makeup, and no jewelry except a fake wedding band to deter male advances. When she thought Milan's attention was diverted, she whispered to me, "You must be my bodyguard."

Milan heard it and swung around. "She's mine," he snarled at me. He gave her a sinister smile. "I'll put you in a ninja suit and a chastity belt, chain you up so no one else can have you."

"What are you talking about?" she said. "I told you I have a boyfriend. You're so drunk."

"I may be drunk, but I'm not stupid. Don't underestimate me."

She looked at me for help, and I felt like I was trapped inside a Charles Bukowski story set in Africa.

We ate dinner. Frank had cooked pasta and red sauce with seafood, and fried up some meat. Being allergic to seafood, I ate meat. Frank said, "The West is now looking to Africa for answers. This liberal thing we have. We are bored, dissatisfied. We think Africa has can fix the hole inside us. These fucking celebrities with their African babies! Unbelievable shit."

The golf pro said, "Let's get naked and party, party, party."

We finished our plates and went back to drinking. I was on beer, so was Lisa. Frank and the golf pro had already polished off a bottle of Konyagi between them and were into the next one. Maddy cast a sober and heavy-lidded eye across the room. She had such dignity. I tried to engage her in polite conversation with a journalistic undertow. Why had they left Zimbabwe? How was the journey? What were the differences between Zimbabwe and Tanzania?

Maddy looked bored. Lisa sighed. The golf pro was drawing a picture of something on a piece of paper. He finished it and held it up for us to see. It was the female genitalia.

Maddy sighed, stood up, and cleared away the empty bottles. As she turned her hips, the golf pro slapped her hard across the ass. She spun around in a fury. I braced for the slap or blow, but she regained her composure and let out another long sigh. She said, "You remind me of me when I was drinking. I can see you have a problem."

The golf pro dismissed that with a bleary wave of his arm, and Lisa fell off the couch onto the floor and collapsed in helpless laughter. She lay on her back and rolled from side to side, tears streaming down her face. Finally she raised herself up on her elbows and said, "Oh, oh, oh. What else can I do? Frank thinks he is a professor. Melanie looks like she is in church.

Milan is crazy. Richard, you try to be nice and polite, but everyone is in their separate worlds. We are not connecting at all. Oh,
it is just so funny."

On the way back to the house, the taxi driver took a shortcut
through the slum, weaving recklessly through the potholes and
puddles. Melanie was just enduring, waiting for the night to be
over, to lock her door and never never never make this mistake
again, and the gin-soaked golf pro was leaning across her, bellowing out the window for pussy in four different languages.
And I was thinking: How did this happen? What am I doing
here? Didn't I come to Africa to run a river?

A MUTTERING squawking man approaches a tethered goat
with a toothbrush and toothpaste. He brushes the teeth of the
protesting goat, then applies lipstick and makeup to its face.
He goes back into his hut and two men appear at his fence, one
of them wearing a floppy pink hat and cowboy boots. They
sneak in, steal the goat, and lead it into town. A policeman
stops them. He knows this goat and accuses them of theft. No,
no, they insist. They lead the policeman into a ladies' clothing
shop. They get a skirt and blouse on the goat and lead it back to
its owner, pretending this was their plan all along.

This was the Bongo Superstars Comedy episode playing on
the television in the front room of the house the next morning.
The golf pro was breakfasting on a plastic bag of gin and aggressively rejecting the suggestion that he had a drinking problem.
He cut open a second bag of gin. "You can't pinch an insect
with one finger," he said. "Hah! That's right, bro."

It pained me to see my friend and trusted guide like this,
especially on the morning of our good-bye. He had looked after
me so attentively, taught me so much, and his company had
been a pleasure nearly all the time. I gave him money to catch

the ferry back to Zanzibar, and a hundred dollars extra, which he accepted only on the condition that it was a loan. I entered his personal cloud of gin fumes for our final embrace, and then we stepped apart and shook hands like gentlemen. "You'll be fine," he said. "The river, Burundi, Rwanda, the president. *Hakuna matata*, no problem. You are protected, my friend."

"All right," I said. "And please, try and take care of yourself. Get some rest, man. Go easy. You haven't been eating."

"Oh, don't you worry about me, bro. My star will shine again, bro."

I hefted my pack and walked through the gates to the waiting car with sadness and relief.

4

The Road West

Traffic—Hunter's den—Departure—Banditry—
Fever and larceny—Gogo—Cattle culture—Dodoma—
Bush mechanic—Forebodings

THE DRIVER WAS a tall, strong, gentle man in his fifties with a slight croak in his voice. His name was Mustafa Omari, he was Ryan Shallom's right-hand man, and over the weeks to come, I grew to like and respect him immensely. He had deep reserves of patience, an unerring sense of direction, and his judgment was always sound and wise. In the lawless hinterlands of the far west, he was steady competence personified, and you couldn't ask for a more soothing or insightful companion in the mighty traffic jams of Dar es Salaam, as I found out that first morning.

In one sense the traffic was crippling the city, making it increasingly difficult to live, breathe, or do business here. But its very awfulness also opened up new economic opportunities, and the worse it got, the better it was for the people exploiting them. First came the little *bajaj* auto-rickshaws. Designed in India by the Bajaj Auto company, they had no seat belts and no doors, which meant the passengers were chewing acrid, gritty dust all the way, but the drivers could fit through gaps in the traffic that were too small for a taxi, and use the sidewalks, alleys, and slum lanes, and the fares undercut a four-wheeled taxi by about 50 percent.

As the Dar traffic reached the next stage of awfulness, *bajaj* jams started forming, and the first motorcycle taxis appeared, with the passengers riding pillion. They were even cheaper than a *bajaj* and able to maneuver through even smaller gaps. The latest development was bicycle taxis, weaving in and out of the traffic with the passengers' legs dangling over the rear wheels. As Mustafa pointed out, every one of these new developments was more dangerous to passengers than the last, but this did not affect their popularity. The price point was far more important, and whether you died in a traffic accident, or made it through safely, was a matter preordained by fate, destiny, Allah, God, or the spirits.

Growing multitudes of vendors worked the jams. From the window of your car, you could now buy a wide variety of snacks, including grilled meats, fresh fruit juices, and cold bottles of water—once emptied, the plastic bottles had a further use for male drivers trapped in the three- and four-hour traffic jams. You could buy gifts for your wife, toys for your children, cigarettes, newspapers, phone credit, clocks, live chickens, *kangas*, flip-flops, T-shirts, caps, and mirrors engraved with the sanctified image of Tupac Shakur. If you were feeling pangs of lust, there were prostitutes available in all shapes and sizes. And all the vendors and prostitutes had their own small needs and desires for food, drink, cigarettes, condoms, knockoff Viagra from India, gifts for their relatives, toys for their children. The boulevards and avenues of Dar es Salaam, designed by the colonial authorities to speed vehicle-owning Europeans from one part of the city to another, were turning into thriving African markets.

Eventually we reached the house of Mr. Ryan, or Mr. Lion as Mustafa pronounced it. Dogs barked, the *askari* opened the gate, and we parked in the small front courtyard. Mustafa stayed out there with the *askari* and another servant, and I walked into a large, air-conditioned living room with big comfortable chairs, various antelope heads mounted on the walls, and a gigantic set of Cape buffalo horns. Ryan Shallom came out to greet me from the kitchen, a short, burly, tough-looking man in his late thirties with brown skin, a goatee beard, and one gold earring. He had a snub nose and a short broad neck, and his hair was razored down to black stubble. His body was like a cannon, his head like a bullet.

"So, *bwana*, you made it," he said with a friendly grin. "I hope you like hartebeest. I've got some tenderloins going here."

"I've never had it before. It smells fantastic."

"What will you have to drink?"

"I'll start with water, if you don't mind."

His wife Lily was half-Dutch and half-Tanzanian, from the Sukuma tribe up by Lake Victoria. She worked in software and held an adorable, nut-brown five-month-old boy in her arms. During the course of the evening, she let it be known that she was not fully enthused about my idea of going down an unknown river with her husband and the father of her firstborn child.

"Of course Ryan's always in dangerous situations," she said. "It's part of being a professional hunter. We had one trampled to death by an elephant just a few days ago. I know he'll be careful, I know he's got plenty of experience. It's really the hippos I don't like thinking about. And the crocodiles."

As the wife of a professional hunter, she knew well that hippos kill more people than any other animal in Africa, except mosquitoes. And if a hippo overturned your boat in the river, you were very much in play for the crocodiles.

Ryan said, "I've talked to a couple of fishermen who have boated different sections of the river. They say the mosquitoes come out fifteen minutes before sunset and are active all night. The tsetse flies are very bad, and there is sleeping sickness in the area. We'll take plenty of DEET [high-strength insect repellent] and tiger balm for the bites. Tsetse flies are attracted to dark clothing, so bear that in mind when you're packing."

I had met tsetse flies, also known as spear flies, in Zimbabwe. They came in numbers, were extraordinarily resilient, taking five or six firm whacks to die, and each bite felt similar to the prick of a doctor's needle. Sleeping sickness, a disease that's fatal if untreated—you get more soporific as the parasite takes over your body until you never wake up—is transmitted by tsetse flies in the same way that malaria is transmitted by mosquitoes. During the 1970s and 1980s, World Health Organization initiatives dramatically reduced the prevalence of sleeping sickness in Africa, to the extent that it became unprofitable for drug companies to manufacture the treatment for it, and in the 1990s the disease started spreading again. In 1999, by pure serendipity, a pharmaceutical researcher found that the same drug, eflornithine, could reduce unwanted facial hair in women when applied topically. Production of the drug ramped up again for cosmetic purposes, and under pressure from the WHO, the manufacturers started donating quantities of it for the treatment of sleeping sickness in Africa.

Ryan had secured the latest maps of the Malagarasi and the surrounding area—one bore the date 1978, the other 1956—and he unrolled them on his coffee table. He jabbed at the middle section of the river with his stubby forefinger. It flowed through a large, unpopulated, government-protected "wildlife management area," which he said was now almost a euphemism in Tanzania for "heavy poaching area." Much as he disliked poaching, the poachers would know the country and the river better than anyone, and he thought we should find one and hire him for a guide.

"I don't think we'll have any technical problems in this section of river. We'll see about the hippos, but otherwise it looks pretty straightforward. Our first big problem will be a place they call the blockage, where the river is totally blocked up with a papyrus swamp. There might be some channels big enough for the raft, but I seriously doubt it, so we'll bring a support vehicle and go around it."

Below the swamp lies the village of Malagarasi, on the old slave and ivory caravan route that Burton and Speke traveled. Then the river swings west, and the next village is Uvinza. "Below Uvinza and all the way to the lake, you're in the unknown," said Ryan. "There might be a waterfall, or series of waterfalls. It's unclear on the maps. It looks like a long, deep canyon, and once we're in there, there'll be no way to get out. No one knows what the river is like there. No one has gone down that stretch in a boat before."

"Which means that no one has ever descended the whole river source to mouth," I said.

"Correct," he said. "I don't think anyone has run the upper river either."

"Why not?"

"Maybe no one has thought of doing it before. There'd certainly be no reason for any of the local people to try."

To my great disappointment, Ryan could not be persuaded into attempting the first full descent of the river, although I had to admit his reasons were sound. The security situation was still extremely unstable on the border with Burundi. We could get all the way up there and find only a trickle of water in the river. There was also the question of time, money, other priorities and responsibilities. He was used to earning a lot more than I could pay him, from the wealthy Texans who dominated his clientele of big-game hunters, and he didn't want to be away from Lily and the baby for more than three weeks.

Both of us were attracted to the idea of going down a river that no one had fully explored before, but beyond that our motivations diverged. I wanted the whole river from source to mouth, for the full linear adventure, and because I wanted to claim my little piece of history and write about it. I was willing to try my luck on the Burundian border, since I was going to Burundi anyway, and was prepared to walk alongside a trickle for forty miles if that's what it took. But I wasn't foolhardy enough to go up there by myself, or attempt the river without an experienced guide.

My prior experience in the African bush amounted to about twenty days of canoeing, hiking, and camping under expert supervision. I had picked up only the most elementary basics of African bushcraft. Above all, I had learned how much there was to learn in a place where survival might depend on reading an animal's body language correctly, knowing the language of footprints, the alarm calls of other animals and birds that might tell you a predator was approaching, knowing what to do if you ran across armed poachers, how to pick a safe campsite on a riverbank, what to do if you found yourself between a hippo and a river.

African bushcraft was an encyclopedia I had barely opened. I could go confidently by myself with a backpack into the mountains of Montana for a week, or the Arizona deserts, but that experience and knowledge was irrelevant among hippos, crocodiles, lions, hyenas, elephants, buffalo, black mambas, green mambas, spitting cobras. American rattlesnakes were so modest and polite compared to the big, aggressive, deadly African snakes. Plus there was malaria, sleeping sickness, dengue fever, African river blindness, bilharzia, tick bite fever, and half a dozen other fevers to worry about.

So I needed Ryan, and he didn't want to spend more than three weeks away from home. His main motivation was to scout

out the more accessible areas of the river for possible future rafting trips for his clients, and he didn't want to be without a support vehicle or a team of assistants to do the camp chores. I thought about saying no, it's the first descent or nothing. But after a year of thinking, dreaming, planning, and worrying about the Malagarasi, I decided to take as much of the river as I could get.

The hartebeest was perhaps the best game meat I've ever eaten, and served with a good South African red wine. Ryan said he had eaten so much game meat over the years that he had become afflicted with gout, and this plus a sprained ankle accounted for his slight limp. "You'll find gout is surprisingly common in Africa, especially among hunters," he said. "Wild meat has got more purines than domestic meat, and it's the purines that crystallize in your feet and give you the pain. I've got some pills that work pretty well, so it shouldn't be a problem on the river."

He was trying to get a permit so we could hunt our own meat on the Malagarasi. I had mixed views on hunting and kept them to myself. Since I loved to eat meat, I considered it dishonest of myself, and a point of moral failure, that I had never killed an animal for food. But trophy hunting—killing the biggest males for the pleasure and competitive satisfaction of killing such a big one—aroused a kind of revulsion in me, and trophy hunting was Ryan's business and his passion.

I've met many hunters who were ardent conservationists, and Ryan Shallom was one of them. What I cared most about was the future existence of wild places and big wild animals on this poor, beleaguered planet of ours, and I agreed with his argument that trophy hunting, if managed well, can help preserve these places by generating the income to hire game scouts and fund anti-poaching programs. I respected his views, but I didn't want to know how many elephants he had looked in the eyes while they were dying from his gunshots, or the gunshots of his clients.

Above all other animals, I have always loved and admired elephants, in the kind of urban, romantic, sentimental way that hunters usually scorn and most African villagers don't understand at all. The traditional attitude of East Africans toward wildlife conservation is well expressed in the Swahili language. The word for wild animals is *nyama*. The word for meat is *nyama*. And for an African villager, elephants are not just potential food but a menace to crops and people.

AFTER DAYS OF preparation and seemingly endless delays, the morning for departure arrived. I was expecting one support vehicle, but Ryan had two bush-worn Land Cruisers stuffed like *daladalas* with gear, supplies, and men. Ryan and Mustafa would share the driving of one of them, and there was a second driver called Omari, a big man with a deep, rasping voice, and a hard potbelly that he patted regularly and opened shirt buttons for—big bellies denote wealth and status in Africa, and their owners are proud of them. Ryan had brought three trackers/camp assistants from his hunting concession in the Kilombero Valley in southeast Tanzania: Hebron Mlachu, thirty-four, Alanus Ngalalika, thirty-four, and Tito Sanga, twenty-four. I never got used to the fact that he referred to them as "the boys," or "my boys."

Hebron, known as Heblon or Hebloni, was slightly built with sleepy, vaguely sinister eyes under the bill of his cap and a long wisp of hair growing from just below his lower lip. A born joker with a quirky sense of humor, he was also a deadly hunter. Alanus was short, strong, solid, loyal, and dependable, the sort of man who does well in the military and doesn't grumble about stupid orders. Tito was handsome and immensely strong, with a medium muscular build and a premature bald spot on the crown of his head. He was younger and more naive than the two others, and had less emotional camouflage. Laughter overwhelmed him completely, and he had a strong need to shine, to prove his eagerness, loyalty, and value. Both his parents had died when he was a child, and Ryan and his staff had taken him in. Tito had a lot of heart and courage, and there would come a time on the river when we saw exactly how much.

None of them spoke more than a few words of English. All of them were married with children except Tito, whose wedding night was still a fresh memory. Heblon and Alanus had grown up together in the Kilombero, when Ryan's Israeli father was the big hunter there. Among their duties now were fetching Ryan's lighter or cigarettes and looking after his guns: a shotgun, a thirty-ought-six, and a .470 that he assured me would take down a charging hippo.

As we, or rather they, loaded up the last of the supplies, including our iodine-purified plastic barrels of Dar es Salaam tap water, Ryan looked at the map. He pointed to Dodoma, the capital city in the middle of Tanzania, some three hundred miles away. "We need to get there by four or five in the afternoon, or we're there for the night," he said.

"Why's that?" I asked.

"Bandits," he said. "They block the roads with logs and rocks. The police won't let you drive out of Dodoma after dark."

Somehow, in the course of my research, I had failed to find out anything about bandits in Tanzania. I had always thought of it as the safe country in East Africa, dirt poor, famously inefficient, but peaceable, friendly, and laid back. Ryan said that was broadly true. Since independence there had been no intertribal violence in Tanzania, no insurrections against the government, and no wars, except when Julius Nyerere's army invaded neighboring Uganda and removed Idi Amin from power. Tanzanians were indeed the friendliest, most laid-back people in East Africa, but there were still bandits among them.

The government made sure to keep the bandits away from the national parks and surrounding areas, where half a million foreign tourists came every year for their safaris, and kept the national economy afloat. That pretty much used up the government's law enforcement budget, to the extent where lawmakers themselves couldn't drive out of the nation's capital at night because of bandits at the edge of the city.

"How far does the bandit area extend?" I asked.

"Let me put it this way," said Ryan. "We're not going to reach the end of it. And it only gets worse across the border in Burundi and Congo. We'll be careful, stay off the roads after dark, and if the worst comes to the worst, our boys know how to shoot straight."

In the scruffy outskirts of Dar es Salaam, as we started to break free of the traffic, we stopped at a supermarket for whiskey, then gathered speed on the road west, passing outlying shantytowns, tethered goats grazing the roadside to dust, and sacks of charcoal propped upright like tombstones. There were the usual fantastically overloaded bicycles that one sees all over Africa, and we passed one stacked up with fifteen cases of Coke in glass bottles, another with an equally enormous load of palm fronds. All the trucks and buses on the road were painted up in bright colors and named in English: "Soul Power," "Jesus Power," "Stone Cold," "Big Boss," "Mr. Handsome," "Mr. Number One," "The Don." It's a cheap shot to make fun of Swahili-speakers for making mistakes in English in their own country, but I couldn't resist writing down some of the misspelled shop signs: GROSSARY for grocery and OIL LUBRICUNT.

A female pedestrian, wrapped in *kangas,* had the business end of a sledgehammer balanced on her head and the handle sticking upward at an angle as she walked. Other women walked under hoes, suitcases, crates of fruit, crates of chickens. Researchers have attempted to measure these extraordinary head-balancing skills and concluded that the average African woman can carry up to 20 percent of her body weight on her head, and burn no more calories than if she was carrying nothing at all. They start head-carrying in girlhood. Their posture becomes so perfectly aligned, and their gait so smooth, that the load rests on the bone column of the spine and requires no muscular effort to keep it there. The researchers also discovered that when Western women try to learn the skill in adulthood, they almost invariably hurt their necks.

Half an hour out of the city, in a region of semiarid deforested hills with occasional lone termite mounds rising out of the earth like sentinels, we were flagged down by a policeman standing on the side of the road in a white uniform. I envisaged the search, the finding of the guns, the improperness of our permits, the bribe. But it turned out that he knew Ryan, recognized his vehicle, and wanted to hitch a ride, so we scooted up to make space for him. He was a road safety officer, and his department could not afford to buy vehicles, or even bicycles, so he and his fellow officers hitchhiked up and down the highways every day, handing out traffic tickets to violators, collecting "fines," and then hitchhiking back home again. We took him ten miles and left him by the side of the road, waiting for a traffic violator who lacked the sense to drive straight past him when he whistled and held up his arm.

"A traffic cop needs a good connection to get a busy highway like this," said Ryan. "And he has to pay a percentage of what he makes to the guy who got him the job, and another percentage to his boss. There is a genuine problem with overcrowded buses, speeding truck drivers, and traffic fatalities, but instead of paying the twenty-thousand-shilling fine, the driver gives five thousand to the cop on the ground and goes on his way. For the police, it has nothing to do with road safety or enforcing the law. It's a business, an enterprise. The most coveted position is to get the speed gun, because you can make a lot of money with that thing."

Ten miles up the road, Omari got stopped by a different *polisi*, and we pulled over next to him to show support and solidarity. "It's more intimidating for the cop to see he's dealing with two vehicles full of people," said Ryan. "Especially with you here. It always helps to have a white guy around. See now, the cop is letting him go."

We reached the first baobab trees towering above the thorn scrub on a wide straw-colored plain, and this was a happy moment for me. The sight of these improbable trees always renews my faith in the strangeness and wonder of the world. According to an Arab legend, the devil went around Africa ripping certain trees out of the ground and sticking them back in upside-down, with their roots in the air. It's this wrong-way-up look, combined with the grossly distended trunk, knobby warts, and elephant hide bark, that places the baobab so firmly in my affections. My eyes had been trained by the safari bubble to expect elephants and giraffes where there were baobabs, but here they searched in vain. The roadsides were scorched black from cigarette fires and strewn with trash. I had yet to see a single bird.

Jagged mountains appeared on the western horizon, and as we neared them, the land formed into hog-backed hills and swales with a good covering of leafless dry season trees. It looked like good wildlife habitat, but Ryan said all the game had been trapped out with wire snares and eaten years ago. Fires were burning in the mountains above the town of Morogoro, and the highest peak rose up through the smoky haze like a rhino horn. Schoolchildren in navy blue and white uniforms ran and scampered along the side of the road, which was now following the old slave and ivory route.

Morogoro lay in a lush and fertile valley under the mountains. It seemed like an exceedingly pleasant and relaxed town, with gardens and shade trees and a university where scientists were training mice to detect tuberculosis, with a 97 percent success rate, and dogs to sniff out land mines. We stopped for homemade cakes and excellent coffee at Ricky's Café, while the others went to get a new battery for their ailing Land Cruiser. "This is where I want to move to," said Ryan. "I've got in-laws here. I could get some land here, a small farm. Dar is chaos, man, a constant battle, and it will only get worse."

We drove on through drier, hotter, sparser woodland on the vast, uplifted central plateau of Tanzania, and during the afternoon I developed a headache, aching muscles and joints, a mild queasiness, a sore throat, and swollen glands under the hinge of the jaw. The feeling is an integral part of African travel: a low-grade fever, a clammy forehead, the worry that some ghastly disease is taking hold, and the optimistic voice in your head that says no, it's just the dust, the heat, dehydration, too many drinks the night before, side effects from the malaria pills, too many nights of not enough sleep in noisy rooms with holes in the mosquito net.

The air conditioning wasn't working in the Land Cruiser. The windows were open and the hot dry wind buffeted my face, reddened the rims of my eyes, roared and pounded in one ear of my aching head. Trucks and buses swam past in the heat haze: "Royal Obama," "Lap Top Machine." And I thought to myself: this is luxury. Savor it. There goes another nine miles like nothing.

BY THIS STAGE of their journey, Burton and Speke had crossed over into some other country of the mind. Since landing on the coast at Bagamoyo, they had suffered one attack of malaria after another, and possibly tick-borne and other fevers as well. Their heads boiled and their limbs trembled. Burton's mouth filled with ulcers, and it became difficult for the great linguist to speak. Both of them went temporarily deaf and fell into long periods of wild delirium. Burton thought he could fly, and Speke had such violent, insane, jabbering fits that they had to take his beloved weapons away.

In 1857, no one knew that malaria was contracted by mosquito bites, but it was obvious that the disease was most prevalent and virulent in swampy, marshy, mosquito-infested areas, where soaking rains alternated with fierce tropical heat, and places like this came along with awful regularity in the first few months of Burton and Speke's journey. For prevention and treatment they relied on a concoction called Warburg's Drops, a mixture of opium, bitter aloes, and small amounts of quinine that was completely ineffective against the disease but probably looped out their heads a little further. Burton was a strong believer in the medicinal powers of alcohol, so he was probably dosing himself from the dozen bottles of brandy they carried, with four dozen more to follow in a resupply caravan. Prim, proud, prudish Speke was a teetotaler, so no threat to the brandy supplies at least.

Ever the keen observer and vigilant diarist, Burton made detailed notes on the appalling condition of his health. He made a distinction (probably spurious) between the malarial attacks and a "marsh fever" that followed and laid him out for twenty days, producing unusually vivid hallucinations: "I had during the fever-fit, and often for hours afterwards, a queer conviction of divided identity, never ceasing to be two persons that generally thwarted and opposed each other;

the sleepless nights brought with them horrid visions, animals of grisliest form, hag-like women and men with heads protruding from their breasts. My companion suffered even more severely, he had a fainting-fit which strongly resembled a sun-stroke, and which seemed permanently to affect his brain."

As if fever wasn't enough to contend with, they were also tormented by red ants, festering mosquito bites, tsetse flies, and inch-long pismire ants that preyed on rats for a living and delivered a bite that "burns like a pinch with a red hot needle." Termites ate their way through cloth and paper. The humidity made mush of their books, turned their matches to paste, rotted their boots. And to cap it all, they were traveling with a mutinous, quarrelsome, larcenous caravan of Baluchi guards, Goan servants, African porters, donkey-whackers, slaves, and in some instances, the slaves of slaves.

The caravan master was a shifty operator called Said bin Salim, an Afro-Arab who charged an outrageous fee for his services, traveled with concubines of both genders, stole as much as he could of the expedition's supplies, and gave away even more to the aggressive beggars and demanding local chiefs along the way. He was afraid to haggle with them, it wasn't his property, and he was planning to desert anyway. The translator was a drunk, either sunk in maudlin self-pity or spoiling for a fight. The porters were always dropping or losing vital pieces of equipment, and the Baluchis—mercenary soldiers from Baluchistan—were a constant source of trouble and aggravation: "Their objects in life seemed to be eating and buying slaves; their pleasures, drinking and intrigue. Insatiable beggars were they: noisy, boisterous, foul-mouthed knaves . . ." To general disgust and bewilderment, Burton insisted on paying the slaves, and the slaves of slaves, in cloth and beads, which were the universal currency of the land.

Meanwhile, the porters were pilfering and deserting the expedition singly and in small groups to go back to the coast. Burton soon discovered that the biggest mistake he could make with his men was an act of kindness or generosity. Almost invariably, it would be taken as a sign of weakness and lead to bolder and more aggressive demands for more food, less work, more cloth and beads so they could buy more slaves.

In Zungomero, a squalid settlement and caravan stop that has disappeared off the maps, Burton and Speke lay shaking with fever in leaky huts while the Baluchis and the slaves went on a drunken looting spree and attempted to rape various local women. Burton managed to smooth it over with gifts and diplomacy, and hire some more porters there. Leaving Zungomero, after the usual delays, squabbles, and malingerings, his caravan numbered 132 people.

In the lead went the guide, wearing a ceremonial headdress and carrying the red Flag of the Sultan of Zanzibar, and behind him marched the drummer. The cloth and bead porters came next with their bolster-like bundles on their heads, then the men carrying the camp equipment, and their women, children, and cattle. The armed guard [*askaris*] was dispersed along the line, each man carrying a muzzle-loaded "Tower musket," a German cavalry sabre, a small leather box strapped to the waist and a large cow-horn filled with ammunition. Many of them were accompanied by their women and personal slaves . . . Almost every male member of the expedition had a weapon of some kind together with an assortment of pots and pans and a three-legged wooden stool strapped to his back. A continuous and violent uproar of chanting, singing . . . and shouting accompanied the march, for it was thought important to make as much noise as possible so as to impress the local tribes. If a hare chanced to run across the track all downed burdens at once to go in pursuit of the animal which, if caught, was eaten raw.

IN THE REAR of the procession, balanced on donkeys, or when they were too sick to ride, swinging in hammocks carried on poles by two porters, came fever-ravaged Burton and Speke, the only two Europeans on the expedition.

Not far from Zungomero, they passed through the outwash of a smallpox epidemic. Fresh corpses and skeletons littered the trail, then dying men, women, and children appeared, staggering forward, doing everything in their power to stay upright as long as possible, because they knew that ravens, vultures, and foxes would finish them off once they fell. Burton and Speke understood why the sick had been driven away by their friends and relatives, and refused shelter by local villagers, but to see them die like this seemed like one more example of the harshness of Africa.

Further down the road, one of the men in the caravan bought a female slave. When he discovered she couldn't keep up the pace, he cut off her head. Why not let her go? Because then someone would get his property without paying for it. By the time this happened, Burton wasn't even shocked. It was the sort of thing he had come to expect.

For Speke, all this and more was explained by the innate savagery and racial inferiority of the Negro. He believed, and through interpreters, often tried to explain to Africans that they were condemned to slavery because of the Biblical curse on the dark-skinned "sons of Ham," in the book of Genesis, a notion that Burton rejected as "beastly humbug."

Like nearly all Europeans of his era, Burton also thought that Africans were racially inferior to whites, but he thought it was because they had evolved in such a debilitating climate, where nature was so hostile and deadly diseases so prevalent. And he made a distinction between the primitive aspects of Africa—the lack of written languages or stone buildings, the deep sway of superstition and suspicion of change—and the cruelty, which he saw as resulting from centuries of the slave trade. "The traffic practically annihilates every better feeling of human nature," he wrote, and it had "brutalized the souls of the inhabitants." He was also aware that by leading a rich caravan along the main slave route, he was seeing Africans "at their worst."

At the village of Dut'humi, instead of the usual outstretched hands and belligerent demands, leading to four, or six, or eight days of haggling, Burton encountered African hospitality for the first time. The villagers offered cozy thatched huts to the Englishmen, which Burton gladly accepted and Speke refused, preferring his damp British tent to native quarters. "Though with swimming head and trembling hands," Burton repaid the kindness by taking some men and rescuing five of the villagers who had been captured as slaves by a neighboring tribe. "I had the satisfaction of restoring the stolen wretches to their hearths and homes, and two decrepit old women that had been rescued from slavery thanked me with tears of joy."

On a normal day, the procession got underway soon after daybreak and traveled until late morning, when the sun became too hot. Then thorn-brush was arranged in a wide circle to keep the livestock corralled and the lions and thieves out. Tents were put up, unless there were existing huts or shelters, and people dispatched to the nearest village to start bargaining for food, while Burton and Speke, whose instruments kept breaking and getting lost, endeavored to measure longitude, latitude, elevation, temperature, wind strength and direction, and write detailed descriptions of the geology, climate, topography, botany, zoology, ethnography. The campfires were lit, dinner was eaten as the sun went down, the Englishmen retired to their tents, and the porters, slaves, donkey-whackers, and women would begin the nightly revelry, singing, dancing, fighting, squabbling, drinking *pombe* beer brewed from maize, holcus, or millet, and smoking the *Cannabis Indica* that Burton saw growing outside every hut in the villages.

Then it would be up before dawn and two hours of chaos and pilfering, shouting and complaining, until finally men and beasts were loaded and lined up in disarray behind the drummer. So the unruly caravan proceeded, averaging nine miles a day.

IN OUR HUMMING Land Cruisers we entered the devastated moonscape of the Gogo people. The land was dust, and the few people remaining were thin and ragged as scarecrows. The air was a dusty haze lit to an apricot color by the enormous sinking sun, which seemed to pulsate and wobble as it went down behind the horizon. Heblon and Alanus wanted to know where all the trees had gone. Ryan said there hadn't been many trees here, and now they'd all been cut down and turned into charcoal. What about the grass?

Ryan explained to them and translated for me: "This used to be a big cattle center. But the people had too many cattle and when the drought came, they totally overran the carrying capacity of the land. Now those people have migrated to other areas with their cattle, and they're doing exactly the same thing. It's happening all over East Africa. You cannot explain to these tribes that they have too many cattle. It's like telling someone they have too much money."

Traditionally, the tribes have subsisted on the milk and blood of their cattle, and slaughtered them only for special feast days. The cattle also provided skins to lie on, dung for plastering on huts, urine for brewing into beer for some tribes, and the bride-price for a young man who wanted to get married. Cattle were objects of love and devotion, with individual animals named and sung to, and cattle were the measure of a man's wealth and status. His herd was like a checking account, a savings account, a trophy wife, and a Cadillac all rolled into one. The more cattle a man had, the more proud, secure, satisfied, and successful he felt. It made no sense to sell them, because what use was money except for buying more cattle, and maybe an AK-47 to protect them against raiders from the neighboring tribes?

I found these attitudes so hard to understand. I was steeped in the idea that you raised cattle in order to sell the meat and make money, but under the African pastoral system, cattle were very seldom turned into meat. I had seen the destructiveness of this system in northern Tanzania and northern Kenya. I had read about it in Uganda, Ethiopia, and Sudan, and here it was again.

Most of East Africa is semiarid. Drought is a normal, predictable part of the climate cycle. Every five years or so, one of the two seasonal rains will fail. Every ten years or so, both will. Despite their predictability, the droughts cause terrible suffering and famine among the pastoral tribes, because even when the grass is withering, the waterholes drying up, their children crying with hunger, they still won't sell or eat their livestock. That would be like withdrawing the contents of your savings account in hundred-dollar bills and using them to set fire to your Cadillac.

When drought comes to the Karamojong in Uganda, they stop feeding their boy children, throw their corpses out for the hyenas when they starve to death, and give what food there is to their daughters. Why? Because girls can be traded for cattle when the drought is over. In northern Kenya, I met a female chief of the Gabbra tribe. She had been away to school and university, and become a modern person. She read and heard the urgent government warnings that drought was coming. Her people had far too many cattle, goats, and camels for their sandy, thorny land; they had built up their herds as large as possible during the years of normal rains, and the land was already overgrazed. She tried everything she knew to persuade the men to sell their animals before they starved to death, at least slaughter them and jerk the meat, and she got absolutely nowhere. "All they see is livestock at the end of their nose," she said. "And now the drought is here, everything is dust, the animals are dying, and we are all living on food aid."

The solution that seemed so glaringly obvious to me—keep smaller herds in balance with the land and sell or eat the increase—required too much change too quickly from a conservative tribal culture that loved its cattle as fiercely as we love money. So they sucked in grasslands and breathed out dust bowls.

"Probably the most destructive tribe in Tanzania at the moment is the Sukuma, my mother-in-law's people," said Ryan. "They're the largest tribe, seminomadic, farmers and herdsmen, very smart, cunning, determined, with good political connections. They've turned a huge area south of Lake Victoria [in northern Tanzania] into a desert. And that was lush grassland, not semiarid like here. So now they're moving with their livestock into a lot of other places, and unfortunately one of them is the Kilombero Valley. A lot of people think poaching is the big threat to wildlife in Africa, but it's nothing compared to cattle encroachment."

IN SWAHILI, the prefix *wa-* is used for a tribe or people. So *muzungu* for white person becomes *wazungu* for white people. The Tutsi are the Watutsi, who gave their name to the 1960s American dance craze the Watusi, and Burton, because Anglicized versions of tribal names hadn't yet been invented, refers to the Gogo as the Wagogo in his account. They impressed him more than any tribe he had encountered so far, which wasn't saying much.

Their principal livelihood in the nineteenth century was extorting tribute from the slave and ivory caravans that passed through their territory, which Burton, even on the receiving end, thought was reasonable and showed initiative. They kept prices high by occasional, devastating attacks, and they also bartered their own ivory and salt for slaves. The biggest market for slaves in East Africa was among the tribes, and recent scholarship has concluded that "only a small portion" of all slaves captured or sold in the region reached the coast.* The reason why Africa as a whole played such a major role in the international slave trade, some historians now argue, is because slavery was already so widespread and institutionalized on the continent, with established systems of buying, trading, and transportation. With the growing international demand for plantation slaves in the American colonies, French Pacific colonies, and Arab countries, it was easy for African traders to extend these networks and increase supply.

The Wagogo, like most African tribes, favored female slaves and kept them as concubines who also did domestic and agricultural work. In addition to collecting tribute and trading, they also grew fields of grain, mainly for brewing into *pombe* beer, and kept large herds of cattle and goats. The men filed their teeth into sharp points, removed the two lower incisors, stained their skin with ochre, and slathered their bodies and hair with dripping quantities of ghee butter—this was a popular look among many tribes in the region at the time. Their

---

Slavery in the Great Lakes Region of East Africa, edited by Henri Médard and Shane Doyle (Athens: Ohio University Press, 2007).

earlobes were so elongated from the use of plugs and discs that they hung to the shoulders and looked like handles to the owner's head.

Burton, feeling slightly better now in the drier climate, although still far from healthy, liked the fact that they had so few witch doctors, and he suspected less of "wizardhood and witchcraft" than any tribe between the Atlantic and the Indian Ocean, perhaps because they were so focused on the cold, hard realities of caravan extortion. They were the only tribe so far to express any curiosity about him and Speke, the first white people they had ever seen, and ask questions about where they came from and what life was like there. For Burton, who was driven by curiosity above all else, it was a welcome change from the disinterest and apathy displayed by the other tribes, and he took the Wagogo curiosity as "proof of improvability—of power to progress."

His caravan was detained by Sultan M'ana Miaha, or "Shortshank," the most powerful of the Wagogo chiefs and a full-time drunkard: "he becomes man, idiot and beast with clockwork-regularity every day; when not disguised in liquor he is surly and unreasonable, and when made merry by his cups he refuses to do business." Burton was kept waiting five days to see him, and despite the tsetses, biting ants, and swarming bees, despite the hyenas that kept killing his donkeys in the night, he seems to have thoroughly enjoyed himself. There was a new language to learn, plenty to drink and smoke, and he greatly admired the lithe, graceful young Wagogo women, who went about almost naked. He hints fairly broadly at some sexual activity: "The women are well disposed towards strangers of fair complexion, apparently with the permission of their husbands."

Needless to say, Speke did not approve of Burton's indulgence in the local intoxicants or native women, and he wrote later that Burton had "gone to the Devil" in Africa.

Speke was revolted by the very blackness of African skin, and morally and physically disgusted by the way Africans lived and behaved. Burton writes about them with withering scorn sometimes, but he was also compelled and attracted by them, sexually and otherwise.

In her fine biography of Burton, *The Devil Drives*, Fawn Brodie sums up the difference perfectly when she says that Burton was a sponge and Speke was a stone.

ONE LONG DAY as a passenger in a Land Cruiser on a paved road, with a headache and a mild fever, had put a serious dent in my energies, and I marveled afresh at Burton's ability to lead such a fractious expedition and function as a geographer, geologist, linguist, diarist, and field anthropologist when his head was boiling with fevers, his mouth swollen with ulcers, and his body racked with pain and exhaustion.

We reached Dodoma in the dark, and policemen had already blocked off the outgoing roads because of bandits. "That's what you get for putting your capital in the middle of bloody nowhere," said Ryan. Dodoma lies in the geographical center of Tanzania, and for this reason, in 1973, President Julius Nyerere decided to make it the capital of this multitribal nation, despite the fact that Dar es Salaam was the biggest city and the existing capital and the added detail that Dodoma was an obscure railway outpost in the middle of desert nowhere, known if at all for its terrible heat and the ferocity of its dust storms.

Now it was a medium-sized, bland, dumpy provincial town containing a retrofuturistic spike-domed Parliament building, "where all the things Tanzania needs doing don't get done," in Ryan's words, "and the people who should be doing them keep getting acquitted on corruption charges." Politicians came out here once or twice a year to legislate, and the ministries and embassies that one associates with a political capital all stayed in Dar es Salaam, citing the water shortage in Dodoma and the transportation costs for getting there and back. The streets were dimly lit—a rarity in East Africa, where the streets are usually not lit at all, and the flashlight feature on your phone gets a lot of use—and they seemed to contain few vendors and many children. Mustafa was dispatched on foot to ask around about a cheap place to stay where we could lock up the vehicles, and he took to heart my facetious suggestion to find out where the corrupt politicians drank.

It was an open-walled, indoor-outdoor bar and grill with plastic tables and chairs, and its name was Chako Ni Chako, meaning Yours Is Yours, or You Earned It, Now You Spend It. The politicians, or so we presumed, were the big fat men in straining suits devouring skewers of grilled meat and crowding up their tables with empty one-liters of beer, while prostitutes laughed at their jokes and jostled for position on their laps. They were big, happy, charismatic men who knew how to enjoy themselves and looked delighted with life.

I pulled the chunks of beef and goat meat off my skewers in silence, feeling too wiped out to walk over there, introduce myself, and hope that someone spoke English. Listening to Ryan and the rest of our group talking in Swahili, understanding only the occasional word, I thought about Speke's linguistic shortcomings and how sour and disgruntled they made him. Burton, with his fluent Arabic, Swahili, and Hindustani, and the vocabularies of tribal languages he was rapidly accumulating, could converse with almost anyone they met in East Africa, and he took great pleasure and satisfaction in doing so. Speke, who spoke only a little schoolboy French and a smattering of Hindustani that he had picked up while stationed in India, was dependent on Burton to translate everything for him, and I would be similarly dependent on Ryan. Already, it seemed like I was constantly asking him to translate for me, and that he was likely to get fed up with it.

At the end of the meal, feeling a little better with meat in my stomach, I wrenched the conversation into English. I wanted to know how Tanzanians remembered Nyerere, the man who built modern Tanzania, anointed Dodoma as its capital, translated Shakespeare's plays into Swahili in his spare time, and was widely admired as a great statesman all over independent black Africa, even though he kept more political prisoners than the white apartheid regime in South Africa. From independence in 1961 to his retirement in 1985, Nyerere had pursued an idealistic vision of brotherly African socialism that kept Tanzania at peace and averted tribal conflict, but led to an apathetic and ruined economy.

"To us he is still *Mwalimu*, our Teacher," said Ryan. "He's the father of our country and we remember him with great affection and the utmost respect. Sure, he made some mistakes. No one had tried socialism in Africa before. It was an experiment that didn't work out as he thought it would, but there's no question that he was a great man, a true leader. You have to look at what he was up against, and what he managed to achieve."

Nyerere was up against the usual African recipe for disaster, so clear now in hindsight and so obscured in the 1960s by the joys and hopes of independence. Following centuries of tribal warfare and the slave trade, this part of Africa had gone through the humiliation, oppression, and economic enslavement of colonialism. Then it was granted an independence for which it was completely unprepared. When the British left in 1961, there were twelve doctors in Tanzania and 120 university graduates. Eighty-five percent of the population was illiterate and living under tribal chiefdoms. The nation itself was an artificial colonial creation, with its borders decided at conferences in Europe, without any regard for the tribal territories on the ground.

The same set of problems faced leaders all over newly independent black Africa, and almost alone among them, Nyerere was able to build a cohesive nation with no ethnic or religious conflicts and a sense of patriotic pride about this achievement. Tanzania was proof that African tribes lumped together awkwardly in a post-colonial nation could overcome their historical animosities and live together in a friendly, peaceful way, if they had a leader who was actually serious about making this happen, instead of steering favors and patronage to his own tribe in the usual disastrous way.

WE SPENT THAT night in a big, looming, echoing, Catholic mission building and were shown to our spartan rooms by wimpled African nuns who clucked at the lateness of the hour and the largeness of our party. There was no hot water, so I took a cold shower, dispatched a few cockroaches with my shoe, and climbed under the mosquito net. Two hours later, I woke up with sweats and chills from a lurid nightmare about African nuns and detachable flesh. Then it was 4:00 a.m., time to get dressed and drag my aching carcass down to the Land Cruisers.

At five in the morning the police opened the road west. In the fading starlight we could make out eerie rock formations by the side of the road—hoodoos, boulders like enormous eggs, lumpy towers—and ghostly figures carrying sacks of charcoal suspended from a pole across their shoulders, moving at a peculiar shuffling trot, perhaps to ease the weight of the enormous sacks somehow, perhaps to reach Dodoma before the sun inflicted its power on this desert. Some of them still had twenty miles to go. Other men were pushing bicycles heavily laden with charcoal sacks, and indeed the main use of the bicycle in these lands is for transporting loads. It is a beast of burden that requires no food or water.

The sun came up fat, squat, and malevolent, and revealed a trash-strewn roadside and a vast expanse of dusty, burnt orange plains. We stopped for breakfast in Manyoni, a small straggle of a town along the highway. The only place open at that hour was the New Rau Lodge, where flies by the dozen crawled over the greasy plastic tabletops. We ate beef soup and sweet, cold, congealed rice balls fried the day before, washed down with milky chai, and one by one, at discreet intervals, we tried and failed to brave the toilet and later mocked each other's cowardice. Tito allowed that it might be the worst toilet in Africa, or at least a contender.

Manyoni was the end of the paved road, and after breakfast we drove all morning through deep washboard ruts and flying dust. By lunchtime you could have grouted tile with the substance in our nostrils, and the electrics had gone out in the Land Cruiser that Ryan was driving. We had no horn, then no lights, then no indicators, then no radio. We pulled into Singida, a highway town raked by a gritty wind, and found a small mechanic's shop between a gas station and a small bar packed with drinkers and prostitutes. Seeing the Land Cruisers and my white face, a crowd of excited young men appeared, trying to take my elbow and steer me into the mechanic's shop twenty yards away, angling for a guiding fee for showing me the way. Then five big trucks got themselves stuck in a jam while jockeying for position at the gas station, and the young men rushed over there with a similar plan in mind.

The mechanic's shop was a mad dangling labyrinth of wires and cables. Ryan said, "Don't make contact with anything. It's all live." There were fish drying from a ceiling wire, heaps of scrap metal and old plastic, and a man heating up two wrenches on a charcoal fire who said the mechanic would be back soon. I watched him melt some plastic bags and the bottom of an old plastic soda bottle to seal a new plate over a battery. As we waited for the mechanic, there was a steady stream of would-be guides and blustery drunks with important reasons why we should give them money. Morose eleven-year-old beggars eyed us hopefully while an aggressive six-year-old chanted, *"Muzungu! Muzungu!* Give me my money!" Polite, well-dressed young men came one after another to introduce themselves and ask if I could help with the expense of their education or sponsor them for American citizenship.

The mechanic was called Saidi, and he was tall, elegantly poised, precise, and unhurried in all his movements. Below the chest, he was dirty and oil-stained, but his head, shoulders, upper chest, and neck were immaculately clean, his hair freshly barbered, his eyelashes long and curling. In this town of unemployed men, he worked with a permanent audience, hoping to cadge some small task from him, but happy enough just to pass the time observing the master in his domain and studying his techniques. There was a definite theatricality about him, an air of cool confident command ramped up just slightly for the audience.

He determined that our alternator was not charging, or not holding a charge. He removed the regulator and then gave us a three-hour performance with soldering irons, voltage regulators, tubes of liquid gasket-maker, assistants dispatched here and there, two false starts, and then a triumphant grand finale with all electrical circuits fully functioning and smiles all around, from us and the audience. For an encore, he replaced our broken taillight with one he had in his midden pile and didn't charge us extra for it.

Leaving Singida, we drove through brutally overgrazed land on the escarpments of the Rift Valley, the great trench that runs down through East Africa from Ethiopia to Mozambique, where homo sapiens and his apelike predecessors likely first evolved. Sukuma herdsmen in blue tartan robes drove cattle and goats before them on the eastern escarpments. The goats cleared away any shoots or sprigs that the cattle were unable to eat. There were also Gogo herdsmen dressed in black robes with broad-brimmed bush hats, and with the sticks they carried, it gave them a Grim Reaper look. Seven years ago, said Ryan, this was a prime hunting area for gazelles, lesser kudu, and buffalo. But then the Sukuma had come down from the dust bowl they had made in the north, and the Gogo from their dust bowl in the southeast, and it didn't take a witch doctor to divine the future here.

The atmosphere in our Land Cruiser turned quiet and somber. In two long days of driving across Tanzania, our keen-eyed hunters and trackers had yet to spot a single wild animal, and to see the cradle of mankind turning to dust put me in a gloomy frame of mind. Sometimes I thought the problems with Africa were simply the basic problems of human nature—greed, anger, envy, sloth, cruelty—magnified by a particularly harsh arrangement of history, climate, and disease. Sometimes I thought the cultural systems and attitudes developed by African tribes were particularly unhelpful and self-defeating when taken out of the traditional tribal context. There was too much credence in witchcraft, too much fatalism, too much worship and obedience toward power, because power in Africa has always contained a frightening supernatural element, and chiefs and presidents have always been careful to maintain it. Also, the best and the brightest people were so often over-extended in trying to support their ever-expanding extended families. I saw this sort of sharing as a method of spreading poverty, of enabling your worthless second cousin to keep drinking and mooching. Africans saw it as a moral duty that could bring them disgrace, violence, witchcraft, and other reprisals if they failed to discharge it.

Sometimes I blamed everything on colonialism, which had obliterated so much of what had preceded it and warped so many of the cultural traditions that survived. But most of the world has been colonized at some point in its history, and there were bleakly amusing claims from Liberia and Ethiopia that their lack of development stemmed from the fact that they *hadn't* been colonized, and so had missed out on its benefits, like transportation networks, health and education systems, administrative structures.

The problems of Africa were thorny indeed, because in addition to all the beggars and moochers drawn toward me, the "wallet on legs," in Paul Theroux's memorable phrase, there were so many talented, energetic people. It seemed to me that the average African was superior to the average Westerner in basic mental sharpness—short-term memory, alertness, mental arithmetic, reasoning skills—and it was rare to meet an African who didn't speak at least three languages and have a positive, optimistic attitude. Then, of course, there was the whole racially charged, cliché-ridden arena of physical stamina and coordination. I had never been anywhere else in the world where it was normal for people to work in the fields all day in brutal heat without eating or drinking water, normal for a woman to walk ten miles with a crate of chickens balanced on her head.

Burton and Speke's idea that Africans belonged to an inferior race seemed absurd and ridiculous, quite apart from being offensive. If you were going to look at people in terms of racial stock, Africans seemed hardier, more resourceful and talented than most. And yet their continent was a shambles and a disgrace. People suffered more and died younger here than anywhere else on earth, while the *Benzi* elites gorged themselves on luxury goods and amassed fantastic fortunes in offshore bank accounts, apparently without shame or regret. Why? And what, if anything, could be done about it? Why did our best ideas keep failing here, and producing unintended consequences?

Ryan had a short, blunt answer to these questions. "I'll tell you the trouble with Africa," he said. "Common sense gets trumped by tradition, belief, taboo. It's starting to change, but too slowly."

5

Waking into Nightmare

**River fetishists—Kahama—Albino body parts—
Nyakanazi—Upper Malagarasi—Bandits and poachers—
Kagera Nkanda—Floating—Terror**

WE HAD VEERED NORTHWEST of the old caravan route, in
order to intersect the Malagarasi up near the Burundi border,
so I never got to see Kazeh, where Burton and Speke stayed for
five weeks and fell into open disagreement for the first time.
Founded by Omani Arabs in 1825, Kazeh was the crossroads
hub of the East African slave and ivory trade, a trading post way
out on the plains with supply lines extending for hundreds of
miles in four different directions. Nothing remains of the town
today, apparently, except some crumbling adobe walls, a strong
Islamic influence in the nearby town of Tabora, and a few of the
mango trees and coconut palms planted by the Omani slavers.

They were tall, elegant, graceful men with beards and turbans and long white robes, living in well-made mud buildings
with enclosed courtyards, slave quarters, and large harems.
They had vegetable gardens, rice fields, and a bazaar where elephant tusks and the "human commodity," in Burton's phrase,
were traded, and chains, ammunition, and other tools of the
trade were sold at vastly inflated prices. The Omani traders welcomed the two Englishmen with warm and generous hospital-

ity, which came as a sharp contrast to the hassles, threats, and demands in the African villages. Burton spoke their language flawlessly, knew their customs, literature, and religion inside out, and had earned the title *Haji* by his pilgrimage to Mecca. The Omanis were astonished and delighted to meet such an Englishman at Kazeh, of all places, and Burton felt great relief at being among civilized men again.

Elsewhere in his narrative he refers to Arab slave traders as the scourge of East Africa, "a flight of locusts over the land," but in Kazeh he was able to shunt these views into a quiet compartment of his brain and enjoy long hours of conversation and burgeoning friendship with these cultured, courtly dealers in human flesh and misery. Perhaps he simply put them in their context and recognized them as part of a two-thousand-year-old slaving tradition that Arabs had always considered honorable and in accordance with Allah's will.

The traders at Kazeh were an invaluable source of information on the geography and ethnography of East and Central Africa, and Burton compiled extensive notes there in his tiny handwriting. The main purpose of the expedition, as specified by the Royal Geographical Society, was to investigate the rumors of a huge lake, or inland sea, in the middle of the African continent. Burton now discovered that there were four lakes, and two of them were of oceanic size. If they marched west for thirty days, they would reach the Sea of Ujiji, or Lake Tanganyika. Fifteen days to the north was the Sea of Ukerewe, soon to be renamed Lake Victoria.

About the source of the Nile, the great obsession of European geographers, the Arabs were as almost as vague and disinterested as the African porters and slaves that Burton had questioned. Perhaps rivers flowed out of the lakes, or perhaps into them. The Arabs weren't sure. Perhaps the lakes were joined by a river, and yes, there were mountains whose streams and rivers drained into the lakes. What difference did it make if one of these streams was the beginning of the Nile? It was a piece of knowledge that altered nothing, furnished no material gain, held no practical or spiritual significance. For the Arabs, it certainly wasn't a question worth dying over, but that is exactly what Burton and Speke, ravaged by a fresh round of fevers and almost blind from swollen lumps growing on the insides of their eyelids, were prepared to do. "We never relinquished the determination to risk everything, ourselves included, rather than to return unsuccessful," Burton wrote, and he reiterated it several times.

Dr. Livingstone, whose long history of compounding folly in Africa ended with a fatal quest for the Nile source, described it in his last, recovered journals as a sort of madness that had possessed him. Later in life, Burton came to a similar conclusion about his own search for the coy fountains. I agreed with this diagnosis—it was lunacy—and yet here was I, another restless Englishman drawn toward the Nile source and prepared to risk everything, self included, to explore a more obscure river. In the same way that some African tribes ascribe an unnatural power to bundles of feathers, carved figures, hanks of fur and bone, and the like, so do some white men fetishize the abstract geographical details of African rivers.

I could see the lunatic aspects of my own quest, but it seemed like the chance of a lifetime, and already I had started to think of the Malagarasi as my river. I knew this was absurd and outrageous, but I couldn't prevent it from happening. It was an echo of the egomania and colonizing impulses that drove exploration, the claiming of geographical features in other people's countries, and the dubious notion that they were "undiscovered" until some European came along with a pen and paper.

Speke became convinced from the vague, conflicting hearsay at Kazeh that there was a river flowing north out of Lake

Victoria, that this river was the Nile, that they should go up there immediately, claim the glory of discovery, and return to England posthaste. Burton thought Lake Tanganyika was more likely to be the Nile source, and since he was the expedition's leader, and since Tanganyika sounded like the lake they had been sent to discover, he overrode the fuming Speke and took them west instead.

Meanwhile Burton had developed an interesting new symptom. His legs were paralyzed. He was now crippled, fevered, and going blind. Speke was also sick, but at that stage he was the stronger man. He became convinced that Burton was about to die, and that this was why he refused to go north: to prevent Speke from discovering the Nile source and returning to England as the sole living hero of the expedition.

IN OUR HUMMING Land Cruisers, we drove on through sunset, dusk, and darkness, until the air felt more humid and smelled of green vegetation and moist earth, and in the distance we saw a gold mine lit up like a fairytale city on the plain at night. There was a town next to this Canadian-owned mine, and its name was Kahama. We found a small guesthouse there with lock-up parking, and I fell exhausted and feverish into bed without eating.

It seemed like minutes later when the alarm rang on my phone at 5 a.m., but I felt slightly improved, as though my immune system had made some headway against whatever was wrong with me. A television was blaring in the front room and the news was about cattle encroachment, land issues, another politician cleared on corruption charges, and the albino killings, which were bringing Tanzania the sort of global publicity it earnestly wanted to avoid.

Up here in the north and northwest near Lake Victoria, and across the border in Burundi, there was a new and spreading belief, started by witch doctors and swallowed wholesale by credulous elements of the population, that the body parts of human albinos brought luck and financial success. Burton had been struck by the high prevalence of albinism in this part of East Africa, and geneticists think the mutation first occurred here, a reminder that evolution is blind and random. Albinos lack the gene that produces darkening, protective melanin in the skin, and under the East African sun, regardless of the body parts trade, it is a condition that drastically reduces life expectancy. Most albinos in Tanzania die before the age of thirty from skin cancer, which does nothing to dispel the widespread folk belief that they are living ghosts who cannot die but know how to vanish. In the last two years, more than sixty albinos had been killed and hacked into pieces, although not necessarily in that order.

In Burundi, where the trade was on a much smaller scale and guns were readily available, the harvesting killers generally shot the albinos before dismembering them and draining their blood into containers. In Tanzania, however, they would often hack off hands, arms, tongues, ears, genitals, breasts, and gouge out eyeballs while the victims were still alive. Most of the victims were women and children, and several children had been chopped up alive in front of their families.

Demand had now increased to the point where an albino hand was worth $1,500 and a "complete kit" of body parts fetched up to $75,000, according to the Red Cross. In a country where the average income was $800 a year, this created a serious economic incentive, and the market was now spreading into neighboring Kenya, where an albino woman had just had her tongue, eyeballs, and breasts removed, and the Congo, where albino skin was particularly prized. Here in Shinyanga province, the heartland of the trade, a fisherman had been caught trying to sell his albino wife to Congolese traders. Albinos couldn't walk down the street without hearing taunts and catcalls about how much their body parts were worth. In Dar es Salaam, following a protest by albinos demanding government action, one of the protesters was followed and had an arm hacked off, but she managed to escape and survive.

The killers and dismemberers sold their grisly harvest to witch doctors, who added value by making blood potions, body-part amulets, lucky shoes sewn from albino skin, and lucky fishing nets interwoven with albino hair. They also sold bones, dried hands, and genitalia. Their main clients were small businessmen, fishermen on the shores of Lake Victoria, and artisanal miners digging for gold and other minerals, although rumors abounded of politicians using albino body parts to win elections.

The Tanzanian government, horrified by the killings and the international attention they were attracting, had responded by outlawing all "traditional healers" except herbalists and asking the public for anonymous tips. President Jakaya Kikwete had called for the albino killers to be killed "to ensure the problem is eliminated and the country's image to the international community is cleansed." Over two hundred arrests had been made, including five policemen found profiting from the trade, and the first trial had just concluded here in Kahama.

The judge found four defendants guilty of murdering a thirteen-year-old albino boy; their DNA was on his severed legs, which had been found in a bush used for soothsaying. The judge sentenced all four of them to death by hanging, and that wasn't good enough for the Tanzania Albino Society, which demanded a public hanging to set a proper example.

The courts in Shinyanga province were also busy with witch murders. An old woman a week was being stabbed, bludgeoned, or hacked to death on suspicion of being a witch. Red eyes were the telltale sign, and in a place where women did the cooking over smoky wood fires, there was no shortage of old women with inflamed eyes. The fact that they were sometimes murdered by their own family members indicated to some Western researchers that it was really an economic issue: they had outlived their usefulness, and their families and communities didn't want to feed them anymore, so they came up with the justification of witchcraft in order to murder them. Was it really that logical?

Six cases were in the courts relating to the new belief, also emanating from local witch doctors, that raping disabled girls made you rich. Meanwhile in Eastern Congo, government troops from the 85th Brigade were raping male pygmies in order to gain supernatural powers. I don't mean to present these news items as a balanced, nuanced portrayal of African spiritual beliefs, which mostly offer hope, solace, and the illusion of power and control to people who need it. But there was undeniably an ugly, vicious side to it that encouraged men to victimize and terrorize the powerless—old women, children, albinos, pygmies, handicapped girls—and it was on the increase all over sub-Saharan Africa, confounding the predictions of Western anthropologists and aid workers. "It was previously believed that these beliefs and socio-cultural practices would disappear over time, but the current situation indicates the contrary," a recent UNICEF report stated. "Far from fading away, these social and cultural representations have been maintained and transformed in order to adapt to contemporary contexts." Witchcraft and ritual murder were a staple theme of the schlocky Nigerian B movies that were watched avidly all over Africa, and some researchers thought this could be a factor too.

It was always difficult and awkward for me to talk about witchcraft with Africans. For the ones who believed in it, it was a dangerous realm best kept private, hidden, and secret, especially from white strangers. For the ones who didn't believe in it, because they were among the small minority of Christians and Muslims who had disavowed "traditional healing" (most syncretized witchcraft into their Christianity or Islam), it was an embarrassment because it made Africans look primitive. No one wanted to hear my comparisons to the witch hunts in Salem or medieval Europe, my musings on the current popularity of Harry Potter or the New Age movement, or the fact that Catholics believed that they were actually drinking the blood and eating the flesh of Jesus at communion, which struck me as being as weird and macabre as any belief or magical practice I encountered in Africa. It was a charged subject, and most Africans preferred to avoid it.

I saw no signs of it among our group, except discomfort when I talked about it. Heblon allowed that he had met a certain game scout from Tanga on the coast who had nine lives and kept a second heart in his bag. Heblon had seen the heart and touched it, and there was no doubt that it was alive and beating. Mustafa, a good Muslim, said that people on the coast were manipulative about these things. "They talk and talk, they work up your mind, they get you ready to believe, then they show you a frog wrapped in a red cloth. You touch it, and it's alive."

Heblon thought about that and didn't say anything more.

"It's not a skeptical culture," said Ryan in English. "It's rude to question anyone older than yourself. You're supposed to say, *'Ndio mzee.' '*Yes sir.' Elders are respected, and the old beliefs hold strong."

DRIVING AWAY from Kahama at first light, we saw that the plains had turned green in the night and sprouted more trees. There was dew on the ground and a light mist over the swampy areas, the "miasma" that Burton thought caused malaria. Just after dawn, we saw a jackal crossing the road, the first wild mammal of the journey, and these trackers and hunters were greatly cheered and relieved. Soon afterward a water bird called a Hamerkop refused to get out of the road, and Ryan said, "What's wrong with that bird? These guys would say it's a spirit, an omen to be read." But they merely looked at it and said nothing.

We drove on through thickening woodland. The land started to undulate and form hills, and the soil turned from a burnt umber color to a rich terra-cotta red. The mountains of Rwanda and Burundi became visible on the far western horizon, a separate and distinct geographical region rising above the great plains and Great Lakes of Africa, with its own history and culture. Arab slavers never penetrated these remote highland monarchies, and Rwanda was unseen by Europeans until 1894, when a German count arrived with some news to impart to the Rwandan king and his people. Eight years previously, at the conference in Berlin that divided up Africa among the European powers, Rwanda had been awarded to Germany as a colony. I hoped to end my journey in those mountains, but it was too soon to think about that. We were getting close to the Malagarasi now.

A goat's tail and a peeled goat leg were nailed to a plank above an open doorframe at the Marangu Grocery in the highway junction village of Nyakanazi. Braced for the worst, I filed inside with the others and sat down at a plastic table on the dried mud floor. Ryan found out that they had real coffee, instead of the usual instant or milky chai, and it turned out to be locally grown, freshly roasted, brewed strong, and intensely delicious. Then came a plate of fresh, hot, perfectly made chapatis, soft and pillowy, instead of the usual cold, stiffening, greasy discs of disappointment, and I ate them drizzled with some honey we had bought by the side of the road, while the others gnawed away at a goat soup they said was particularly good.

It was one of those moments when something lifts away from

you and the world reveals itself as a place of charm and beauty again. It was a bright sunny morning in the green hills of Africa, and there was nowhere else I wanted to be. Choral gospel music played from a transistor radio. The women who ran the place patted out the flour for the chapatis in good humor, chatting away in a warm, unaffected way with the customers, laughing at some crazy joke made by one of the regulars. They came around again with the coffeepot and another plate of chapatis that released little puffs of steam when you tore into them.

I noticed the others in our party smirking and chuckling. "The people here speak Swahili with a very different accent," Ryan explained. "The boys are finding it funny." Then a young man with strange, haunted-looking eyes wandered in through the doorway, went out, came back in, went out, and turned in a small circle. Hebron made some quip, and they all tried to stifle their laughter again.

"Heblon says he must be a Rwandan who saw the genocide," Ryan translated. "Sometimes his sense of humor gets like that. There are a lot of refugees in this area, from Rwanda, Burundi, and Congo. They've decimated the game, unfortunately, but hopefully there'll be some left where we're going."

After breakfast, he called us together and spread out the maps. "We should get our first look at the upper river in a couple of hours," he said, "and we'll see how much flow we've got." I wanted to find a good flow of water there so badly that I slipped over into magical thinking. I was trying to will water into the river. I was praying for it when I said to myself, "Please let there be water."

Next to the Marangu Grocery was a tiny kiosk selling pirated CDs and DVDs, and we bought some music for the last stretch of road: a Bob Marley album and some Congolese music. Tito, who spoke more English than he had been letting on, was astounded when I mentioned to Ryan that Bob Marley's father was British.

"A white man?" Tito asked.

"Yes," I said. "A captain in the Royal Marines."

"Bob Marley is half-white? Like Obama? No, no, no. I cannot believe this. Bob Marley is black man hero, African hero."

"So if his father is white, he can't be a hero in Africa?" I said. "Even though the music and the message are the same? Even though Bob is still Bob?"

Tito thought for a moment. "No, he can still be a hero," he said. "But this is a very big surprise. You are sure?" He delivered the astonishing news to Heblon and Alanus, who looked mildly surprised but basically disinterested.

The Congolese music was by L'Orchestre Empire Bakuba, featuring the late Pepe Kalle, a three-hundred-pound singer who wore shiny suits and spangled robes, performed with a dancing dwarf who died of malaria, and then with three dancing pygmies. It was impossible to imagine a better sound track for the drive to the river—a red laterite road with thatched huts and lush roadside forest, women carrying baskets of bananas on their heads, children everywhere (*"Muzungu! Muzungu!"*), bicycles with the spokes turning like the irresistible, cycling, soukous groove, and that shining, ringing, amplified Congolese guitar sound, notes rippling out of the guitarist's fingertips with such suppleness and delight as big Pepe crooned, chanted, exhorted, and demanded what could only be a party. One of these days, I promised myself, I would ignore all the dangers and warnings and travel across Congo from dance hall to nightclub to recording studio, and look deeper into the miracle of the human spirit that produced Congolese music.

Every hill we crested with anticipation, hoping for a view of the river, and in the usual way of these things, we kept getting another hill instead. Ten or eleven hills later, we stood by the side of the road and looked out over a vast green basin steaming with equatorial heat. There in the dead center of the view, revealed by a parting in the trees, was one broad gleaming curve of river. We couldn't tell from this distance how deep the water was, but it was certainly more than the trickle I had feared and altogether a bigger and more impressive river than I had been expecting.

After relieving ourselves, as men are wont to do in high places with panoramic views, we got back in the Land Cruisers. I longed to be down there on the water, out of the vehicles, away from the noise of engines. Impatience chewed away at my insides, and Africa has a way of punishing the impatient.

A produce truck had broken down in the middle of the narrow rutted road. Another truck had tried to get around it—oh, the irrepressible optimism of Africa!—and was now slumped with a broken axle in the roadside ditch. Vehicles were backed up in both directions, and a man in civilian clothes was walking toward us with a short-stock AK-47.

"Who's this guy?" I asked.

"I'm guessing police," said Ryan. "Let's have a word with him."

The man said there was a problem with disorder in the vicinity. Burundian refugees had been robbing and killing people on the roads and in the villages and there were also problems with homegrown bandits. The government was taking steps to curb these problems, and there were now armed police like himself patrolling the roads during the day and stationed in the villages. "Crazy," said Hebron. "Is this my country?"

He pulled his chin wisp, his eyelids sank to half-mast, he shook his head slowly from side to side. Like me, he had never heard of bandits in Tanzania until this trip. He had never imagined that it was possible to drive all the way across Tanzania and see only one wild animal, that jackal on the road this morning. A conviction was growing in him that this whole expedition was ill starred and foolish, a reckless courting of danger, and that the wild west of Tanzania was no place for decent folk.

Bush mechanics got one of the trucks moving, and we made our long winding descent into the Malagarasi basin. The trees closed in and blocked out the views of the river. The air grew progressively hotter and more humid, and the insect noise increased to a shrieking metallic whine. We passed a group of anti-poaching game scouts in green uniforms and sunglasses, waiting out the midday heat under a shade tree. Somewhere poachers were doing the same.

"There are two kinds of poaching," said Ryan. "There are hungry people who want meat, and they use wire snares, or bows and arrows, because they can't afford guns or ammunition. And there are well-armed, well-organized poaching gangs who are in it to make money. In a place like this, they would normally send in two shooters, with one or two guns. When they make a kill, they call in the porters and cut off the animal's tail for tradition's sake. The porters carry out the meat, and you cannot beat or bribe the names of the shooters out of them. And if you do, you must then protect that porter, because someone will find out that he talked, and he will be killed."

It was a system designed to separate the guns from the meat, because only when the two were found together could you prosecute an act of poaching. The weak point of the system was that the shooters could also be prosecuted if they were found in possession of the tails. So why keep the tails?

"It goes back to the old colonial days. When they were shooting elephants or other large game, white hunters would cut off the tails and bring them back to the porters, so they would know how many animals they were supposed to find and carry out."

Ryan thought most of the poached meat in this area was probably sold locally, although bush meat could now be bought in cities all over Africa, where it was prized for its supposed strength-giving properties. Ten metric tons of it were reportedly entering London every day, with similar quantities reaching Paris, Brussels, and other European capitals with large African communities. The bush meat trade was having a devastating effect on African wildlife populations, although cattle encroachment was an even bigger problem.

The closer we got to the river, the more blue-and-black fabric cubes we saw hanging in the trees. These were tsetse fly traps. Reluctantly, because it was so hard not to hate the little bastards when they were biting you, Ryan had come to see tsetse flies as his best friend and ally in the cause of wildlife conservation. Where the flies lived, cattle died of a tsetse-borne disease related to sleeping sickness, and the native wildlife, which had evolved with the tsetse fly and had immunity to the disease, still had grass to eat. The famous national parks and hunting areas in East Africa nearly all owed their majestic herds of game, and the predators that fed on them, to this mean little fly, which had kept the cattle tribes at bay for thousands of years. Now, with tsetse eradication campaigns funded by aid money in full swing, these ancient barriers were falling, and cattle were displacing wildlife in new areas.

Two hundred yards from the river's edge, we hit another traffic jam. This one was emanating from a broken-down truck on the steel bridge spanning the river, and two men with AK-47s were patrolling it. I got out and made my way down to the river through the gauzy heat. The water was a murky, greenish, tan color, and it was gloriously deep and wide, moving at a stately pace through a riverside gallery of trees. All our worries and plans for the upper Malagarasi at the end of the dry season had been founded on an error. But no matter. We had a raft, and we had water in the river. We had all the gear and supplies we needed and two vehicles to resupply us when necessary. There was a nice gentle slope leading down from the bridge road to the river, and a perfect spot on the bank to inflate the raft, rig it, pack it, and get this expedition underway. It was true that Ryan was planning to launch the raft some forty-five miles downstream, but surely that would change when he saw all this water in the river.

I walked back to the vehicles in a state of high excitement. I sat down next to Ryan in the Land Cruiser and gave him the good news. He said nothing and refused to look at me. He got out of the vehicle, stood with his back to me, and ordered Alanus to fetch his cigarettes from the dashboard. At first I was just surprised. I assumed he thought I was being flighty and inconsistent, a greenhorn who knew nothing and was now trying to change his carefully laid plans, which of course I was. But I was also paying for everything, and I had been so clear from the beginning that I wanted to run the whole river, and Ryan's plan was clearly based on a faulty assumption about water levels, and I thought all that gave me the right to change it.

As Ryan continued to pretend that I didn't exist, and talk only in Swahili to Alanus and Hebron, my frustration turned to rage and fury. I wanted to stomp on his gouty foot, bury my fist in his face. I had been so patient for so long, through so many delays and disappointments and sidetracks. Now I could see the goddamn river and this stubborn little bastard had the nerve to stand in my way. Both of us fumed in silence, pretended it wasn't happening, and later that it had never happened. I took myself off for a walk in the swampy heat, stopped to scribble furious notes. Basically, I realized, I was feeling like Speke: closed out linguistically, lacking experience but convinced that I knew best, and seething with unexpressed resentment.

I went back across the bridge. Ryan was now back in the driver's seat, and I sat down next to him. "Well?" I said.

"It would put another week on the trip," he said.

I thought three or four days, but I hadn't yet seen how slow and meticulous Ryan was about setting up and breaking down camps. My personality type was always telling me to pack light, run fast and loose, don't ask permission, beg forgiveness instead if things went wrong, and improvise your way out of trouble. Ryan liked to have everything squared away, all boxes ticked, no loose edges flapping. The desk at his home office was frighteningly neat, clean, and symmetrical.

"We need the blessing of the local authorities," he said. "They know we're coming, and it shouldn't be a problem, but we need to meet them face-to-face, and line up all our favors in a row. I don't want to risk a surprise confrontation on the river. If that happens, this whole trip could be over, and it could cost us a lot of money to stay out of jail."

In particular, he wanted the blessing of the district game office in Kasulu, three hours down the road. By the time we got there, my anger had curdled into a dull, sour depression, aggravated by the extreme heat and the return of my aching, feverish malaise. I thought about finding a doctor, but it seemed like one more obstacle and delay. I was taking Malarone, so it couldn't be malaria, right? It was probably some snotless African flu, trying to take advantage of an overtaxed immune system. Breathing all that dust, it was no wonder my throat was sore. After eight hundred miles in an aging Land Cruiser on bad roads, it was hardly surprising that my kidneys ached.

Kasulu was a fast-growing town with a raw-bitten feel. Some 35,000 people lived here without electricity, except for a few dozen private generators. There was a grimy market run by women in bright, clean *kangas*, the usual surplus of idle, unemployed young men on the corners, and packs of children chasing and whacking the scrawny pariah dogs with sticks. "We need to watch our vehicles close here, or something will happen," was Ryan's appraisal. "Too many smart people with nothing to do."

The local government offices and district game headquarters were in the same compound. It was quiet and deserted except for two dozing security guards and an elegant, courteous man with glasses who spoke English, described himself as an urban planner, and declined to give his last name. "I prefer my first name," said Victor. Standing there in my dirty, sweat-drenched safari clothes, wondering if I was going to pass out from the heat, I looked in absolute amazement at his white polo-necked sweater and sports coat.

We exchanged pleasantries for a while in his office. He said there were a million people now in the district, including 130,000 refugees from the wars in Congo and Burundi, and populations were growing more rapidly here than anywhere else in Tanzania except Dar es Salaam. The average Tanzanian woman had six children. Here she had eight, and this created obvious challenges. By the time one school was built, you needed three more.

He tried to reach the district game office on the phone, with no luck. He got through to one of the game officers, who said he would meet with us that afternoon. I struggled through that meeting, which took place at a table outside a small hotel. There was a small shifting patch of shade and I tried to keep my aching head in it, while Ryan expertly charmed and small-talked the deputy, casually mentioning some of the members of parliament he knew in Dar es Salaam and musing lightheartedly about getting into politics himself. "What you need is a good boot with soft soles, so they feel the weight but don't get any bruises," he said, at which the deputy howled with laughter and spluttered into his beer. "The trouble with the guys in power now," Ryan added, "is hard boot, hard sole."

By the end of it, he was on our side, but he couldn't, or wouldn't, grant us permission to boat the river. He said he would arrange a meeting with a second game officer and suggested we check into a motel. I lowered a bucket into my well of patience, and it came up dry. I felt like screaming and running around in circles until I collapsed in the terrible heat. I had stood on the banks of the river, and now it was getting further and further away. I consoled myself by thinking of Burton. It had sometimes taken him eight days of haggling and negotiation to get permission to cross a chief's territory, and he had been a lot sicker than I was.

At the motel there was a rule against two men sharing a room with two beds. It was printed and framed on the wall. Only men and women were allowed to share rooms with two beds. I couldn't understand it at all. "What if we bring some prostitutes to the rooms?" I said to the manager, resisting the urge to ask if he could supply us whores from his family. He smiled politely, a tall dandy in a gray suit with a Nehru collar. The rule appeared to be a ploy to extract more money, but we had offered more money and that hadn't worked. I sat down in the lobby with a book and left it to Ryan. It took another hour, but we got our rooms.

I collapsed fully clothed on the bed and woke up in the same position three hours later, saturated with sweat and shivering. Ryan had good news. He was off to meet with the second game officer, and there was no need for me to come along. I took a shower and went back to bed. By the time I woke up, Ryan was back from the meeting, Mustafa had been out buying supplies and gathering information, and all the arrangements were in place for us to leave in the morning.

We had a final briefing in the motel restaurant, with maps spread over the table. The game officer had confirmed that no one had ever run the river before in a boat, only small sections of it. On the upper river, the main obstacle was bandits and poachers. The bridge where I had been so eager to launch the expedition was a particularly notorious spot, and the police wouldn't let you drive that road after four in the afternoon unless you had armed guards. There used to be a big pod of hippos at the bridge, but the poachers had got them and wiped out all the hippos from the upper river.

This is why I hired Ryan, I thought to myself. Left to my own devices, I'd probably be on a riverbank right now somewhere near that bridge with everything stolen, money belts and passport gone, standing there in my underwear being feasted on by the mosquitoes and tsetses.

We would be putting in our raft, as planned, on the edge of the Moyowosi Game Reserve. It was a remote area and there were still hippos in the river and big game on the banks. The game officer thought the swamp was impassable by raft, and he knew very little about the lower river. There were no roads leading in or out of it, and he had never heard of anyone going down it in a boat.

"After Uvinza, we go into the unknown," Ryan said in both languages. "We either come out alive or we come out in pieces. So speak up now if anyone's got a problem with that."

Heblon, Alanus, and Tito conferred. "We only have a problem if you ask us to kill someone," said Alanus.

"If it comes to that, it will happen so fast there won't be time for asking," Ryan said, smiling at the look of alarm that spread across their faces.

Then he spoke to me. "You are not, repeat not, a journalist. If he gets the idea we're investigating poaching, or hunting, or anything like that, we'll be straight off the river. You are a safari client that likes to travel in different, out-of-the-way places in Africa where the *wazungu* don't go. I told him we wanted to open up tourism in the area, and you were a trial run."

THE GAME OFFICER who had given us the clearance turned up the next morning wearing a green camouflage uniform and a blue foam baseball cap that read "I ♥ Tanz." He was carrying a rolled-up foam pad and suffering grievously from gout. He would be joining our expedition, to give it his official seal of approval, make sure everything went smoothly, and find us reputable local guides along the river.

"He wants to keep an eye on us," Ryan whispered. "And he wants money. We've had the preliminary negotiations already, and he'll probably try to renegotiate when he leaves. I've also promised him some of my gout pills. You can't get them out there, and the poor bastard can hardly walk from the pain."

Off we went in the Land Cruisers, first north, back up the familiar road, and then east for two hours on a rough track toward the river. We bounced and jolted through a cattle- and goat-grazed woodland with man-high termite mounds and the first few tsetse flies—four, five, six hard slaps and still they came back biting.

Five miles from the river, we reached the rough little bush town of Kagera Nkanda, a straggle of huts and shacks and tobacco fields awaiting the rains. It smelled of goats, goat shit, and goat stew. There were a few small mud-walled shops selling Cokes and cigarettes, a two-table restaurant under a thatch awning, chickens scratching, occasional mango trees. Forty or fifty children came charging after the vehicles, and when they caught sight of me, they stopped in their tracks and stared in silence.

"I think they have never seen a white person before," said Mustafa, chuckling softly. "I think you have scared them." But a bold young boy of eight or nine made his way to the front of the crowd at the passenger side window, gave me a big smile, said "*Muzungu!*" and pointed at my plastic water bottle. I made the mistake of taking a photograph and handing out a few empty plastic water bottles, and the children became wildly overexcited, shouting, yelling, climbing all over the vehicle, leaning in and touching my hair, trying to snatch at things on the dashboard, tugging, pulling, yanking at the door handles and bumpers, until Mustafa boomed out an admonishment, and they all stopped and went quiet, and a drunk man with an AK-47 appeared. He wore a red T-shirt, and he was the village policeman.

I waited in the Land Cruiser, a continuing object of study and fascination to the children, while Ryan, Mustafa, and the game officer went through the interminable process of exchanging greetings and talking things over with the policeman, the village elders, various passers-by and hangers-around. The game officer wanted a certain fisherman to be our river guide, but he wasn't in the village, so someone was dispatched to track him down.

Tito waited with me, and with Ryan gone, we had our first real conversation. His parents had been killed when he was four years old, he said, and his biggest regret in life was that he had missed his education because of it. When I complimented his English, his eyes shone, and he thanked me profusely. He had attended some school, loved it, and done well in his lessons, but then came the necessity to work for his food. Hearing this gave me a sharp, unexpected pain in my chest.

"You don't need to go to school as a child to become a wise man," I said. "You can learn a language by talking to people. You can teach yourself many things. I see you are an intelligent man who learns quickly."

"You are my friend," he said. "I see this. And I will work hard for you."

"Yes, we are friends. But you don't need to work for me. I am happy to do my own work."

"No. You write your words. This is your work. I do everything else, and you are my friend, so I work very hard for you."

"Do you want to make me fat and lazy?"

"Oh yes! It is better you have big belly like Omari."

He tried to engage some of the children and villagers in conversation, but they couldn't understand him. "They no speaki Swahili," he said. "Very few words. Bush people, very bush people. I don't know what language."

When Mustafa returned, he told us that the people here spoke Kiha, the language of the Muha people, the dominant tribal group on the borders of Burundi. It was a mark of the village's remoteness that so few people spoke Swahili as well.

"These people are suffering very much from bandits," Mustafa said. "Whenever they sell their tobacco crop, bandits come and take everything from them."

To have a corrugated aluminum roof on your hut is a sign of wealth and status all over rural East Africa. When the bandits started raiding here, their first targets were the huts with metal roofs, and now the villagers had all gone back to grass thatch. One of the local shopkeepers, who lived in a partitioned room behind his shop, no longer slept there at night. He kept his money in his underwear and went off to sleep with the wild animals and the ghosts.

The last bandit raid had been two weeks ago. I should have been more concerned, I suppose, but all I cared about was getting the raft in the river. I had run out of patience again. I was a sick man losing self-control. The sun pounded down with unbelievable force, and I sat there roasting in the Land Cruiser, basting in my own sweat, ears ringing from fever. My mood swung around wildly and I had no control over it anymore. I fumed with rage, plummeted into despair. I was hollowed out by great upwellings of sympathy for these poor villagers, who were not quite poor enough to avoid getting preyed upon. I was desperate to get away from them.

The infernal heat was boiling my brains. I tried to relax into it, to breathe slowly and calmly and evenly, to dissolve the boundaries and become one with the heat. That worked for about five minutes. Then I got out to find better shade, and the children came after me. Some of them had worked out that I was a potential source of money and things, and their hands were outstretched, the murmured pleas getting louder and more insistent. Others were simply curious. They wanted to touch my skin, feel my hair, stare at my blue eyes, shake my hand over and over again, which I consented to, not wanting to be rude, but I was also acutely aware that their hands were smeary with snot, grime, fecal matter, both human and goat, and a rich selection of African bacteria.

I got back into the Land Cruiser and tried boiling again. Tito passed me a cold bottle of water. Could I pay for his education? Sponsor this fine young man for U.S. citizenship? Then he started saying again how honored he was to be my friend, and how he would work so very hard for me, and I had a sudden urge to scream, "For chrissakes, man, stop polishing my balls! They're shiny enough already."

That was the whole goddamn problem with this continent. Men with power wanted their balls polished to an insane luster, and there were too many people eager to shine them. No, I decided. That wasn't just Africa. That was corporate America, too, and the reason I had walked out of my last salaried job in London twenty years ago. I poured the rest of the cold water over my head and handed the empty bottle to the delighted children outside the window. I pleaded with my mind to shut up and stop thinking.

Ryan and the game officer returned with the fisherman

guide, and then we were off and moving again. Air was moving, dust was moving, tsetses were biting again. Twenty minutes passed. We stopped and I got out and took my second look at the Malagarasi River. It was a greenish brown, a khaki color, and it looked heavy, sluggish, torpid, without the magisterial flow it had shown in its upper reaches. There were patches of floating lilies, thickets on the other side knitted together with creeper vines, a gallery forest of acacia trees, fever trees, palms, and sausage trees with dangling phallic fruits.

I sat in the shade on the riverbank, feeling queasy and spaced out. Sweat dripped from my face onto the pages of my notebook and poured off the men who were unloading the vehicles. There was a constant drone and whine of insects, and some fearsome bug that was ten times louder than the others and sounded like a circular saw cutting through a sheet of metal.

Now came the long, slow, frustrating process of inflating, rigging, and loading the neoprene raft in the worst heat of the afternoon. No one had done it before except Ryan, and he couldn't remember exactly how it all fit together. There was a lot of trial and error with the straps and buckles, the oarlocks, ropes, carabiners, ammunition cans (for dry storage), and several times, when it looked like the raft was almost fully loaded, it all had to be unloaded again and rerigged. A Sukuma herdsman appeared from the bush wearing a blue blanket like a toga, and he sat on the riverbank to watch this novel spectacle. Three hours later he was still sitting there contentedly, with a patience I would never match or understand.

With our oars, paddles, life jackets, camp chairs, kitchen table, propane stove and lanterns, buckets, rifles, ammunition, axe, hatchets, machetes, tents, sleeping bags, dry bags full of clothes, binoculars, satellite phone, GPS, expedition first-aid kit, maps, books, food, and twenty gallons of water, we had too much gear for the raft. By the time Ryan, Hebron, Alanus, Tito,

John Gangara our fisherman guide, and me were in there, the *"boati,"* as everyone called it, was dangerously low in the water. We strapped on our life jackets regardless, and I dunked my hat in the water and put it on my head. Finally, I was afloat on the Malagarasi River. My fevered head swung over to the ecstatic, and my haggard face twisted into a crazy grin.

Ryan had to heave mightily at the oars to move the overladen raft downstream. He instructed Hebron and me to scan the river ahead through binoculars, looking for those small dark shapes disturbing the pale surface of the water that would turn out to be the bulbous eyes, snouts, and swiveling circular ears of hippopotami. I had performed a similar lookout function on the Zambezi but never worked out why hippos were so defensive and aggressive. They were herbivores who grazed on riverside vegetation at night, and they had no predators. An adult hippo was longer and taller than a Jeep Cherokee, weighed twice as much, and could bite a twelve-foot crocodile in half. So what were they so worried about? Were they just big, paranoid vegetarians?

"It's territorial and it's male aggression," said Ryan. "A male hippo has to win a lot of fights and showdowns to get control of a territory and a pod. He is primed to defend it against other male hippos, and that aggression carries over to rafts and canoes. Also, they get really tired and cranky after feeding all night, and they don't want to be disturbed in their river."

In the riverside trees there were spur-winged geese, big dark-brown birds with red faces, and glossy black open-billed storks sunning their extended wings. Ryan stopped rowing to admire the birds, and I could see him start to relax and enjoy himself. I could feel the same process taking place in myself. Huck Finn was right. There's something mighty free and easy about floating down a river, even if it does have hippos and crocodiles in it.

"What's the name of this *boati*?" I asked Ryan.

He thought for two seconds. "Jimmy Hendrick," he said, and I laughed in agreement. I had never met the legendary Jimmy, but I'd heard dozens of stories about him. He was an ex-Marine who had found his way to the bottom of the Grand Canyon, where he rowed tourists through the big whitewater rapids and worked with a good friend of mine, who describes him as follows: "Jimmy's about half-crazy, and he likes to run hard, and fuck." Then Jimmy had turned up in Tanzania, and Ryan had made the first raft descent of the Rufiji River with him and another American river runner, surviving nine hippo attacks on the raft in the process. Jimmy had then married a young African woman, supposedly a tribal princess, and was currently in Malibu writing a screenplay about his life for some Hollywood mogul who had heard his stories on a rafting trip through the Grand Canyon.

Hebron spotted the first crocodile after half an hour on the river. It was an eight footer off the bank that slithered into the water at our approach. Our fisherman guide John said that an average of one fisherman a year was taken by crocodiles in this stretch of the river. He was a lean and strong man with prominent cheekbones and gave every indication of being honest, reliable, and intelligent, although shy and reticent at being thrust suddenly into this company of strangers. Forty-five years old, he was from the Nyakanda tribe, and he lived in Kagera Nkanda with his wife and five children. He said he knew the river well all the way to Uvinza, including channels through the big swamp, but he was used to a dugout canoe, and he doubted that our big *boati* would fit through them.

At the motel in Kasulu, one of the guards had told us there was an elecric fish that lived in the Malagarasi, and it would give you a shock if you touched it. I had filed this in the mythical beasts column, but John said it was true. The fish was called a *nyika*. It reached fifteen kilos, with a fleshy head, a body like a catfish, an elongated split tail, and it would give you a mild, buzzing electric shock. Ryan had never heard of an electric fish in Tanzania, and we wondered if it might be an undiscovered species.

As the sun went down, John guided us to a fishing camp on a raised piece of land inside a horseshoe bend of the river. It was a beautiful place with a tributary stream entering on the far bank through a lush green marshy wetland, the river unwinding below us into a long straight avenue lined with big trees, and long-necked birds flapping against the sinking orange sun. A pod of hippos was grunting and snorting at a safe distance downstream, and on a sandbank thirty yards away, a little too close for my comfort, a fourteen-foot crocodile surveyed us. I remembered Burton's phrase about "small malignant eyes, deep set under warty brows," and how big crocodiles waddled down to the river "like dowagers on their horrid claws."

The fishing camp was a simple lean-to structure containing two woven reed mats, a tiny three-legged stool, some woven baskets in disrepair, and a stick-and-mud fish smoker buzzing with flies. It was set back from the river, and to get away from the flies, we made our camp closer to the water's edge. It came as no surprise to see that Mr. Ryan wanted everything done in a certain order and arranged just so. The tents were pitched in a circle, encircling the fire. The kitchen was off to the side with a table, a dish line of three steel buckets (one hot, one bleachy, one cold), and a garbage bag. Propane lanterns were hung around the perimeter of the camp, camp chairs unfolded for me and Ryan. All lumps, roots, and intruding branches in the campground were removed with the axe, hatchets, and machetes, so no one would trip in the dark, and the three rifles leaned up against a tree behind Ryan's camp chair. "The pump-action shotgun makes a big noise, and is good for birds, bandits, and scaring off hippos," he said. "The .470 is for putting a hippo down. The thirty-ought-six is for meat, if the game officer will let us shoot any."

Fanning out from the campsite, Alanus and Hebron found signs of lion, buffalo, hyena, reedbuck, and bushbuck, and we collected enough wood to keep a big fire burning all night. "For safety," Ryan clarified. "Nothing works better with unwelcome visitors in the night."

From our food stores he selected a packet soup mix and a can of stew. He lined up a cutting board, a knife, two onions to enhance the flavors, salt, and pepper. One of the onions wobbled slightly out of line, and he put it back. Then came the first slow, meticulous slice of his knife across the first onion, then a pause while he stepped back, admired his handiwork, took a drag on his cigarette. Then he made the second slice. It was well after dark by the time we ate, and the talk had turned back to bandits. We were all getting jumpy at the rustlings, snapping, sudden cries, and other sounds one hears at night in the wild places of Africa.

"Better sleep light tonight," Ryan told his staff. "Or you'll wake up as someone's wife." This was the expression for male rape, and it produced giddy peals of laughter from Hebron, Alanus, and Tito. Then John quietened the mood by saying the bandits had recently made two men their wives in Kagera Nkanda and raped women, too.

After eating, doing the dishes, and packing everything away, we sat around the campfire and started quizzing John in detail. He said the bandits had raided Kagera Nkanda three times in the last six months. They would come in the night with guns blazing and then go shop to shop, hut to hut, taking anything of value. In the raid two weeks ago, he said, there were four gunmen, and they all had automatic rifles. You could buy an AK-47 for thirty dollars in Burundi.

"Let's hope they haven't got wind of us," said Ryan. "Because if they're that well-armed, I don't think they can resist having a go."

"How do they travel?" I asked.

"By foot, sometimes bicycle," said John.

"This is a pretty remote spot," I said. "We'd be very unlucky if they found us here."

"There's a bad place a short way down the river," said John. "A group of Tutsis have their cattle there, and other people try to steal them. They all have guns. We must be careful going through there."

"It would really be a sad case of coincidence if we ran into anything," said Ryan. "It's such a pity, man. Africa is blessed with so many beautiful things."

"Kagera Nkanda," intoned Hebron, shaking his head with a wisp of a smile. He reminded Ryan that we were supposed to be promoting tourism in the area, and then we all dissolved into laughter. "Enjoy the sights of Kagera Nkanda," said Hebron. "Bring the whole family."

"Come experience the exciting nightlife," I said. "AK-47s are cheap, and you can marry a bandit."

Suddenly there was a big splash in the river, and I spun around. "Hippo," said Ryan. "He won't bother us if we keep the fire burning." A few minutes later, we heard the yawning groan of a lion and then the ascending whoop-whoop of a hyena. As jumpy as I was, sickness and exhaustion overtook me, and I crawled into my tent and passed out.

SHE WAS AN Englishwoman in her thirties, and she was blonde and beautiful, and I wanted to get away from her because I knew she was trouble. Then we were in her bed, and her clothes were off, and she was wet and ready. She insisted on a condom, so

I got out of bed, found one in the bathroom, rolled it on, and came back to her bed. She sighed a faraway sigh, said she had to check on something, then she was out of bed, putting on her clothes, and *boom!* I woke up from the dream drenched with sweat. *Boom!* There it was again, a high-caliber rifle way too close. Was that Ryan's gun?

Then the sound of tent zippers frantically unzipping, and we were all scrambling out into the firelight, and Ryan grabbed his .470 with a look of deep alarm on his face, and then came *BOOM! BOOM! BOOM!* from behind us on the other side of the river. I had a splitting headache and was shivering uncontrollably, and more than anything I was desperate to kick out the fire and smash the lanterns, to hide in the darkness, but Ryan said, "No. We need the fire. There are lions out there."

"The fucking lanterns then," I hissed. "For fuck's sake, man."

"Okay," he said. He told Hebron to turn out the lanterns, and he took some wood off the fire. "Hebron," he said. "You take the shotgun and go outside the circle. If I need to shoot, I'll put the first one in the air. Alanus. Get the thirty-ought-six."

Boom! Another one from upriver, closer this time. *Boom!* Another one from across the river, out in that tributary marshland. I huddled next to the fire, craving the warmth, cringing from the light, and running through my mind like the broken white line in the middle of the highway was the eternal traveler's question: what am I doing here? What in the living holy fuck am I doing here?

6

Chapter of Accidents

**Bad night—Hippo meat—Tutsi cattle—Hunting camp—
Swamp—Malagarasi town—Lord of the Ferry—
Underwear Rapid—Trapped**

"NOT GOOD," SAID Ryan. "I don't like one bit of this."

Twenty minutes had passed without a gunshot, and now we waited with eyes and ears straining into the darkness. Normal life was resuming in the nocturnal animal kingdom, with twigs snapping, rustles in the undergrowth, strange calls and cries, a sudden heart-stopping splash in the river just behind us. Then I heard something or someone advancing toward us with slow, cautious, stealthy footsteps.

Our night vision was maimed by the firelight. I thought we should use the old cowboy and Indian trick, leave the fire as a decoy, and wait thirty yards away, but I said nothing because I had been wrong about so many things lately, and lions and hyenas were out there. The sinister footsteps came closer, raising the hairs on the back of my neck. Then a dog barked, and my heart filled up with dread.

The bandits had heard from the villagers that we were heading to the river and they had brought their dogs to find us. Now they would fan out, surround us in the darkness, and suddenly appear all at once in the firelight with their AK-47s pointed at us. Another dog barked, or was it the same one?

"You hear that?" I hissed to Ryan.

"It's a bushbuck," he whispered.

"That's a fucking dog, man. They've got dogs."

"Alanus?" he whispered. Alanus confirmed that it was the doglike call of a bushbuck, a small spiral-horned antelope. Then, by the weak starlight, we saw that the sinister footsteps belonged to a grazing cow. Then there was another gunshot. It was closer this time and on our side of the river.

I hadn't even registered the absence of John, but only now did he emerge from his tent. He looked concerned, but not gripped like the rest of us. John didn't think they were bandits. He thought we were caught between two different groups of poachers, one going after hippo in the river, the other hunting impala and reedbuck in the tributary marsh on the other side. Another shot boomed in the darkness, followed by a big splash. John nodded. That was the sound of hippo poaching. Then, from the same direction, came *boom-boom-boom!* That was the sound of a shooter who had missed and was now blasting away in frustration at a hippo submerged in the river. "It is very dark to be hippo poaching," John said. "Normally they do it when there is moonlight."

How much of a threat were the poachers to us? John said it depended. If they thought we were fishermen at the fishing camp, they would leave us alone. If they had heard about us in the village, they might be tempted to rob us. If they thought we were game scouts, they would want to kill us. There was open warfare now between game scouts and poachers in this area. Both sides shot at each other on sight. John's younger brother was a game scout in Kagera Nkanda, and when poachers came for him a few weeks ago, they riddled his hut with bullets and burned it down. His brother had been warned that they were coming and kept them in a running gun battle for most of the night before finally they gave up.

I was writing all this down in my notebook by the firelight, thinking that they must have heard about us in the village and guessed we would have reached the fishing camp, and would soon come and try their luck. John saw me scribbling and became concerned. "I know you're trying to bring tourists here. I hope I haven't said anything wrong."

"No," said Ryan. "The truth is most important."

"Kagera Nkanda is a notorious village," he said. "This is a dangerous area. The Tutsis downstream are dangerous. I didn't want to say anything, because he is a big man, but I don't understand why the game officer let you come here."

The first gunshot, the one that woke me up, had been at half past midnight. At four in the morning, the gunmen were still blasting away at regular intervals, but further away from us. At four-fifteen, Ryan called in Hebron from his post in the darkness. Crouching by the fire with his hands extended, Hebron said laconically that he preferred that nice breakfast place at Nyakanazi to this riverbank. Ryan got out his satellite phone, called Mustafa, and told him to come and get us.

"We're pulling out," he told me. "I don't need another night like this. You need a military expedition to run this river."

I couldn't argue. My judgment had been proved faulty too many times in the last twenty-four hours. I crawled back into my tent, too sick and exhausted to care that my plans had collapsed once again. The gunshots were far away now, and less frequent, and I sank down into a deep, dark well of sleep.

THEN IT WAS DAWN and the gunfire had stopped. Walking behind the tent toward the nearest bushes, I saw fresh hyena tracks. He came, he saw, he sniffed the smoky air and turned around. Ordinarily, the idea of a hyena so close would have given me a shudder. These ugly, slinking, powerful creatures can drive a lion off its kill, and they have a nasty if occasional habit of breaking into unsecured tents and ripping people's faces off with their teeth. But worrying about hyenas seemed absurd under the circumstances. The entire animal kingdom seemed harmless compared to homo sapiens with guns.

Scanning the river downstream through binoculars, I was relieved to see at least two hippos left of the three or four we had heard at sundown. They were no longer the big menace of the river but beleaguered comrades. We had bonded in fear of a common enemy, and they had my sympathy for their trauma and loss. Like elephants, hippos grieve for their dead, and I have read accounts and seen video footage of hippos holding a kind of funeral service. A group will stand vigil around the corpse for hours, gently nuzzling and licking it at regular intervals. That wouldn't be happening here this morning. Any dead hippos would have been hacked up into chunks, carried away by porters on foot, and then handed over to porters with bicycles at the nearest road.

Back in the camp, Ryan was talking to his wife on the satellite phone, asking if baby Ruben was all right, telling her that he loved her, saying there was a poaching problem on the river, and he might be home early. There was a kettle boiling over the fire, and I made myself some instant coffee and oatmeal, depriving Tito of an opportunity to serve me. "Too much guns," he said. "Safari over."* I sat down on the riverbank and added to my fire-scrawled notes from the night before, while the others took down the tents and started deflating the raft.

The sound of Land Cruiser engines announced the rescue

---

*In Swahili, the word *safari* means journey, and Sir Richard Burton is credited with introducing it to the English language party led by Mustafa. He had found his way here through a maze of overgrown bush tracks and was now weaving in and out of gaps between trees and termite mounds. With him were the game officer, a local pygmy, and Omari following in the second vehicle.

There ensued a long debriefing and discussion in Swahili between Ryan, the game officer, John, and Mustafa. Omari leaned against his vehicle and opened some shirt buttons to air his belly. I stood silently on the sidelines with the pygmy. He was about four feet ten, wearing denim shorts that hung down to his ankles and chunky plastic sandals. He was probably a Twa pygmy from Burundi. The better known pygmies from the Ituri forest in Congo seldom get that tall.

The game officer came up to me afterward and said he was sorry we had experienced such a disturbed night. The curse of his district, he added, was its proximity to Burundi, "These Burundians have nothing, they have seen terrible things, their children do not go to school and do not speak Swahili. They come down here from the border to farm, or graze cattle, and some of them go bad. Guns are so cheap. On the last sweep we did through Kagera Nkanda, we confiscated thirteen submachine guns."

He had only four game scouts at his disposal, and he needed twenty at least. He would report last night's poaching activity, but he didn't like sending his men into this area, because it so often led to a gun battle and threatened to leave him with less than four game scouts. "How is the elephant population?" I asked.

"We have lost thirty this year," he said. "They are all gone from this area, but there are more than a hundred left in the other areas."

"And the hippo populations?"

"One good population in the swamp. The rest will be gone

soon." He said this in a blank, unconcerned, matter-of-fact way, as if it were a situation over which he had no control. He thought there were probably fifteen full-time poachers operating out of Kagera Nkanda, plus porters, and Ryan said, "That's all it takes to wipe out the game in a large area. It's very hard to stop a committed poacher, because that is his life."

John pointed out that it was more expensive to live here now, and this was a further incentive for poachers and also for thieves and bandits. "Why is it more expensive?" I asked.

"Phones and phone vouchers," he said. "Also people grow less food than they used to, so they have to buy more."

"Why do they grow less food?"

"The government tells them to grow tobacco so they can sell it and have money. But the bandits take the money."

We packed everything away in the Land Cruisers. I was already planning my doctor visit and convalescence in Kasulu and then an overland route to Lake Tanganyika, Burundi, and Rwanda, but Ryan said he wanted to try one more thing before abandoning the Malagarasi.

About twenty miles to the south, the river flowed through an area managed for hunting and fishing by a foundation called the Friedkin Conservation Fund, which fielded its own teams of anti-poaching game scouts. Ryan said he was willing to drive down there, inquire about the poaching and bandit activity in the area, and if it seemed safe, we could at least raft down to the swamp.

The road took us back through Kagera Nkanda. The name of the village had become a byword for infamy and craziness in the mind of Hebron, and he kept repeating it in a low, spooky, ironic voice, stretching out the syllables like an incantation. We stopped there for lukewarm chicken stew and sour-smelling rice in a filthy hovel crawling with flies. Congolese music was playing through fuzzy, blown-out speakers on a small boom box as we talked over the economics of the hippo poaching trade. The meat from one dead hippo was worth a thousand dollars, said John and the game officer. It was sold in three-kilo chunks, for five dollars each, and distributed by foot and bicycle through dozens of local villages and across the border into Burundi. The poor couldn't afford such pricey food. It was for the better-off families.

"What does it taste like?" I asked.

"It's extremely chewy with kind of a musky smell," said Ryan. "It needs special cooking techniques with marinades to make it palatable. The meat is very fatty, and the fat is not separated through the meat."

The worst way to cook hippo meat was slowly over a fire, which gave it the consistency of a rubber tire, but this was the way Tanzanian villagers cooked it and every other kind of game meat. "They're not particular about the flavor, and they don't mind chewing," said Ryan. "*Nyama* is *nyama*. Meat is meat, the best food there is for keeping hunger away." The notion of cuisine didn't exist and perhaps couldn't exist where hunger was still the main concern.

Hebron had regained his sense of humor. "Don't go to the Serengeti, don't go to Kilimanjaro, come to Kagera Nkanda for your African vacation," he quipped. "We have twenty-four-hour armed police for your security, and he sleeps very well when he's drunk."

Leaving Kagera Nkanda, where most of the dwellings are square or rectangular, we passed a cluster of round huts with conical thatched roofs. These were Tutsi huts, belonging to Tutsi refugees from Burundi, and further down the road we saw Tutsi cattle with their extraordinary horns. Five or six feet long, immensely thick at the base, they curve upward to form lyre shapes, crescents, and occasionally an almost perfect circle. This ancient African breed of cattle, also known as Ankole, is able to shed heat by circulating blood through its horns.

They were grazing, or more precisely overgrazing, a lightly wooded savannah west of the Malagarasi designated as the Uvinza Open Area. We saw no wildlife whatsoever until we got further from the villages and closer to the river. Then the trees thinned out, the cattle disappeared, the grass grew thicker and greener, the sky seemed to yawn open, and a family of elephants trooped across the flat horizon line.

Herds of hartebeest and topi came into view, then impala, reedbuck, buffalo swinging their heavy horns, warthogs running with their tails aloft, another group of elephants involved in knocking over an isolated tree. There had been no fences or gates, but we had crossed over into the hunting area managed by the Friedkin Conservation Fund, a nonprofit organization bankrolled by a Texas billionaire and big game hunter named Thomas H. Friedkin.

"You see?" said Ryan. "This is what I'm talking about, *bwana*. This is what hunting can do for conservation."

The Friedkin strategy was a mixture of stick, carrot, and education. They had well-armed, well-trained, well-paid game scouts, recruited from local communities. They funded community development projects, and their education campaigns focused on explaining the economic benefits of conserving wildlife, and the income and employment it could generate for local villagers. I had seen similar conservation projects fail elsewhere in Africa, and in Asia and Latin America, but this one appeared to be working.

As we drove, Hebron and Alanus were exhibiting their highly trained visual awareness, spotting animals at incredible distances, identifying antelope species from an ear or a horn protruding from the grass three hundred yards away or a shape of a haunch in the dappled shadow under a tree, where I could stare for five minutes and see nothing at all.

I was watching elephants through my binoculars. "I agree

that hunting can work for conservation," I said to Ryan. "But I could never shoot an elephant. They have such intelligence and understanding in their eyes."

"My dad has the same sentiment, and he's an avid, lifelong hunter," said Ryan. "He killed one once, and said he'd never do it again. There's something about an elephant. They cry."

"Jesus. I didn't know that."

"I never tell a client to take a heart or lung shot with an elephant. Always a head shot so it ends cleanly. We used to have five thousand elephants in the Kilombero. Now they've been so decimated by poachers that we don't hunt them anymore. They don't hunt them here either."

The river came into sight below us, making its way through a corridor of trees at the edge of the plain. The road led us to a lodge and a compound on the riverbank where the Friedkin people were headquartered, and a young, clean-cut, white South African in safari gear came out to meet us. His name was Dale Wright, and Ryan at first refused to believe that he was South African. "Are you sure?" he whispered to me. "He seems too nice."

Dale had heard from his bosses that we might be showing up, but he was expecting us by river. We told him what had happened, and where, and he said, "Yah, that's really a hot spot, I'm afraid. We lost a game scout not far from there two weeks ago. Our guys surprised some poachers, there was a gun battle, he was hit and died from loss of blood. Terrible, eh. But it happens, unfortunately."

"And how is it down here?" asked Ryan. "It looked good driving in."

"Yah, they got an elephant a couple of days ago, but it's pretty much under control here. You're not going to have bullets flying around like that. How long were they shooting for?"

"Most of the night," I said.

"Jeez," he said. "If they were shooting that much, they can't have been shooting very straight. When we put our anti-poaching patrols up there, the activity ceases, and then the moment our guys leave, the poachers go straight back in."

Dale had talked with a friend about running the Malagarasi in a canoe, and one thing that had put them off was the amount of pollution in the upper river. "It's supposed to be the most polluted stretch of river in Tanzania from all the villages at the headwaters," he said. "Then the poaching got bad up there, the crime. I don't know, we might still do it one day."

On a map, Dale showed us a place about twenty kilometers upstream where we could camp by the river and launch the raft in the morning. "It's a beautiful stretch of river," he said. "Fantastic birds, some hippo, some big crocs. You'll have a great time. You can run the river all the way to swamp and you shouldn't have any trouble."

"What about the swamp?" I asked.

"It's the most inhospitable place for a human being I've ever seen," he said with a grin. "You've got bullrushes twelve feet high in knee-deep water, or you've got solid walls of papyrus. Lots of mosquitoes and tsetses. A lot of weird-looking insects I've never seen anywhere else. I have to wade in there on foot and cut canoe paths for our fishermen. There's no way you'll get a raft through there."

And what about the lower river below Uvinza? "No idea. On the map it looks like a big canyon going through the mountains all the way to the lake. I've heard there's a big waterfall, and some hydro project getting built there. I don't think there's much game left below the swamp, so you won't have to worry about poachers."

Like the game officer, Dale identified Burundi, and the availability of cheap guns there, as the biggest problem for wildlife in this part of Tanzanzia. "We sweep the villages and a year later they're full of guns again. SMGs, AKs, G3s. Muzzle-loaders too for hippo. Some of them are antiques, but they also know how to make muzzle-loaders from scratch. The ivory guys use semiautomatics, and they are really at the bottom of the food chain in that business, doing it for peanuts. The ivory goes to China and the Far East."

One thing he didn't understand was how the poachers always seemed to know when his game scouts were going to switch locations. "They have very good intelligence, which is a little worrying," he said. "I don't know where they get it from."

The game officer stared at his gouty feet. There was an awkward silence. The information was either leaking out of the Friedkin anti-poaching operation, or it was leaking out of his department.

WE DROVE UPRIVER on a bumpy track through swarms of tsetse flies and discovered that Alanus knew more English than he had been letting on. Receiving two bites on the ear in quick succession, he let out a vehement, exasperated "Oh fuck!" We all crowed and laughed, and were inspired to teach him other useful English phrases like "Fuck you, motherfucker" and "Shit goddamn, get off your ass and jam." We were in that giddy, brittle territory that lies on the other side of deep fatigue, slapping ourselves silly trying to kill the tsetses, denouncing them with mangled English oaths. The warthogs looked particularly comical, and every five minutes or so Ryan would stop the lead vehicle, Hebron could creep out with the shotgun, stalk through the grass with a hunched-over, high-stepping gait, and kill another red-necked spur fowl for dinner.

I was still a little feverish, and my head felt thoroughly rattled and wrenched around by recent events. At one o'clock in the morning, I was in mortal terror. At five in the morning, I was unhappily resigned to the failure of nearly two years of planning and expectation, but relieved to be alive. Now it was four in the afternoon, and the Malagarasi River expedition was a live prospect again, at least as far as the swamp.

"Exploring is a series of mistakes," wrote Burton, and African adventure "a chapter of accidents." Our expedition would not be a linear, orderly progression, in which things unfolded as planned, but something more in keeping with Burton's definitions. An expedition in Africa, he said, was unimaginable without "the maladies, the weary squabbles, and the vast variety of petty troubles."

We parked the vehicles and inspected the riverbank camping area. There were two muddy hippo trails coming up from the river, fresh tracks of buffalo and hyena, and a big pile of lion shit, all of which cheered Ryan immensely. This was his beloved African bush as wild and pristine as he wanted it. He was entirely comfortable and familiar with the risk from dangerous wild animals, and although accidents did sometimes happen, if you made a good tight camp, kept the fire burning all night and a .470 rifle to hand, there really wasn't that much to worry about.

As we set up camp, I started gathering firewood, even after Tito asked me to please sit down on the camp chair he had set out for me. I wanted to feel useful, more like an expedition member than a client. I started putting up my tent and then realized I wasn't making things easier for Tito, but more difficult. I wasn't sparing him a chore but making him look incompetent and encroaching on his usefulness. He came from a hierarchical culture—big men and little people, as Africans call it—and I was ingrained with the egalitarian culture of the American outdoors, so ingrained that I ended up helping Tito to set up my tent, thereby making him look as though he was incapable of setting up a tent by himself. Meanwhile Ryan was sitting in a camp chair while Hebron and Alanus put up his tent and fetched his cigarettes. And it never occurred to the game officer to lift a finger around the camp. He was a big man, and he expected to be waited on hand and foot.

Dale was right. It was a beautiful stretch of river. The Malagarasi flowed along at a good clip, generating a few white-capped riffles where it ran over submerged rocks. On the west side of the river, where we were camped, there were scattered thornbushes, a few stunted trees, and the vast expanse of savannah grassland we had crossed in the vehicles. On the opposite bank there was an impressive gallery forest of sausage trees, fig trees, acacias, palms, and yellow fever trees. Before the link between mosquitoes and malaria was understood, European explorers suspected these trees, with their bilious looking yellow-green bark, of emitting the vapors that caused the disease.

At sunset, a pod of hippos started up their low honking grunts. There were herons and storks and ornate geese in the air, and a magnificent fish eagle. A twelve-foot crocodile lay motionless in the river. It resembled a log almost exactly, except a log would have drifted downstream with the current, and the croc held its position with a little riffle of water flowing over its snout. This was the Africa I had fallen in love with: the riverside safari Africa of tents, boats, storytelling, campfires, incomparable birds and wildlife. But I hadn't understood so clearly then that its continued existence depended on armed game scouts willing to kill and be killed to foil the hungry appetites of a desperately poor and rapidly expanding population—a million people were living in ninety villages within easy reach of all this grass and bush meat.

Ultimately I thought it was a good idea to keep them out, and so did the eight Tanzanians around the campfire that night. To let those appetites run unchecked over this land would not improve life for the rural poor. It would enrich a few individuals, waste an immensely valuable resource, and lead instead to overgrazing, dust bowls, migration, and the enlargement of future urban slums.

Hebron plucked and gutted his birds and arranged them on a metal grill over the fire. In the usual African fashion, the fire consisted of four longish pieces of wood laid flat on the ground and fed into the burning center. European and American fires are more architectural, with their scooped out firepits, broken-up pieces of wood arranged in latticed stacks, or conical teepee shapes. The advantages of the African fire are that it requires less time and labor to build, consumes wood more slowly, and is better for cooking, because the heat level can easily be adjusted by sliding in or removing a piece of wood. Its disadvantages are that it gets more smoke in your eyes than the classic teepee-shaped American fire, which funnels smoke upward in a column, and it's also less efficient at warming you up on a cold night.

Hebron laid down some cassava strips next to the game birds. "What if we'd had to shoot someone last night?" he said.

"What if we've been shot?" countered Alanus.

"Kagera *Nnn-kaaahn-dah*," intoned Hebron, producing a round of soft chuckles. One by one, we started to admit how scared we had been and how we had seen and heard things in the darkness that weren't there. Ryan, Hebron, and Alanus, the three men with guns, had also imagined shooting a man for the first time. Once on the Mozambique border, the three of them had been removing snares and had found a poacher's hut. They set fire to it, not realizing that there was ammunition buried under the floor. The resulting explosion had been the most frightening moment of their lives until last night.

Hebron and Alanus started reminiscing about a young bull elephant that became habituated to people at one of their permanent camps in the Kilombero. He learned to open the fridge door to steal vegetables, and he loved the radio. "In the off season, he would come to the window and stand there for hours listening to the radio," said Ryan.

"Is he still around?" I asked.

"Nope," said Ryan. "Poachers got him. We don't even have a camp there anymore. We've lost that whole area to cattle."

He produced an after-dinner bottle of Scotch, but I had no desire for alcohol, a sure sign that my organism was in ailing health. I got up from the fire and said good-night. "You might want to take an empty water bottle with you," said Ryan. "We've got elephant, hippos, buffalo, hyena, and lion in the area. It's not a good place to get out of your tent at night."

These were exactly the words I needed to hear. I don't quite know how to explain it, but I sleep more soundly in wild places, knowing that wild beasts are prowling around in the night. I give up control, abandon myself to fate, let the animals decide what will happen, and sleep comes more easily than it does in my nice, safe, comfortable bed at home.

IN THE MORNING I felt much improved. There had been no drenching sweats or shivering chills in the night, my joints no longer ached, my head no longer felt like it had been parted through the center by a hatchet. Apart from a sore throat, swollen glands, an inflamed eye, two painful mouth ulcers, a dozen welted tsetse bites, and the mouthparts of a tick in the back of my neck, I was good as new. Ryan wanted us all to inspect our tsetse bites. The first sign of sleeping sickness, he said, was a yellow ring around the red bite, in which case we would need to get to a well-supplied medical facility or find a tube of women's facial hair removal cream and eat it.

Ryan was limping badly. His recently sprained ankle had healed poorly, and now it was swollen again. When I suggested that he should wrap some tape around it, he gave me a hostile, bristling, scornful look, as if taping up a sprained ankle was something for puny weaklings. He had decided to run the river to the swamp but pack light and send most of the gear ahead in the support vehicles, along with the gout-stricken game officer and a disappointed Tito. Five of us climbed into the raft—Ryan, me, Alanus, Hebron, and John—and we carried only the bare essentials: some food and water, a first-aid kit, the .470, and the shotgun. Ryan pulled at the oars, Hebron and I were the hippo lookouts, and John and Alanus had short paddles to give us added momentum.

It was a fresh sunny morning filled with birds and birdsong. We saw our first Goliath herons, the largest herons on earth, and at first sight easily mistaken for pterodactyls or small airplanes. We saw Egyptian geese, sacred ibis, open-billed storks, a fish eagle with a fish in its talons. Around every bend, another crocodile splashed in from the riverbanks, and bushbucks darted away from us in alarm. We came upon six hippos who all submerged themselves as we made our way past them. To dissuade them from surfacing under the Jimmy Hendrick, or next to it with their enormous jaws open, Ryan told John and Hebron to slap the water aggressively with the flat side of their paddles.

John thought our paddle-slapping technique was overly cautious. The hippos were not that aggressive, and he couldn't remember any fishermen getting killed by them. "We go around them," he said. "If he is very grumpy, we get out and pull the canoe along the shore. But crocodiles are a problem, and they have killed many people."

Did the crocodiles kill in the shallows, as the fishermen were getting in and out of their canoes? "No, they attack the canoes in the water. They know it is a way to get food."

I tried asking him, via Ryan, what it was like to live with the risk of being eaten by a crocodile, but it was a difficult question to get across. It was like saying to a Californian, "How does it feel to drive in a state where nine people are killed every day in traffic accidents?" It was a risk you accepted as part of life.

We floated past a grove of dead trees in the river, standing up with their branches still mostly intact, but the leaves long gone and the bark turned bone white. Both shores were thickly forested now, and despite the hippos and crocs, and the occasional bite from a tsetse, there was a deep, soothing, ancient serenity about the river. We stopped for lunch and spent an idyllic two hours lazing around on the east bank, eating a meal of luncheon meat, crackers, and canned cheese that I was hungry enough to enjoy. I took a delicious snooze in the shade of a big fever tree, checking its lower branches for snakes until my eyelids got heavy, and the warm, whispering breeze soothed away the last resisting nub of consciousness. I woke with a start to the sounds of a male hippo surfacing next to the moored raft and snorting, curious about this big, strange, passive intruder into his territory. I watched him sniffing and studying it, then he submerged and used his great weight to walk away along the riverbed. With the others still asleep, I made a tentative investigation inland and found lion tracks and elephant dung and a grassland that grew over my head. A game trail went into the grassland, and I managed about fifteen paces before a feeling of foreboding overwhelmed me, that it was a mistake in all ways to disturb the soporific, heat-drugged torpor of the bush in early afternoon.

On the river it was slightly cooler. We spent the afternoon paddle-slapping our way past hippos, perhaps thirty in total, and slapping ourselves in a futile effort to make some headway, or at least extract a measure of revenge, against the voracious and building swarms of tsetse flies. It was Alanus who first noticed that he was getting bitten more than I was. "These tsetses are racists," he said with a smile, and here he identified the lone physiological advantage of having white skin in Africa. Tsetse flies are attracted to dark colors, and I definitely suffered less than my dark-skinned companions, including cinnamon-brown Ryan.

The first sign of the swamp was a slowing down of the current. The raft seemed to gain a new heaviness, and Ryan had to pull harder on the oars to keep us moving. Then there was no discernible current at all. The surface water was mirror flat, reflecting the white clouds in the blue sky, and the river had turned into a kind of elongated lake dammed up behind the blockage.

We camped that night just above the swamp and I went back to talk with Dale Wright about the Friedkin conservation strategy. "Education is really the biggest challenge," he said. "These are rural tribal people, and they're extremely conservative. Their way of thinking is, why should we listen to these white people who are here now and will soon leave?"

First we brought colonialism, and we wrapped that up in promises and rhetoric about making African lives better. Now it was NGO uplift schemes that followed the latest NGO fads—water projects one decade, microfinance loans the next, eco-tourism lodges, women's basket-weaving cooperatives. Our world in the West is constantly moving from one fad to the next, chasing the next new thing, but rural Africa has a deep resistance to change and never more so than when some *muzungu* comes waltzing in, holds a workshop, and tells people their relationship with the land needs to be improved for their own good.

The Friedkin fund had supplied a local medical clinic with a solar electricity system that was having some maintenance problems. It had set up and funded beekeeping cooperatives, fish-farming initiatives, tree nurseries, and replanting programs, and it had expended many hours preaching about the benefits of wildlife conservation and explaining that hunters bring money and job opportunities to the area.

"Some of it is getting through, I hope," said Dale. "But they know that we don't have to live here, and that we can't handle the hardships of their daily lives. They know how to survive these hardships, and it goes back to the ancestors, and it's handed down, and it's tried and proven, and it's sacred, and it's hedged in with taboos. It's God's plan, and they want to stick to it."

"So it's frustrating for you?" I asked.

"Sometimes but not really," he said. "I love it here. I find it fascinating. I mean, who wants to live in a world where everyone thinks the same way?"

THE PAPYRUS BLOCKAGE extended for about ten river miles, and it was flanked with broad marshes and swampy wetlands where the blocked river had spread its waters laterally. We drove around it on a big, flat, treeless floodplain grazed by herds of Tutsi cattle. It felt like one more failure, one more blow to my original hopes of running the entire river from source to mouth. As we approached a village, the sound of the engines brought families out of their huts, and they stood there staring at us as we drove past. They were dressed in ragged cast-off Western clothing, and they looked proud and wary.

We rejoined the river at a bridge outside the town of Malagarasi. Having seeped its way slowly through the swamp and gained the tributary waters of the Moyowosi, it was now flowing steadily again and about forty yards wide. Small boys were fishing on the bald, dusty riverbanks, observed by young men in baseball caps lounging back on their bicycle seats. Thin yellow dogs slept in the slatted shade under the bridge, and over their heads passed the main road west and the tracks of the Central Line, Tanzania's east-west rail artery, which runs from Dar es Salaam all the way to Lake Tanganyika. Built by the Germans before World War 1, and expanded by the British, it had been out of commission for more than a year because of a dispute between workers and the new Indian management. This was a disappointing situation all around, and among the aggrieved parties were the thieves and bandits who had made their living robbing the passengers on the western part of the line.

When Burton and Speke reached the Malagarasi, "a swift brown stream . . . swirling through the tall wet grasses of its banks," there was a ferry system in place to get the slave and ivory caravans across the river, and it was controlled by a chief called Mzogera. This "Lord of the Malagarazi" (Burton's spelling) lived downstream in Uvinza and sent envoys to negotiate for his crossing fee. After a day of negotiation, the envoys left with forty cloths, six coil bracelets, and a hundred necklaces of coral beads, all of which was worth fifty pounds sterling in London. Burton assumed he had now bought permission to cross the river, but there was also a Lord of the Ferry, who commanded a fleet of flimsy bark canoes, and he demanded a further thirty cloths and two coil bracelets plus a quantity of beads for each load to be ferried across.

Speke at this point was almost blind from inflammation of the eyes, but otherwise in slightly better condition than Burton, who was still unable to walk and half-blind himself. The ulcers in his mouth were so bad that it was difficult for him to eat, drink, or speak. He had just survived an agonizing paralysis of all his limbs that the locals attributed to mushroom poisoning, and leaving Kazeh, he had come down with a malaria attack so dire that he was unable to write anything in his journal for two weeks except "Unyanyembe and Kapunde. Too sick to observe. Climate precisely the same."

By the time he sat on this stretch of riverbank, watching elephants in the reeds on the far bank and great numbers of crocodiles, "delayed by the scabrous question of how much was to be extracted from me," by the Lord of the Ferry, he was able to write again and noted down what he had learned about the Malagarazi. Geographers in Europe knew of its existence, but they had corrupted its name to Magrassie, Magozi, and Mdjigidgi, and heard wrongly that it flowed out of Lake Tanganyika. Burton correctly asserted that its source lay in the mountains of Burundi—Urundi as it was then—and flowed into the lake. Presumably he got his information from the same Arabs at Kazeh who were so vague and conflicted about the Nile source.

The Lord of the Ferry settled for half his original asking price, but after Burton and his men gingerly lowered themselves into the wobbly little seven-foot bark canoes—identical to the canoes used on the river today—the boatmen began extorting yet more cloth and beads from him. When he protested at these new demands, they poled their canoes away and waited on the bank until he understood that he had no choice. Then they landed at a dry outcropping of rock in the middle of the river and demanded a second fee to take him from there to the far riverbank. Burton was impressed by the skill of the boatmen in threading their way across the rocky, braided channels, and he couldn't help but admire their boldness and ingenuity as they exacted their exorbitant fee.

Before launching our raft again, we drove into the town of Malagarasi to replenish our food supplies. Ocher dust lay deep in the rutted streets, where sheep and goats outnumbered motorized vehicles. There were some mango trees and date palms, possibly planted by Arab slave and ivory traders, and a small market of plank stalls and tiny mudbrick shops. People here were more reserved, and no one came after us offering their services, wanting money or sponsorship for U.S. citizenship. The children looked at me without the usual excited cry of "*Muzungu!*"

Men sat behind whirring Chinese sewing machines, and vendors were selling *pemba*, a mineral soil said to be good for pregnant women, Obama T-shirts, nylon women's underwear in the colors of Liverpool football club, and tables and boxes and piles of the usual flimsy Chinese plastic crap. The stuff was so worthless in my eyes that it took an effort of will to actually look at it and determine what it was pretending to be. Here was a gentleman's watch retailing for 26 cents, a purple comb designed to break instantly with first usage, a pair of child's orange sunglasses designed according to the same principle, flip-flops that might last a week if you walked slowly and carefully in them.

In the food section, there were dried fish and dried catfish heads, plastic buckets filled with cassava flour, rice, cloves, and cardamom for flavoring chai, and five different kinds of beans. Ryan bought a bag of yellow beans and a big sack of rice. Talking to the vendor, he discovered that rice was a new crop in the area. "They only started growing it here two years ago after the Sukuma moved in," he said. "Unbelievable! All that land on the edge of the swamp is perfect rice paddy."

We stopped for a lunch of rice and beans in a little hole-in-the-wall restaurant in the market. It was a clean, efficient, friendly operation, run by two sisters with at least one child clinging to their legs at all times. The sisters were originally from Kagera Nkanda, and John piped up that he had lived here in Malagarasi for eleven years and fished near the bridge until the fish got too scarce. Below the bridge, he added, there was a stretch that canoes couldn't get through because rocks blocked the river and then some bad rapids. Ryan and I looked at him, looked at each other, wondering why the hell he hadn't mentioned this before.

"Can the raft get through these rocks?" asked Ryan.

"I don't think so."

"What about the rapids?"

"I don't know. I only know canoes. A canoe cannot go through without flipping."

IT WAS HARD TO TELL from our 1956 map where exactly these rocks and rapids were, relative to the nearest road, and John was used to finding them by canoe. We turned down a likely track, which led to the riverbank and then dead-ended at a small subsistence farm hacked out of the bush. An elderly Sukuma man appeared, and Ryan and Mustafa spent about twenty minutes talking to him.

When they told him we were on a safari down the river in a boat, maybe all the way to Lake Tanganyika, he said that there had been a *muzungu* who tried to run the river in 1962, and we should be careful of the big rapids downstream. "What happened to the *muzungu*?" Ryan asked.

"He wrecked his canoe, and got stranded on a rock in the middle of the rapids. He was badly injured. He survived by eating his clothes. Then they airlifted him out seven days later."

Hebron couldn't get over this story. The idea of a white man eating his clothes was irresistible to his sense of tragi-comedy, and he said we should bring extra clothes in case the same thing happened to us. The old man pointed out a place where we could camp and put our boat in the water. He said to be careful around Uvinza—it was full of unemployed salt miners and Congolese refugees trying to sell their aid goods—but we would be safe here. Our main problem, he reiterated, would be the rapids.

We set up camp, and inflated the raft, and people started

arriving in twos and threes to watch. They stood in their ragged clothes, looking shy, uncertain, and curious. We were unloading objects and luxuries they had never seen before. I went with one group to the river's edge and kept them entertained for a long time with my binoculars. There were nine hippos in the river on the opposite bank, and when one boy of eight or nine saw them in the binoculars, he jumped backward, provoking soft laughter in the others. Then he raised the binoculars again and stared spellbound.

These "very bush people," in Tito's phrase, were Sukumas who had migrated down here from Shinyanga three years ago. They had trekked on foot with their cattle and goats, their dogs for hunting game meat, and a tradition of sprinkling powdered poison in carcasses to get rid of predators. They had cut down trees to make charcoal and to clear ground for their huts, and they had planted small patches of cassava, sweet potatoes, maize, and tobacco.

Ryan didn't think they would come for us, or our possessions, in the night, but just to make sure, he told Alanus and Hebron to sleep with their rifles, and he asked the Sukumas if anyone watered cattle or gathered water on this part of the riverbank at night. They said no, and he said, "That's good. Because we'd probably shoot them, and we wouldn't want that."

That night, over drams of Famous Grouse at the campfire, with hippos honking in the river, Ryan told the story of the Sukuma invasion of the Kilombero Valley, where he had grown up with Hebron and Alanus. He spoke with tightly marshaled facts for nearly two hours, although sometimes he had to pause and stare into the fire for a few moments to keep his emotions under control. In 1992, when his father secured the hunting concession for the Kilombero Valley, this vast seasonal wetland contained one of the most impressive concentrations of wildlife in East Africa. There were 30,000 buffalo, 60,000 puku antelope, a rare wetland species, 8,000 hippo, 5,000 elephant, 500–600 lions, plus leopards, sable, waterbuck, eland, hartebeest, reedbuck, bushbuck, and zebra, all in prodigal abundance.

In 2003, fleeing the dust bowl they had made of their homeland, Sukumas brought hundreds of thousands of cattle to the edges of the floodplain, began poisoning the predators, hunting the grazers for meat—puku antelope was a particular delicacy—and bribing local leaders to let them stay. It became a national scandal, and Operation Clean the Valley was launched to remove illegal cattle. But the Sukumas had political connections, and two weeks later the operation was shut down. More people poured into the valley with more cattle. Since the Kilombero was an internationally recognized wetlands site, there were protests from the Belgian government and other international agencies, but still the Tanzanian government failed to take action.

Ryan tried all the usual strategies to fight it. His safari company had invested heavily in game scout patrols and community development. It had donated nearly all the meat from their hunts to local villages, built classrooms, donated school desks, sponsored promising students, dug wells, donated medical supplies and equipment to win the support of the local villages, all of which counted for nothing when Sukumas offered direct cash bribes to village leaders. "Sometimes it wasn't even cash," Ryan said. "Sometimes the bribe was enough beer for a good party. But the real problem was that the authorities never acted, never sent in police to enforce the laws or went after prosecutions. I don't know what else we could have done. When we tried to stop it, by putting in our own anti-poaching patrols, the authorities stopped us, promised they would do something, and then did nothing. Maybe we should have exposed it internationally much earlier. Now it's too late. There's nothing left to fight for, our resources have run out, it's a lost cause."

The 60,000 puku were down to 5,000. The 30,000 buffalo were 3,000. There were 12 lions at best from the 500–600. The eland were gone completely. The zebra, hartebeest, hippo, and waterbuck were almost gone. There were 50 elephants left of the 400, and they were diminishing rapidly with the booming market for ivory in the Far East.

For Alanus and Hebron, who grew up in the Kilombero allied to Ryan's family hunting business, it has been extremely difficult. "They're seen as enemies in their own communities," said Ryan. "They've had death threats. Their families have been intimidated. I've had to pull them off anti-poaching patrols for that reason. They're strictly trackers now. And they're depressed about it. Their villages have been taken over by Sukumas, their leaders have been bought, their livelihood is disappearing, and they want to get out of there."

For Ryan, there was some irony in the fact that he had married into the Sukuma tribe. "Even by the standards of other cattle tribes, Sukumas are incredibly hard on the land. For them, wildlife is food, predators should be exterminated, cattle have priority, this is how they're brainwashed as children. The Masai kill lions, but not with the idea of exterminating them. They recognize that lions, and dealing with lions, are an integral part of their culture."

His Sukuma relatives—his mother-in-law and brother-in-law—are well educated and modernized. They still keep a few cows for milk, and old times' sake, but they are teachers, fish traders, landlords. When he tells them what Sukumas are doing to the Kilombero, his mother-in-law insists these are not real Sukumas but outcasts who should know better.

Seeing him there in the firelight, bottling up his sadness and grief, my heart went out to him, but there were no consoling words to give. The place he loved above all others had been destroyed, and all he could do now was accept it and mourn.

THE NEXT MORNING, we pulled into the riverbank above the big rapids to seek advice from an elderly couple hoeing a field. When they heard what we were doing, they offered a different and more convincing version of the story about our clothes-eating forerunner. He was not a *muzungu* but a local canoe-builder called Paolo Bahaye, and the year was 1968, not 1962. People who didn't know Paolo got the idea that he was a *muzungu* because of that first name of his. The river was high after the rains. Paolo had just built an especially fine canoe. His plan was to take it through the rapids and all the way to Lake Tanganyika, sell it there where the prices were higher, then catch the bus back.

He took a colleague with him, and they came right past here in that fine new canoe. They made it through the first rapid and flipped it in the bigger, more difficult second rapid. The colleague was unhurt and managed to swim to shore, but Paolo was badly injured, stranded on a rock in the middle of the rapid, and barely able to move. He was there for many days, and by the time he was airlifted out, he had eaten his tank top and underwear to keep the hunger pangs away.

"I wish you luck," said the old man. "There's a hidden rock in the second rapid where people usually flip their canoes. I don't know about that boat of yours. I've never seen one like that before."

His wife, who wore a yellow *kanga* wrapped around her head, leaned on her hoe and said, "You men are going to get hurt, but we wish you well, and God's blessings on you."

Ryan asked, "Are there any hippos to watch out for below the rapids?"

"Hippos?" snorted the old man. "That's their main production ground. You'll find some hippos all right. Crocodiles too."

We thanked them, wished them luck and blessings, and carried on down the river. When we heard the first distant roaring of the rapid, Ryan pulled in the oars and passed out paddles. As we checked our life jackets, he explained the basics of left-turn, right-turn on a paddle raft, with one side forward paddling and other side back paddling to make the turn. This was old hat to me, but no one else had paddled a raft before. "As we go through the rapid, keep the body flexible, and above all try to stay in the boat," Ryan shouted over the increasing roar. "If there's a bump from a rock, that's when you might be ejected. If you fall out, stay with the boat and we'll pull you in."

We slid down over a rocky lip into the first rapid and got through it with no problem. But our inexperienced crew fell into confusion approaching the big second rapid. The current seized the raft and whirled it backward into the rapid. In the foam and roar, I caught brief flashes of panicked faces, then we slammed into a rock, and I thought we were going over, but we caromed off it, past a lone hippo staring at us from a deep pool, and emerged grinning, chagrined, and fully drenched. We named the rapid Underwear Rapid in honor of Paolo Bahaye, perhaps the only person before us to attempt the river all the way through to Lake Tanganyika.

Below Underwear, there were smaller rapids and riffles and a lively, enjoyable stretch of boating. Then the river changed its character again. It became much broader, perhaps four hundred yards from bank to bank, and correspondingly shallower. The bottom of the raft started scraping over rocks, then rock formations began to protrude out of the water—fins, hogbacks, spires, domes, and many small islands jungled with palm trees, cycads, and thickets of creeper-strewn vegetation. One flowing body of water now split into dozens of narrow channels, and we could find only one that was deep and wide enough to float the Jimmy Hendrick. It became increasingly overgrown with vegetation and hemmed in by rocks until the raft lodged itself in a thick, green dead end.

Hebron pulled out a machete and started hacking away at the branches and vines blocking the way forward. Twenty minutes later, he had cut a gap, and we managed to squeeze through it, only to get stuck again in an even worse place. The channel ahead was blocked by a fallen tree, the raft was pinned and wedged in at the sides by a thick latticework of overhanging branches and thorny vines.

There were two options. We could hack out a passage sideways through thirty feet of thick jungle and then drag the boat through it to the shore. Then we would have to unload all our equipment, carry the boat along the shore to where there was open water again, if there was open water again, then come back for all the equipment, carry it forward, and pack it on the raft again. Or we could get out of the boat, risk the crocodiles, drag it upstream against the current, retrace our route, and maybe find a navigable channel that we had missed.

As we considered these options, the tsetses and mosquitoes were closing in, biting incessantly as the sweat rolled off our faces. A huge spider fell into the raft, and we checked the surrounding branches for snakes. Tito was bitten on the lip by a hornet, and the pain made him double over and stay there for a minute or two. When he sat up, his lip was swollen to twice its normal size.

"Not good," said Ryan. He looked around again, swatted another tsetse. "I'm beginning to hate this fucking river."

7

Fool's Errand

**Sweats to Work—Tito Rapid—Exasperations—Rescued—
Uvinza—Waterfalls—*Boati* dead—Whiskey bottle—
Tanganyika—City of white Land Cruisers—
Traveler's protocols**

RYAN SENT ALANUS wading to shore with instructions to
scout ahead, look for channels leading to open water, and talk
to any riverbank farmers or fishermen. We waited for him in
that sweaty, itchy, thorny, insect-infested little trap. My head
was ducked under some branches, and what was that digging
into my right buttock? Shifting position, which wasn't easy in
such tight quarters, I discovered that it was the business end of
a loaded shotgun that had slipped its moorings.

Ryan had his GPS out, but it was as useless as the 1956 map,
and for the same reason. They both showed the river broaden-
ing and dividing into channels and islands but gave no indication as to which channels might be blocked by fallen trees, or
which we might be able to squeeze through at this water level.

Tito became self-conscious about the enormous swelling
of his upper lip and pulled up his T-shirt to cover it. Then he
took off his T-shirt and wrapped it loosely around his face. This
was too much for Hebron, who started mimicking Tito's efforts

to hide his hornet-stung lips and nicknamed him "Mr. Super-
model."

It was an easy place to grow impatient, and after twenty
minutes we all got out of the boat and waded to the riverbank,
threading our way single file between the rocks and jungle
thickets. Ryan wrenched his bad ankle slipping on the rocky
riverbed. Following Alanus's footprints along the shore, we
came to a small field planted with maize and tobacco among
the tree stumps. Two scarred, yellow hunting dogs, one limping as badly as Ryan, came toward us uncertainly, followed
by five men and a boy, dressed in the usual ragged Western
castoffs, and a woman with perfect teeth. The balding patriarch smiled at us warmly and said, "Welcome! Welcome! How
are you?"

After the initial round of greetings, each of them came forward in turn to shake our hands and give us their best smiles. It
struck me what a shabby thing the European welcome smile is
by comparison, and how false and empty American smiles often
are. One man's jeans were more hole than cloth, and he wore a
black T-shirt with white Scrabble letters that read YO S CK and
underncath in smaller letters "Would You Like to Buy a Vowel?"
I seriously doubted that he could read and write Swahili, let
alone English. Another man wore one pink flip-flop on his feet.
The boy was about twelve and he had on a red and white Santa
hat, and how strange I must have looked to them, a pale giant,
at least a foot taller than any of them, with white greasy smears
across my pink, stubbled face, wearing an unbuckled blue
nylon life jacket and a bush hat with a chin cord.

My camera was in my shirt pocket in a waterproof bag, but
they knew enough about white people to know I must have one,
and the patriarch insisted on a group photograph. We lined up,
with me towering at the back, the men smoking their home-

grown tobacco rolled in newspaper, the woman stern and serious with a necklace of bright green beads. Ryan pressed the shutter and then showed them the image on the camera screen. The woman went bashful, put her hand over her mouth. The men were intrigued and studied themselves carefully. I wondered if they had ever seen a fixed image of themselves before, and Ryan thought maybe just on their national identification cards.

When we asked about the river, the patriarch said, "The channels are closed. The water is too low. You will have to get your boat to the shore and then carry it. We will help you. You are our guests."

Then Alanus appeared with a man in his forties called Kula Kway, meaning Sweats to Work. He was tough and scrawny, with missing teeth in the front and an air of gruff good humor. I tried for a moment to imagine the proud parents that had looked down at their infant son, thinking about his life ahead, wondering what to call him, and agreed that Sweats to Work was a good name. Maybe it was a family name. I could only assume he came from a very long line of men who knew no other means of staying alive but hard sweaty work.

He said there was one narrow channel open, and he would take us to it. There were no negotiations for money, and he seemed delighted to be able to help us. "Come," he said, walking back upstream and wading into the water. "Are there crocodiles here?" we asked. "Let's hope not!" he said with a hoarse cackling laugh. We waded back to the raft and began the hard, sweaty work of pushing, shoving, wrenching, and pulling it upstream through the rocks, miniature rapids, fallen trees, and thickets. The current was strong enough to take your legs out from under you if you lost balance, and the boat was heavily laden with equipment and five-gallon jugs of water.

Tito, with a T-shirt still wrapped around his face, was a lion of strength, courage, and athleticism, plunging into all the worst places, never losing his balance on the loose slippery rocks underfoot, doing the work of two or three men. When the raft got stuck, which was often, it was usually his mighty efforts that worked it loose. When my head was six inches away from clunking into a beehive, it was Tito who called out the warning and then said how glad he was that I had missed it.

It was about forty minutes of hard work to get the raft up to the open channel, and by then it was full of leaves, branches, debris, caterpillars, spiders, various beetles, and other insects. We scrambled into it as the current took it away and snatched up the paddles. We made it around two tight turns and then got stuck in another dead end. Sweats to Work had a look around and decided we needed to get across to the next channel over. In the way were some rock outcroppings and a small island growing brush, undergrowth, saplings, and a tree two feet in diameter. Taking up their machetes and swinging them with fearsome power and precision, Alanus and Hebron felled the tree in fifteen minutes. Then we lifted and dragged the laden boat over the rocks, found the channel open, and a minute later we broke free into open water.

We paddled over to the shore for a rest, and with our feet on dry land again, Sweats to Work took off his T-shirt and showed us his scars. He had been in a canoe fishing with another man. First the crocodile came up underneath the canoe, but they managed to stabilize it. Then the crocodile reared up out of the water and started snapping and slashing at him, trying to get the proper death grip but impeded by the canoe. Sweats to Work was helpless, but his friend grabbed the fishing net and got it over the croc's head, and that confused it into letting go. The thick white scars were up one leg, on his chest, stomach, side, and arms. He pointed to his missing teeth. They were knocked out in the attack. His conclusion was the same as mine: it had not been his time to die.

We walked over to his relatives to say our thank-yous and good-byes, and they all in turn wished us luck and blessings on our journeys. We handed out chocolate-flavored lollipops, and Ryan gave Sweats to Work a five-thousand-shilling note for his help, equivalent to five dollars. At first he was absolutely stunned and speechless to see so much money in his hand. Then a grin took over his face and showed no signs of leaving. He showed the banknote to the others. They had the same reaction: shock and amazement followed by absolute delight.

"They seem like lovely people," I said to Ryan as we paddled away down the river.

"That's the best of Tanzania," he said. "The warmth and friendliness you saw. We've got friends there if we ever come back."

"They were Sukumas?"

"Yup."

THE RIVER was still wide, shallow, and rocky. Larger islands appeared with palm trees and impenetrable walls of jungle, bound together with creeper vines and festooned with white egrets. It wasn't easy to find navigable channels, especially if you kept looking for them in the middle of the river like the inexperienced Hebron. He was leaning out over the front of the boat, scouting ahead for channels and hippos, and calling out "*Shoto!* . . . *Kulea!* . . . *Shoto-shoto-shoto!*" Left! . . . Right! . . . Left-left-left!" Then the crashing bump as we ran aground on rocks submerged just under the surface.

The deepest channels in a shallow, meandering river are nearly always on the outside of the bends, but Hebron didn't know this, and he didn't seem to be learning. What he was seeing as the ripples of the main current were the ripples created by shallow water passing over rocks. Time and again, he called out a course that I could see was going to get us stuck, and I couldn't understand why Ryan, who was paddling in the stern, didn't explain or override him. Was he letting Hebron learn by trial and error, as I had learned in a canoe on a shallow river in Utah? Or was Ryan also inexperienced in the ways of shallow rivers? I held my tongue. Mr. Ryan did not take advice or correction kindly, especially in front of his staff.

In the late afternoon we entered a broad, forested canyon with high red cliffs, and the river narrowed and deepened. We put away the paddles, and I rowed for a while on glassy smooth green water. Ryan took over the oars when we heard rapids downstream, and there followed a pleasant hour of running small splashy rapids and making up some of the time we had lost. When the sun went behind the canyon rim, we started looking for a place to camp and found one on a boulder-strewn beach on the north bank of the river.

I was relaxing in a camp chair with a plastic beaker of Famous Grouse, watching the flickering fire and savoring the soothing taste and effects of the whiskey. Ryan, wearing a red, sleeveless, Nike T-shirt and black Manchester United shorts, gold earring glinting in the firelight, was stirring fried onions and potatoes into a large saucepan of ramen chicken noodles. The tents were up, and Hebron, Alanus, and Tito were standing around joking with each other in Swahili. All of us had that feeling of honest tiredness and relief that comes after a strenuous day's work in fierce heat.

Then Hebron spotted the light of another campfire further down the shore. All the fears and alarms that had imprinted themselves on us at Kagera Nkanda came surging up again. We jumped up and gazed at it transfixed. Then a flashlight started signaling to it from the other side of the river.

Ryan unzipped the .470 from its case. He told Hebron and Alanus to grab the shotgun and two machetes, go down to the fire, and see who was there. If they seemed harmless, ask them for information about the river ahead. "I want them to know we're armed in case they get any ideas in the night."

Fifteen minutes later, our emissaries returned. They had found an old woman smoking by herself, uneasy at the sudden appearance of two strange men with machetes and a shotgun in her firelight. She was fishing here with her husband, and that was him signaling from across the river. About the river ahead, she said there was a big rapid coming up, and then a really big rapid where many people had smashed up their canoes, and we would know it when we saw it. What about hippos and crocodiles? She said there weren't many left now between here and Uvinza and seemed pleased by this fact.

I was losing faith in satellite technology and local knowledge in equal measure. Neither had warned us adequately about the problems we were facing on the river. The GPS was blind when it came to rapids or narrow braided channels in tangled blockages, when so much depended on the water level and the height of the overgrowing branches. The riverbank farmers had been more useful, but the ones who told us about Paolo Bahaye and the rapids ahead hadn't said anything about the rocky blockage. John, our fisherman guide, had mentioned a rocky blockage but it was thirty miles from where we found one. Nor, out of shyness and deference to the game officer, had John explained the full extent of the violent lawlessness in Kagera Nkanda until bullets were flying all around us.

Now there was an old woman saying the risk from hippos and crocodiles was minimal between here and Uvinza. I took no reassurance from this but resolved to redouble my watchfulness for these deadly creatures. She said there was a bad rapid coming up and then a worse one. We would see. This, I realized, was the essence of exploration, and such a rare thing in the twenty-first century: not knowing what lay ahead, and not being able to find out without actually going there. Finally, we had our eyes, our ears, our sense of judgment, and nothing else could be trusted.

THE PROOF came the next morning. Hour after hour, we waded, dragged, shoved, strained, slipped and slithered, cursed, hacked away with machetes, crashed through spiny vegetation, and poured sweat in that monstrous African heat that reaches its crescendo just before the rainy season. It was impossible to do this work and properly scan the surroundings for crocodiles, even though with our legs in the water, they were never far from our thoughts. With brief interludes of deep water, just long enough to get our hopes up, the river had resumed its wide, shallow, many-channeled course through tangled rock gardens, jungled islands, and tight little rapids. A foot more water, and it would have been pleasant boating. Six inches less, and we'd have been stranded. As it was, we were assured of seemingly endless frustration.

Papyrus swamps started to appear, spreading out into the river from blocked-up tributaries, the papyrus heads bobbing and swaying like green fright wigs. We toiled on, knowing that every time we got stuck and had to work ourselves loose, the more likely we were to go without supper. We had eaten all the food on the raft in the blithe confidence that we would reach our support vehicles in Uvinza. Technically speaking, we were getting closer to Uvinza all day, but it felt like Uvinza was getting more unreachable, because the available daylight kept ticking away, our progress was so much slower than expected, and the hazards, blockages, and swamps were steadily getting worse.

In the early afternoon we reached the biggest rapid we had seen so far, perhaps a Class IV. It had to be the place the old woman had warned us about, although she described it as two rapids. Many people had smashed up their fishing canoes here, she had said. I couldn't believe anyone would even attempt to run such a big, dangerous rapid in a hollowed-out palm log or a flimsy little canoe sewn together from two strips of bark. The riverbanks were rocky and densely jungled. They funneled the water into a series of steep, plunging drops, all roaring white water and spume spray, and culminating in a huge churning hole flanked by sharp jagged rocks. That hole looked entirely capable of flipping the Jimmy Hendrick and puncturing its neoprene hide.

Another hour drained away as we studied the rapid from various angles up and down the right bank. "We've got to stay out of that hole," said Ryan, "but everything from this side of the river leads right down into it." From my experience in the Grand Canyon, I thought we could smash right through the hole, so long as we entered it nose first with plenty of speed. But if we got turned sideways, it would flip us for sure, and Ryan didn't want to take that risk. Instead he devised a complicated plan that involved lining the boat to a little island halfway across the river, where the angle was better for entering the rapids without getting sucked into that big hole.

He tied a long line of green cord to the front of the raft. Now someone had to walk halfway across that raging river to the island with the other end of the line. I tried taking three half-steps across the thigh-high river and was nearly swept away. The current was also too strong for Hebron or Alanus, and Ryan was a nonstarter with his bad ankle. But Tito with his strength and balance could hold his own against the current.

Ryan told him to put on a life jacket and looped the line around his chest and shoulders. If Tito could make it to the upstream end of the island and tie the line, we could get in the raft on the shore, push off, and it would swing over to the bottom of the island. From there, he could get back in the boat, and we would have the best possible approach into the rapid.

It was an agonizing and magnificent thing to watch Tito battle his way across the river in waist- and chest-high water, one half-footstep at a time, starting to teeter, then regaining his balance with fierce determination, until he was through the worst of it, then into the calmer shallows and tying the line around a clump of thick, cane-like roots at the head of the island. We let up a big cheer. All hail the mighty Tito, conquering lion of the Malagarasi!

We got in the raft and swung across the river on the tethered line to the bottom of the island. Tito untied his end, clambered his way down the island, and got back in the boat. "Now," shouted Ryan over the roar of the waters. "After the first big drop, we all pull left, left, left as hard as we can to get around this hole. Make sure your life jackets are on good and tight."

We were all fizzing with adrenaline and fear, trying not to think about the hippos and crocs that might be waiting for us below the rapid if we flipped. We plunged down the first big drop, and then it was roaring noise and spray, a desperate heaving failing effort to get left, left, left as the river swept us backward right into the maw of the hole, smashed us into a rock, nearly flipped us, and then spat us drenched and giddy into the calm water below the rapid. It has long been the custom of explorers to name geographical features after themselves or their patrons back home, and let it be recorded henceforth that this rapid, which lies approximately ten miles upstream from Uvinza, now carries the name of Tito Rapid.

It had taken us an hour and a half to make the fifteen-second run, and now we rowed and paddled as hard as we could, in an increasingly desperate bid to make Uvinza by nightfall. Hebron directed us unerringly into a midstream rock garden just below the surface, and I could hold my tongue no longer. "Ryan," I said. "On a shallow river like this, we're not going to find the channel in the middle. We should be looking on the outside of the bends."

Ryan said nothing, but soon afterward he broke an oar on a rock. Then the river got even shallower than before, and for the next hour and a half we were physically dragging the raft over the rocks. Every man grabbed one of the handles on the outside of the raft and braced himself. Then Ryan, or Tito, would count out the chant of *Moja, mbili, tatu, twende!* One, two, three, heave! We would all lift in unison and drag the raft forward, usually moving it about three feet at a time, although sometimes we would heave six or seven times and get nowhere and then have to drag the raft back upstream, or start moving rocks and boulders off the riverbed to create a passage, and throughout this process, the Jimmy Hendrick was accumulating serious signs of wear and tear and in constant danger of a puncture.

With Ryan sitting in the raft, it was too heavy to lift, so he had to get out on his bad ankle and help, and in due course he twisted his other ankle. He halted everything, took a deep breath, and stood there in the water smoking a cigarette. "This river has now fucked both my ankles," he said with strained calm. "It has fucked my oar. It has fucked my boat. Let's hope that's all the fucking it's going to do."

We recruited two boys from the riverbank—actual boys, ten or eleven years old—to show us the best channels through the rocks, and when it started to get dark, we set them down on the shore with money and candy. The towers of the Uvinza salt factory were now visible about two miles down the river, and finally we had some open water. Ryan started rowing hell for leather, with all the paddles churning at the same time, and then, in the very last of the murky dusk, we hit another maze of rocks and shallow channels and got badly stuck in a thickly overgrown trap, much like the one that Sweats to Work had extricated us from after two hours of hard labor.

Alanus and Hebron were hacking away with their machetes when we saw a light bobbing in the darkness, apparently in the middle of the river. We hailed and shouted, and the light bobbed and zigzagged toward us.

It was coming from a flashlight strapped to the side of a man's head. He was carrying a small fishing net, wearing a pair of briefs, a Muslim prayer cap fashioned from a piece of white nylon sacking, and nothing else. He was in his early thirties, a big strong hearty man, delighted to meet us, overjoyed to show us the way through to Uvinza. He introduced himself as Shabani Jumanini. There would be no problem, he assured us. He knew all the channels. He knew where the bad hippos were.

We said, "Hippos?" We hadn't seen one since this morning.

"There is a pod of ten near Uvinza on the right bank and a few others," said Shabani. "No problem. I know where they are. We are fine."

Then he shone his headlamp off to the sides, and it picked up the red eyes of three different crocodiles. "We will stay away from those fellows too," he said.

With the water up to our thighs, we wrestled the boat upstream into another channel and into another dead end. I could write that same sentence five times. Shabani was used to slipping through these channels in a skinny bark canoe. He had never seen a boat as fat, bulbous, and heavy in the water as the Jimmy Hendrick. For the next hour, we were back to *moja, mbili, tatu* again, except now it was dark and clouds covered the moon, and there were crocodile eyes in our flashlight beams.

Grabbing at a branch to keep my balance, I came away with a fistful of needlelike spines. Then I ripped off half a big toenail on a riverbed rock. At one point, I was pulling on the front of the raft, trying to dislodge it, and as it came loose, a rock rolled under my foot, and I slipped and went down and got pinned underneath the raft. If Hebron hadn't pulled me loose, I might have drowned right there in two feet of water.

Oh, Malagarasi, how I loathe thee. Let me count the ways. *Moja, mbili, tatu* . . .

We came to a choice of two options. We could paddle in the deep flowing water near the right bank, where we could hear the pod of ten hippos grunting but not see them. Or we could look for a channel to the left among the rocks and jungle and crocodiles that Shabani thought might be passable with a little light machete work. We chose the channel, came through it below the hippos, and then paddled on open water toward the electric lights of the Uvinza salt factory, bracing for aggressive swarms of unemployed salt miners and Congolese refugees.

But there was only a modest crowd on the Uvinza riverbank, and good old Mustafa and Omari were waiting for us as planned, shining their Land Cruiser headlights out on the river. They had secured a place for us to camp, and with the assistance of John the fisherman they helped us unload the raft. The crowd was waiting for a ferryboat across the river to the salt factory. The ferryboat's engines were broken, or its captain lacked money for gasoline, because men were paddling it across the river toward us. I stared in confused exhaustion at three improbably glamorous young women waiting for the ferry in elegant dresses and high heels. At first, I took them for a hallucination, or an ocular exaggeration in the confusing light of Land Cruiser beams, flashlights, clouds parting away from the moon, and I could feel the fever taking hold again of my aching, weary head. But they were real, they were fantastically beautiful, and why were they going to a salt factory with these other ordinary-looking people at ten o'clock at night? Were they prostitutes? Did their boyfriends work over there?

Ryan slipped some banknotes to Shabani. This I remember clearly. I remember standing there on the dock, still wearing a life jacket and puzzling over those three women. And I remember wondering if I was going to pass out, observing myself wobbling from a distant, distracted, dreamlike perspective.

THE NEXT MORNING, waking up in my tent, I broke out the first-aid kit and took stock of my health. Sore throat, swollen glands, aching joints, sweats and chills in the night, lurid sex dreams, low-grade fever. Abrasions, cuts, and bruises on both legs. Infected abrasion of right knuckles. Painful big toe missing half a toenail, starting to infect at the separation line. Mouthparts of tick now thoroughly infected on the back of the neck just under the hairline. Inflamed eyes like a Shinyanga witch. Sunburn. Mosquito bites. Some forty welted tsetse bites, none ringed with yellow. I patched myself up with antiseptics and Band-Aids, applied eyedrops, took pills to keep the malaria away, pills to bring the fever down, pills to ease the aches and pains.

Emerging from the tent, I saw that we were camped in a dusty field close to the riverbank, opposite the salt factory, but I had no memory of walking over here last night or getting into my tent. My first blackout and not a drop of alcohol involved, at least not that I could remember. I checked with Mustafa. He said I had gone straight into the tent after he set it up. It had been a very long grueling day in the sun with the sickness and fever coming on. A little mild delirium was par for the course. But those women were real. I know they were.

Opposite my tent, about thirty yards away, fat-tailed sheep were grazing, or rather tugging away at tough brown stalks they had previously rejected as inedible. These peculiar animals somehow manage to store their fat reserves in their tails, as men and other sheep store them around their waists. My fat reserves were gone, and being a modern Western person, I liked having a flat, lean stomach again. I patted it through my shirt in the same satisfied way that Omari patted his "investment," as bellies are sometimes known in these regions. Fat is admired on men and women alike, and in Swahili you can say with no hint of irony that a woman is "beautiful like a hippo."

African attitudes toward age are completely different too. To survive all the hardships and perils and reach old age is considered a major accomplishment and an indication of strength, intelligence, luck, and accumulated wisdom. You can flatter a woman of fifty by telling her she looks sixty, and this sometimes gets African safari guides in trouble with their Western clients, especially if the woman in question has gone through cosmetic surgery to look younger. As a general rule, the older and fatter you are in this part of the world, the more respect you get.

Mustafa had been talking to local fishermen about the river ahead, and Ryan had talked to Shabani. The game officer, who had done nothing so far except eat our food, sponge gout pills, and lead us into danger at Kagera Nkanda, knew nothing about the river here, and neither did John, but they weren't about to get off the gravy train, and John at least worked hard and efficiently at camp chores. The game officer hadn't lifted a finger.

Below Uvinza, the river entered a gorge, and the fishermen said the water was too low for even bark canoes to get through. Basically, it was a fool's errand to attempt the Malagarasi River at the end of the dry season. This was now abundantly clear and the major contribution of our expedition to the world's store of geographical knowledge. But at high water, according to Shabani and other fishermen, the rock gardens and dead-end channels are all submerged, "the rapids really roar," and you can have a clean run all the way from Malagarasi town to Lake Tanganyika, except for a long portage around the big waterfalls.

We had been hearing rumors about these falls all along, but now, like the dry gorge, they were a fact that had to be dealt with. The only option was to deflate the Jimmy Hendrick again, put everything on the Land Cruisers again, drive around to the base of the waterfalls, and see how much water was in the river there.

We packed up and went into Uvinza for breakfast. In Burton's day, it consisted of "forty to fifty bee-hive huts, tenanted by salt-diggers." They dug pans in the salty banks of the Malagarasi and its tributaries. The saline water was boiled down, and the residual salt formed into little cones. They were sold all over central Africa and much prized as top-quality salt. The diggers toiled in poverty while three chiefs hoarded all the wealth from this trade. One of them was the Lord of the Malagarasi, who also ran the ferry racket.

Uvinza today was a shabby town of rusting tin roofs, spreading mango trees, peeling Manchester United posters on dried mud walls. Goats and fat-tailed sheep wandered through the dusty brown streets, and those same white cones of Uvinza salt were for sale in the market stalls. We ate our goat soup and chapatis in a place called the Priest Pick Inn. I wouldn't recommend it, but there's probably a worse breakfast to be found in Uvinza.

Wandering the market afterward, we bumped into Shabani. He was wearing a brand-new, freshly purchased outfit: red T-shirt tucked into baggy jeans, leather belt, fake Timberland boots, digital watch, and new white *kofia* prayer cap. I was happy that Ryan had given him enough money to effect this transformation. Shabani was looking good, feeling good, and he confessed with a big laugh that his name wasn't Shabani at all. Now that we were friends, now that we had cemented our friendship by giving him a good sum of money, he was happy to tell us his real name, but it wasn't something you went blurting out to strangers, especially if you happened to be fishing without a license.

Like everyone else we met along that troublesome stretch of river, he had done everything in his power to help us and make us feel welcome. He had made no monetary requests or demands in advance, in the faith that we were decent, honorable people who would give something back and probably give generously. As a traveler, this was the world as I wanted it to be, and these were the Africans I liked best, far from the grasping cities and predatory highways where Africa's future was being formed, far from tourists and the self-appointed altruists working for NGOs. Out here in the remote areas, a deep rural courtesy prevailed, and a sense of hospitality that Burton missed almost entirely because he was traveling on the main caravan route, where begging, stealing, extortion, swindling, and selling people into slavery were well established as the easiest ways to make a living.

STANDING ON THE riverbank looking at the waterfalls, it seemed extraordinary that we hadn't detected them on the satellite maps. It was a question of perspective. The satellites were looking down and so couldn't detect sheer vertical drops. You needed to be here at river level looking upstream to see this big, three-tiered waterfall with a main drop of a hundred feet and only a thin strand of river falling at the end of the dry season. Work was beginning on an American-financed hydroelectric power project, and on the trail up to the falls, I met one of the engineers, a half-German Tanzanian called Michael, who was living with his wife and workers in riverbank tents. He was building a bridge, and before that could happen, he had to disassemble a huge digging machine and transport it in pieces across the river by canoe. He had already completed this operation once, but the machine broke on the other side, and he had to go back to Dar for a replacement. Once completed, the project aims to provide electricity to hundreds of thousands of people living around Lake Tanganyika, and the Malagarasi will be a free wild river no more.

Ryan and Mustafa were talking to fishermen about the prospects of running the river through to Lake Tanganyika. Some said it was impossible. The water was too low. Others insisted that a big canoe had gone through a week ago heavily laden with timber. One said we would be at the lake in four hours, no problem. Another said two days, or four days if the wind was coming east off the lake. When that happens, so much lake water is blown into the river that it reverses the current. I thought about all the conflicting information Burton and Speke had heard about the rivers in this part of Africa, from the Arab slavers and their own porters. I thought about all the witless gas station cashiers I had encountered in America who couldn't tell me how to get to a town ten miles away, and didn't know where the nearest supermarket was, or the number of the highway that went past their place of employment. So much for local knowledge.

We set off downriver the next morning, with thunder and lightning to the east, the sky a bruised mauve color, the short rains of October and November now imminent and palpable in the air. For the first hour, we rowed in calm, deep water through a broad canyon with mountains on either side and a coolness in the air that felt like a gift. It was a Sunday morning and crossing from one bank to the other was a canoe full of churchgoers, the men wearing ties and the women clutching purses. They looked at our boat and said we had no chance of getting through the rocky shallows ahead. Then came a canoeist with no paddles. He held flip-flops in his hands and used them instead. He guessed that we would get through with a few problems, and this turned out to be accurate prophecy. We did have to get out and count to three in Swahili a few times, but it was nothing compared to our trials upriver.

Along the banks of the river, there were beached canoes, grass huts, and the wafting smell of rotting cassava. Like most of Africa's staple foods, this starchy root was introduced from another continent. Bananas and rice came from Asia. Cassava, or manioc, was brought by the Portuguese from Brazil, along with maize and beans. In its raw state, cassava is poisonous. You have to soak the white tubers in water until they start to rot, then peel them and lay them out to dry. Then you pound them into flour and make *ugali* porridge. I ate it a few times, and I can guarantee that it will not be the next ethnic food craze. Nor is it nutritious. Cassava contains very little protein, minerals, or vitamins, but its heavy starches are good at filling a hungry stomach.

There were no roads over the mountains to this stretch of river, no schools or medical clinics in the area, no infrastructure or state presence of any kind. "I don't get it," said Ryan. "Why put yourself out here so far from anything?"

"They've got fish in the river, land to farm," I suggested.

"They're just growing enough cassava to survive, and just enough tobacco to smoke. Do you remember that old guy below Malagarasi town who first told us about Paolo Bahaye? He had a proper field of tobacco, and he was selling it to pay for his children's education.* He said it was his responsibility, and there

---

*The Tanzanian government abolished school fees in 2002 in accordance with the U.N. Millennium Development Goals. But the extra funding was very slow in making its way from the treasury through the ministry of education and far outstripped by the population growth, so schools started charging fees to children for using desks, chairs, textbooks, toilets, and "supplemental tutoring" that is actually the basic course material. The cost of these new fees, on average, is double the fees that were abolished.

was a school his kids could go to. But these children here are born into a totally stagnant situation."

In Dar es Salaam we had met with a doctor friend of Ryan's who was setting up a floating medical clinic on Lake Tanganyika for the rural poor in the surrounding areas. He told me that most babies in these areas are not delivered by village midwives, as I had assumed, but by their fathers. "The village midwife is largely a myth," he said. "Eighty percent of babies are delivered by men who don't know what they're doing. So there's a horrendous rate of women dying in childbirth and infant mortality."

Nonetheless, the number of children on the riverbanks was stupefying, and they grew more numerous as we got closer to the lake. Every hundred yards we would pass another grass hut, with a bark canoe pulled up on the bank, a cassava patch, and eight, nine, twelve, even fifteen or eighteen children standing in front of it, staring at us. Some of them jumped up and down and shouted in excitement when they saw my white face. Others looked bewildered, or horrified, and a few ran off in terror. One group of thirteen children, all of slightly different heights, all wearing mud-colored rags, were lined up next to each other with homemade fishing poles, "Like the fish are just going to swim up to them and climb on the hooks," said Ryan.

We came to an area where big mango trees were being cut down for charcoal; the desire for short-term cash was stronger than the enduring shade and fruit the trees would provide. The lake was only a couple of hours away now, depending on what happened with the wind and the current. Our voyage into the hardly known was drawing to a close, and we crossed over into some new territory where the children were familiar with white people, no longer fearful to see my face, but aggressively demanding money in English. "There's been a lot of aid and NGO activity around here," Ryan explained. We passed a group of fifteen children all jeering and yelling as their aged father stood there with his hand outstretched. "Money!" they shouted. "Give me money! Eh, *muzungu*, I want my money!"

Another group said, "Pitcha! Pitcha! Take my pitcha! Give me money, money, money! Money! Pitcha!" This suggested tourists, unless NGO workers had been taking their photographs and giving them money in return.

The canyon ended, the mountains receded behind us, and we entered the long straight final stretch to the lake. The wind was in our faces now and the river flowing backward. Ryan toiled at the oars. Prisoners in orange jumpsuits were collecting buckets of water for the oil palm plantations on the north bank, watched by uniformed guards with rifles. The lake was close now, just seven or eight miles. We could see the lightning and hear the thunder from a storm out in the middle of it.

Hebron, Alanus, and Tito started reciting the names of all the places we had been on our safari. Lovely Morogoro, and Dodoma where the politicians feasted on meat and women. Manyoni and the worst toilet in Africa. Singida, where Saidi the bush mechanic had performed his magic. Then up through Shinyanga province to Kahama, and that fairytale gold mine. The great breakfast at Nyakanazi, Kibondo bridge, down to Kasulu, and then the dreaded Kagera Nkanda. Down the river to the swamp, and the Tutsi cattle. Malagarasi town, and the long battle through to Uvinza.

Our final camp was at a small town called Ilagala, on the edge of the Malagarasi delta. The GPSi, as it was called in Swahili, showed just three or six miles left to the lake, depending which channel you took through the delta marshlands. Mustafa and John were waiting for us on the busy, crowded riverbank, where women were boiling up palm fruits in fifty-gallon drums, making palm oil, and people were gathering water from the river in filthy plastic containers, and a full-sized passenger bus, bright blue with a chimpanzee painted on the back, was inching its way onto a rusty old platform ferry that worked its away across the river on steel cables. Bicycles everywhere, the usual goats, sheep, chickens, dogs, fires burning, Congolese music playing through blown speakers. I was beginning to entertain the possibility that Tanzanians actually preferred their music played through blown speakers, with that extra fuzz, buzz, and rumble. I thought of those West African wood carvings where the sculptor fashions a smooth figure, then hammers spikes or nails into it for a kind of visual distortion effect.

As we were unloading the boat, we saw that one of its inflatable sections had gone soft and flabby. What a drag, I thought. We'll have to patch it, let it dry overnight, reinflate it in the morning. For Ryan, though, fatigued as he was from rowing against the wind and current, having spent days dragging the boat over rocks on two bad ankles, it was the last straw. Finding the puncture, he exploded with anger and frustration and announced that this was as far as we were going.

"We're getting in the vehicles tomorrow morning, and we'll drop you in Kigoma," he told me.

"*Boati* dead," said Tito. "Safari over. I go back Dar es Salaam, see wife."

I waited for Ryan to calm down. "Come on," I said. "We put a patch on it, and paddle down to the lake in the morning. We'll be there in an hour."

"Against this wind? Against this current? No, that's it. The river has fucked my boat, fuck the river. You'll get a look at the lake from the road to Kigoma."

"Ryan, I've got to see this last piece of river," I pleaded. "I've got to see it flow into the lake. I'll go with a fisherman, come back, then we drive to Kigoma. Ask Mustafa to start talking to fishermen."

He expelled a sharp sigh. "Okay," he said. "We'll rent a motorboat, and take you down to the lake that way. Mustafa!"

Ryan hobbled into camp, and I poured out the last of the Famous Grouse into two plastic beakers. We had had our differences of opinion, we had not become friends, we had not achieved the first descent of the Malagarasi River. But we had run more of it than anyone else, and I was far too depleted to hold any grudges or hard feelings about the things that might have been.

"A motorboat will be fine," I said.

He held up his beaker and said, "Cheers, *bwana*."

We finished our drinks, and I got up with the empty whiskey bottle to find the trash bag. Ryan said, "A local would treasure that bottle. Why don't you give it to one of those women?" I went over toward the blackened lean-to where women were boiling palm fruits and breathing acrid black smoke. A young mother came forward to retrieve her pointing toddler, and I offered her the empty bottle, hoping she wouldn't be insulted by a gift of my trash. At first she didn't understand. She thought I wanted her to go down to the river and fill the bottle with water for me. Then I explained in my atrocious Swahili that it was for her, a gift, and her face lit up with amazement, gratitude, disbelief at her good fortune. It was a fine, strong bottle and would probably be the most substantial possession in her hut.

I walked back into camp, reflecting on all the whiskey bottles I've thrown away in my life. Mustafa predicted that she would still have that bottle years from now, unless of course someone stole it from her.

ON FEBRUARY 13, 1858, having emerged from a region of ghastly swamps and jungle just north of the Malagarasi River, Burton and Speke rode through an area of tall grass, crossed a small savannah, and were then confronted by a big, steep, rocky hill studded with thorn trees. Speke was almost blind. One of the porters walked ahead of him, leading his donkey. Burton had partially regained his sight, but his mouth was still too ulcerated to take solid food, his legs were still suffering intermittent paralysis, and there had been yet more malaria attacks. They had now been traveling for seven and a half months, and had covered nearly 950 miles.

They struggled up the hill. Speke's donkey collapsed and died on the summit, and Burton called a rest for the exhausted animals and porters. Through his clouded eyes, and through a screen of thorn trees, he saw a streak of light in the distance below them. To Sidi Bombay, the one honest, trustworthy man in his caravan, he said, "What is that?"

"I am of the opinion," said Bombay, "that it is the water." Burton was crushed. Instead of the vast inland sea he was expecting, it appeared to be rather a small and nondescript lake. "I began to lament my folly in having risked life and lost health for so poor a prize, to curse Arab exaggeration, and to propose an immediate return, with the view of exploring the Nyanza, or Northern Lake."

Advancing a little further, however, beyond the obscuring trees, the full immensity of Lake Tanganyika burst suddenly into view, and Burton was overcome with "admiration, wonder and delight," and also a tremendous sense of relief that he hadn't failed.

Nothing, in sooth, could be more picturesque than this first view of Lake Tanganyika, as it lay in the lap of the mountains, basking in the gorgeous tropical sunshine . . . in front stretch the waters, an expanse of the lightest and softest blue, in breadth varying from thirty to thirty-five miles, and sprinkled by the crisp east-wind with tiny crescents of snowy foam . . . Truly it was a revel for soul and sight. Forgetting toils, dangers, and the doubtfulness of return, I felt willing to endure double what I had endured. . . ."

Behind the far shore was a high, broken wall of mountains, partially wreathed in white mists, and elsewhere "sharply penciled against the azure air." To the south, the Malagarasi River, swollen and violent from the rains, and ocher-red from all the soil that had washed into it, discharged itself into the lake behind a long, low point. The whole expedition joined Burton in joyful celebration, all except the bitterly disappointed Speke, who could see none of this. "The Great Lake in question," wrote Speke, "was just mist and glare before my eyes."

We climbed gingerly into a leaky motorboat shortly after dawn on October 5, 2009. There was no wind, and palm fronds and storm clouds were perfectly reflected on the river's glassy surface. The boatman started up the engine and assured us that the large hole in the prow was no problem. So long as no one sat in the front part of the boat, the hole would remain above the waterline. And if the lake got choppy? Still no problem. The assistant boatman had a yellow plastic jug for bailing out the water. Water was already seeping in through cracks in the bottom of the boat.

We chugged our way past oil palms, borassus palms, mango trees, waving children, mothers boiling water for chai on Monday morning cookfires. I took a photograph of a long-crested eagle perched on a dead tree as the sun broke through a gap in the storm clouds and fanned out its rays. Then there were no more trees. We followed a tongue of river through bullrushes and papyrus, passed a lone grass hut on the last piece of solid ground, flying an Arsenal flag from its roof, and with a feeling of sweet melancholy release, under an immense African sky, we crossed over from the mouth of the river into the lake.

The water under the boat was returning home. It had begun as evaporation from Lake Tanganyika, formed into clouds that rained on the Burundian mountains on the northeastern flanks of the lake. Collecting in streams and rivulets, it formed itself into a river, flowing northeast along the Tanzanian border and then making a tight arching turn like a scorpion's tail to come south across the great basin where we first saw it. Having flowed through the game reserve and seeped through the swamp with inexorable slowness, the water had then turned west to make its runs through rapids, channels, rock gardens, waterfalls, the long mountain canyon, and now it was rejoining the lake to begin the cycle again. For such a long river, the Malagarasi flows in an unusually closed system.

When you read the rush of purple prose about Lake Tanganyika in Burton's account, you can't help wondering if he was exaggerating its beauty, feeding in all the qualities that the Victorians required to satisfy their ideal of the sublime in nature, perhaps boosting his achievement, or simply overcome by the emotion of the moment. But the truth is that Lake Tanganyika, the longest freshwater lake in the world and the deepest after Lake Baikal, is also spectacularly beautiful.

Its water was jade green under the storm clouds, and when the sun broke through, it turned to a light, soft blue color. Dugouts were silhouetted out on the water, insanely overloaded with huge mounds of marsh grasses. Ahead of us was the dramatic, mist-wreathed, mountain wall of Eastern Congo. Behind us was all of Tanzania. To the north was Burundi, and at the southern end of the lake, beyond our field of vision, was the border of Zambia. I had the distinct sense of being close to the geographical heart of Africa, and I could see why Burton thought this lake was the great reservoir that fed the Nile.

Hebron and Alanus experienced Lake Tanganyika with a feeling of unease. They had never seen such a broad expanse of fresh water, and they lacked confidence in the boat. As the wind started to freshen, and white-capped waves appeared, and the assistant boatman started bailing the rising water around our feet with his yellow plastic jug, I felt uneasy too. But there was nothing to do but fall back on fatalism. If it was meant to be, we would join the hundred-plus people who sank and drowned in Lake Tanganyika every year in unsafe boats. Otherwise, we would be fine. There was nothing we could do about it, so why worry?

We motored out maybe a mile from shore, passing big, long, lake-faring fishing boats painted with black and white zebra stripes, with the assistant boatman bailing casually all the way and the water level rising at our feet. Ryan asked me if I wanted to go further. I said that was far enough, and Hebron and Alanus looked relieved.

As we chugged back upriver to Ilagala, I started daydreaming about Mexican food, the smoky tang of *carne asada*, flour tortillas, the crunch and fire of tortilla chips and fresh salsa. Maybe there would be something good to eat in Kigoma. There would certainly be cold beer, a barbershop to shave away this river beard, and a doctor to see what was wrong with me. I took a photograph of myself that morning as the others packed up our final camp and loaded all the gear into the Land Cruisers. It is the photograph of a sick exhausted ruin.

A STEADY RAIN was falling in Kigoma, the biggest town on the Tanzanian stretch of the lakeshore. I bought a new credit voucher for my phone and sent a text home saying I had survived the Malagarasi. Then, for nearly two hours, I sat parked outside a bank that contained Ryan and the game officer. There was an endless parade of new white Land Cruisers going up and down the muddy street, and I passed the time by noting down the acronyms on their doors: ICAP, UNICEF, UNDP, UNEP, UNHCR, ActionAid, JGI, ISF, CARE, Familia, World Food Programme, and many more. I don't know how much aid money was passing through Kigoma every year, but it was certainly millions of dollars, and there were probably a hundred and fifty foreigners here disbursing it.

They were operating refugee camps for Burundians and Congolese. They were bringing electricity, building water projects, schools, hospitals, running workshops on environmental awareness, conflict resolution, gender issues, information technology, and so on. It struck me that they were all operating on the same principle that nineteenth-century Europeans had used to justify colonialism and missionary work: these poor Africans can't look after themselves properly, it is our duty to help them and bring them forward into the light.

I held a very dim view of missionaries and colonialism, but they had been successful in transforming the continent and bringing it more into line with their arrogant goals and intentions. The same was not true of aid. Forty years of aid to Africa, amounting to $300 billion, had achieved almost none of its goals and quite possibly had made things worse, mainly by inadvertently funding and prolonging wars, propping up inefficient and corrupt regimes,* and fostering dependency on more aid. On the other hand, how could the West sit back and do nothing as Africa plunged deeper into preventable suffering?

---

*According to one estimate, nearly half of the $20 billion a year that Africa receives in aid money ends up in private bank accounts in Switzerland and London.

In Kigoma the most tangible development created by the "international community," as these mostly white foreigners liked to call themselves, was the local economy that had grown up to service their needs. They were renting houses, offices, and hotel rooms. They were hiring local assistants, drivers, maids, cooks, gardeners, security guards, nightwatchmen. They were buying most of the gasoline in town, supporting the Land Cruiser mechanics and computer repair technicians, eating and drinking in restaurants and bars that most locals couldn't afford, unless they had hit the jackpot and scored an administrative job with one of the NGOs.

The game officer came out of the bank, looked around, called John over, said something, and went back inside. He had been acting strangely all morning. At one point the two Land Cruisers were parked next to each other. The game officer was in one, Ryan was in the other. He rolled down his window and began talking loudly on the phone so that Ryan could hear him, saying, "Yes, these poachers in Kagera Nkanda, we must send a team after them."

Later we asked John, who had been in the vehicle with him, who the game officer was talking to. "I don't know," said John. "But he was using my phone, and I don't have any credit on it."

The fact that he would stage this fake call only increased our suspicions that he was involved in the poaching business. He had stared so fixedly at his shoes when Dale Wright brought it up. The policeman in Kagera Nkanda had told Mustafa that he thought the game department was involved. And sadly, it was an unusual game officer in Tanzania who wasn't involved in the poaching business. "There are honest game officers," said Ryan. "A lot of them start out that way, at least."

Back in Kasulu, perhaps unwisely, Ryan had come to a financial arrangement with the game officer. Ryan's bank in Dar wouldn't let him draw money in Kigoma, and he needed cash for the return journey. So Ryan told his bank to wire a thousand dollars to the game officer's account on the understanding that the game officer would draw it out as cash when we got to Kigoma. Ryan would then give some of the money to the game officer and John for their help and use the rest to meet his expenses on the road back to Dar. All of this, I might add, was because the money I had wired to Ryan for the trip hadn't cleared by the time we left Dar.

Now, with Ryan's thousand dollars in his account, the game officer was claiming that he had forgotten to bring his bank card or any personal identification, so the bank here in Kigoma wasn't letting him draw any money. He was also trying to charge Ryan $450 for "rafting through a protected area," plus $250 for John. When John heard about this, he said, "I don't know how much you think is right to pay me, but please don't give any of my money to him. I will get none of it. He will drink it all."

Without ever getting angry or confrontational, without ever questioning the game officer's outrageous assertions, Ryan went into the bank, explained the situation to the bank manager, and using a strategy of calm, patient, unyielding forcefulness, got the game officer to call his bank manager in Kasulu, who okayed the transfer. "Ah, here's my money," said Ryan pointedly as it was counted out. Once he had it in his hands, he explained calmly that he needed to get five people all the way back to Dar, pay for their food, their accommodations, and all the fuel for two Land Cruisers (gas was $8 a gallon in Tanzania at the time). Almost apologetically, Ryan said that normally the game officers they worked with charged a much lower rate for their services, and here was what he had budgeted for (putting $200 in the game officer's hand). Then he walked over to pay John separately.

With that settled, Ryan put his crew in a cheap hostel and drove me up to the Hilltop Hotel, where we passed a tame zebra on the grounds and a team of Scandinavian aid workers in the lobby. "Well, *bwana*, that was a hell of a trip," he said as we clinked our beer glasses together in the restaurant.

"It was indeed," I said.

We had clashed egos and gotten on each other's nerves at times. Our motivations for the trip had never converged, and I disliked the brusque, domineering way he exercised his authority, both over me and the men he called his boys. On the other hand, his decisions had nearly all been wise, erring on the side of caution, and I respected his integrity, his abilities, his judgment. He had reined in some foolhardy and potentially disastrous impulses on my part. Now, as we ate lunch and drank our farewell beers, it was easier to feel the camaraderie of having come through such a difficult and trying experience together, although neither of us felt like lingering over it. A quick beer, a bite to eat, and I was relieved to say good-bye and get rid of him, mainly because I felt so wretched with exhaustion and sickness. Later I found out that I wasn't the only one. On their return to Dar es Salaam, Ryan, Mustafa, Omari, Hebron, Alanus, and Tito all tested positive for malaria—none of them were taking antimalarials like me—and stoic Hebron was also suffering from typhoid.

As for the Malagarasi, it was still there for the taking, but the shine was off it now, at least for me. I had seen all of the river that I wanted to see. I felt no calling to explore its upper reaches or battle my way through its swamp. Whatever exploration was left on my journey would be into human geography and contemporary Africa.

I would be traveling by myself for the first time on this continent, and heading directly into Burundi, one of its poorest and most unstable countries. I would be more vulnerable now and even more conspicuous. Everything would depend on the kindness of strangers, the vagaries of luck, and my own instincts. Language would be a major problem. Until now, Ryan or the golf pro had always been there to translate and interpret, and I had made slow progress in Swahili. In Burundi and Rwanda, former Belgian colonies, people spoke French, and hopefully my schoolboy French, unused in thirty years, would come back to me.

There were some basic traveler's protocols to follow. Don't walk around at night, don't drink the water, don't flash cash. Keep your money, bank cards, and passport under your clothes at all times. Never use the safe in a cheap hotel. Beware of cops and whores who say they don't want money. The best defense against swarms of hustlers and would-be guides is to hire one to keep the others away. Look for the face that appeals most to you, and good luck getting rid of him when the swarms are gone. Always use a condom (although I was still intending to be loyal) and don't buy drugs.

Be alert. When walking down a street, try to notice people before they notice you, especially the people who look like they're up to no good. If you get the first glance on them, it makes you less of a mark. Be alert, but don't be paranoid and stunt the travel experience with overcaution. It's better to plunge in, and get used to feeling off-balance and out of your depth, than to cling to the remnants of your comfort zone. Don't be too concerned about your personal dignity. Accept that you are a fool here, and hope that people will teach you this gently.

If you're fond of drinking and male, this can be a great advantage and also a liability. In most of the world, drinking is the fastest way for men to form cross-cultural friendships and for a traveler to get a street-level view of a place. But drinking also leads to sloppy mistakes and puts you in volatile situations. It impairs alertness, and a slight stumble as you leave a bar is certain to attract the attention of any nearby predators. Remember: you probably look more drunk than you feel, even though you are convinced the opposite is true.

Remember also: there will always be predators, but respect and acknowledgment is what most people in poor countries want from a traveler.

8

Burundi Calling

Sickness—White people—Livingstone—Nkilaha Social Club—The Chinese—Border crossing—Heavy vibes in Mabanda—Bujumbura—Hutu and Tutsi—Sudi's house—Immigration office—The wisdom of Kenny Rogers

AT AN INTERNET place called Baby Come and Call, I checked the latest news and travel advisories coming out of Burundi. Some demobilized child soldiers had rioted in their rehabilitation center and spilled out into the streets, saying they were hungry and demanding that sardines be added to their daily food rations. Grenades were still going off with alarming regularity. An overcrowded boat had capsized on Lake Tanganyika, drowning twenty-eight, and the president, Pierre Nkurunziza, was holding ecstatic rallies in packed soccer stadiums to celebrate his four years in office.

"Down on the pitch, the police is struggling to contain the crowd's fervor," reported Esdras Ndikumana of AFP. "Sandals and loincloths fly as the president's fellow born-agains slip into a quasi-trance. The spectacle reaches a climax when comes the president's favorite song: Nkurunziza rolls on his backside and starts kicking the air, together with his 20-odd dancing vocalists. Then he suddenly rises to his feet and belches in his microphone, 'God is with us! God has supported us for all those years . . . ' Taking no time to rest, he launches straight into his next hit, wiggling his hips to the powerful rhythms of a Congolese *ndombolo,* a kind of mix of rumba, funk and traditional rhythms."

The U.S. Department of State website gave a very different impression of Burundi. "Crime and banditry are still prevalent . . . Crime, often committed by groups of street children or armed bandits, poses the highest risk for foreign visitors to both Bujumbura and Burundi. Visitors should keep car doors locked, windows up, and be careful when stopped in heavy traffic due to the threat of robbery . . . armed criminals are ambushing vehicles, particularly on the roads leading out of Bujumbura."

Bujumbura, the capital city of Burundi, was my next port of call. It lay at the top end of Lake Tanganyika, a hundred miles north of Kigoma, and I was hoping to go there on the MV *Liemba,* a 1913 German steamship that has served as Lake Tanganyika's ferryboat since 1924. I went down to the ferry office, where the clerk spoke English, and asked him for a ticket on the next ferry to Bujumbura.

"I can sell you a ticket, but the ferry is not running to Bujumbura," he said.

"So what is the ticket for?"

"You can go to another place," he said.

"Another place in Burundi?"

"No, you can go to Zambia."

This was probably good advice, but I was bound and sworn for Burundi. I wanted to see what life was like in the world's poorest country,* now that its long, flaring, subsiding, flaring

---

*It depends how you measure poverty and over what period. Burundi was the poorest country in the world measured by per capita income in some years, but not others. In reality Burundi, Liberia, and Zimbabwe were all about as poor as it gets. Congo (DRC) was right down there, too, despite the fantastic mineral wealth enriching its elite and foreign traders and corporations.

Hutu-Tutsi civil war was over, with 300,000 dead. And Burundi was inescapably on the way to Rwanda, where I had my interview with the president and an appointment with the source of the Nile.

"Are there other boats that go to Bujumbura?" I asked.

"There are lake taxis. But the ferry is better."

"But the ferry doesn't go to Bujumbura."

"No. It is coming from Bujumbura."

"Wait . . . It doesn't go back there?"

"No, it goes to Zambia."

Soon after that exchange, as I was leaning against a wall writing it down, my head started ringing with a high unsettling whine and dark flecks swirled around in front of my eyes like black snowflakes or a swarm of tiny bats. I felt faint and sat down, breathing heavily and suddenly drenched in clammy sweat. After a few minutes, I felt better and went back to Baby Come and Call to see if it was possible to get malaria while taking Malarone every day, as I had been without fail.

I e-mailed my symptoms to the travel doctor in London who had sold me the Malarone. He ruled out malaria and side effects to Malarone and said it was impossible to say what was causing my symptoms. The list of likely candidates was "really quite extensive," starting with flus and insect-borne viruses like dengue fever and chikungunya, and tests were the only way to find out. Basically, I realized, I was feeling like millions and millions of Africans felt on a regular basis: feverish, faint, sore, weak, shitty, but not really sick like you got with the big league diseases like malaria, typhoid, yellow fever, sleeping sickness, and HIV.

I revived somewhat after spending a day in bed, and the hotel found me a taxi driver called Sufian who spoke some English. I asked him to take me to a doctor, and he dropped me off at a crowded medical clinic. The people there looked so horribly ill, so dire and ghastly, that I decided the best thing for my health was to get out of there as fast as possible while holding my breath. Whatever I had wasn't nearly as bad as whatever they had.

Out in the street, I called Sufian and told him to take me to Ujiji, the old Arab trading town where Stanley found Livingstone and where thirteen years earlier, Burton had based himself for three months while exploring Lake Tanganyika and searching for the Nile source. Most of his time was taken up with interminable haggling and waiting for a boat and riding out yet more malaria attacks in a verminous hut. "I lay for a fortnight upon the earth, too blind to read or write . . . too weak to ride, and too ill to converse," Burton recorded at one point, but he rallied to make the first ethnographic studies of the Lake tribes.

They contain his usual accurate, detailed observations and descriptions, peppered with his usual scathing remarks and flashes of jaw-dropping bigotry. At this stage in his career, Burton had a low and sinking opinion of Africans, and he considered them incapable as a race of improving themselves. Later in life, having met an African who had graduated from Oxford University, he completely revised his opinions on race and reached an early form of cultural relativism, deciding that it was impossible for people from one culture to judge another objectively, because they were incapable of escaping their own narrow cultural assumptions about the world. But he never lost his caustic sense of humor, and at one time or another Burton denigrated almost every race under the sun, including his own.

Despite his deep respect for Islam and knowledge of Arab culture, languages, and literature, he had no qualms about characterizing the Omanis as "lawless and fanatical, treacherous, blood-thirsty and eternally restless." The Wanyikas on the Swahili coast were "a futile race of barbarians, drunken and immoral; cowardly and destructive; boisterous and loquacious; indolent, greedy and thriftless." Arriving back in England as a young man, he wrote that he had "fallen among grocers," and "the faces of the women were the only exception to the general rule of hideousness." Rome was "a piggery," and America was "Uncle Sham."

The Wajiji, the native people of Ujiji, were "rude, insolent and extortionate," sturdier and stronger-looking than any other Africans he had encountered, extensively tattooed, covered in scarification patterns, glistening with palm oil, and their hair was shaved into tufts, crescents, and little buttons. They stacked as much shell jewelry, brass discs, and other ornamentation as possible around their necks, and each man carried a pair of iron or wooden pincers around his neck. They soaked their tobacco in water, snorted the juice up their noses, and then used the pincers to close off their nostrils so the juice could percolate through their nasal membranes.

The Arabs considered them notorious troublemakers, and Burton judged them the drunkest tribe in a region that he thought was probably the drunkest place on earth. All the way across East Africa, except where Islam had prevailed, it was customary for the men to start drinking *pombe* beer or palm wine when they woke up, work up a good buzz over the course of the morning, sleep it off in the afternoon, then wake up and drink until midnight with drumming and dancing. The only real curb on drinking was when the supply ran out, and people were also smoking a lot of weed—none more so than the Wajiji, who couldn't conceive of paddling a boat or canoe without getting stoned.

Driving through Ujiji today, it was clear that the Arabs had left behind a stronger influence than the hedonistic Wajiji. Bars and beer signs were unusually scarce, and outnumbered by mosques, madrasas, Islamic institutes, and cultural centers. The town was noticeably more decrepit than neighboring Kigoma, with medieval squalor in the side streets and back alleys. Sufian said Ujiji used to be 90 percent Muslim, but now it was more like 70 percent. When I asked him why it was poorer than Kigoma, he said it was because Muslims were lazy and didn't want to develop. I didn't know what to make of that, except add it to the rich and voluminous archives of human prejudice.

The ways in which Europeans have racially stereotyped Africans have been so exhaustively studied, analyzed, and catalogued that I didn't think there was any more to learn on that subject. But I knew very little about African prejudices. How did the different African nations and ethnic groups stereotype each other? How did they stereotype white people? Sufian laughed when I asked him what Tanzanians say about the *wazungu*. "Oh," he said. "We say many things. We say white people do not lie. Is this true?"

"Yes," I said. "We always speak the truth. If we tell a lie, it makes our skin go very pink so we never do it."

"Really?"

"No," I said. "That was a lie. That was a joke. White people are liars like everyone else."

"You don't keep your promises?"

"Sometimes we do, sometimes we don't."

"That is like us. But we say a *muzungu* is more trustworthy than an African."

"Really? Even though we colonized your country, and told you it was for your own good?"

"I don't know about that. But we say you can trust the whites."

"What else do you say about us?"

"Hah! Oh! No! I cannot say."

"Come on. I give you a good tip."

"We say you are weak with your women."

I DIDN'T HAVE TO TELL Sufian where to go. Every *muzungu* who came to Ujiji wanted to go to the same place, and he had never taken a fellow African there. He bumped his taxi down a shack-lined, trash-strewn lane and parked outside the fenced and gated entrance to a large gray-brick memorial commemorating the spot where Henry Morton Stanley, a Welsh-American newspaperman whose mother had cast him into an orphanage workhouse, found the haggard ruin of Dr. David Livingstone, a Scottish missionary explorer who had undergone an equally hard and ambition-forging childhood in an Edinburgh textile mill. Straining to sound like an English gentleman, Stanley stood before the only other white man in central Africa at the time and uttered that immortal and slightly ridiculous phrase, "Dr. Livingstone, I presume."

Sufian had been to the gates many times, but he had never been inside. "Do you want to see it?" I asked.

"It costs money," he said.

"I will pay for you."

"Okay. I will see it."

An elderly guide in a Muslim prayer cap, a sweet and gracious man called Guvuru, welcomed us at the gates and led us past an outdoor table, where an elaborately coiffured woman was sprawled asleep on the registration book. The monument had a map of Africa embossed on its polished gray bricks and a cross deeply incised into the map. Here was the hardshell Protestant style—it reminded me of church monuments and tombstones I had seen in Aberdeen, Scotland, and Abilene, Texas.

Guvuru pointed to a stone bench and invited us to sit down. Standing up to his full height of five foot three and tilting his head back slightly, he recited a summary of Livingstone's career in erratic English, with the usual Swahili suffixes, and an odd way of rising up to a high-pitched squeak at the end of each sentence: "After that journey, he proceededi back to Europe, where he studiedi at Cambridge-i Universi-*tee*!"

This was not the time or place to voice my opinions about Livingstone, which ran sharply contrary to the accepted myth of the noble, virtuous, saintly hero. I thought Livingstone got a lot of people killed unnecessarily, including his long-suffering wife, because he was incapable of admitting that he had made a mistake. And he made so many mistakes. They stemmed from a combination of pride, self-righteousness, and unquenchable optimism, and he could always justify his decisions by saying to himself and others that he was carrying out God's will.

When Stanley found him here in 1871, Livingstone's reputation in Britain was at a low ebb. Fifteen years earlier he had basked in nationwide acclaim for his epic tramp across Africa, from south to central, then all the way west and all the way east. Whenever I think my restlessness is extreme, I have only to remember Livingstone, a man who blew a gasket every time he tried to stay put and could always find a vital new reason to go tramping across Africa again. But African travel was expensive, and to get funding from missionary organizations and the British government, Livingstone had made a series of bold and overconfident claims.

He had hailed east-central Africa as the ideal location for an improving colony of British missionaries and settlers, assured his backers that malaria was not endemic to the region and in any case no worse than a bad cold, that the Zambezi River was a navigable highway into this promised land, that the tribes weren't warring and slaving on each other, and selling captives and children to the Arab and Portuguese slavers. By 1871, all these claims and more had been proved false by the deaths or testimonies of British missionaries who had believed in Livingstone, and in mid-nineteenth-century Britain all this was front-page news. African explorers were the celebrities of their age and subject to the same fickle adoration.

Livingstone had been hailed as a great missionary, but people were starting to notice that in all his years of proselytizing in Africa he had made only one convert to Christianity, who later backslid. He had been hailed as the greatest African explorer, but many of his geographical theories, especially about rivers, had proven faulty, and the Portuguese had already been to most of the places he had "discovered." Now Livingstone had gone back to Africa to find the source of the Nile, certain that it would cancel out all his other failures, and restore his reputation to its former glory, and this is why he became so obsessed with the quest.

His famously iron constitution was worn down to the filings. The man who used to get up, pray for strength, walk through his malaria attacks, and deride others as shirkers and weaklings for not doing the same was now laid out helpless by his fevers and also suffering from chronic dysentery. He was destitute, stuck here in Ujiji without the vital supplies of beads, cloth, and medicines that enabled a foreigner to travel in East Africa, and he was living off the charity of the same Arab slavers that he had thundered against as the scourge of the continent.

Stanley tried everything to persuade him to come back with him to Zanzibar and London, but Livingstone couldn't bear the prospect of returning as a failure, and he felt sure that God would guide him to his prize. So armed with medicines and supplies that Stanley gave him, Livingstone went south into present-day Zambia, when the Nile source lay to the north. He got lost in a swamp in the rainy season, owing to a geographical error he had stubbornly refused to admit some years earlier, and died there of malaria and dysentery. His two faithful servants, Susi and Chuma, buried his heart under a tree, mummified his body, wrapped it in bark, and carried it a thousand miles to Bagamoyo. Then they sailed with it to Zanzibar, where the body was housed briefly above the golf pro's barstool, and on to London.

In the meantime Stanley had maximized his journalistic coup with an artful and shameless piece of mythmaking. The Livingstone he had found in Ujiji was not a deluded old failure but the noblest and most resolute of all the African explorers, a living saint who went alone among the savages, "as close to an angel" as it was possible for any man to be. Stanley's mythological Livingstone was carefully molded to embody all the strengths, virtues, and heroism that Victorian Britain aspired to. The media and the public fell for it wholeheartedly, and all Livingstone's failures and shortcomings were forgotten. When the husk of Livingstone's body was buried with full honors at Westminster Abbey, Britain wept and mourned and came together like it did for Lady Diana's funeral.

Guvuru led into us into a dingy little house that served as the monument's museum. A man and a woman were playing cards in the foyer. A sleeping mat was rolled out in the corridor. He unlocked a door and ushered us into a room with some paintings and photographs and two larger-than-life papier-mâché statues by a local artist. Dr. Livingstone, a red-faced blond, was holding up a blue pith helmet, and Stanley with his muttonchop sideburns was doffing an explorer's cap in return. I stood between them doffing my own bush hat, and Guvuru obliged by taking the photograph. There was also a photograph of Burton, looking very fierce and swarthy with his long mustaches.

On the way out, the woman at the registration desk was awake, and Sufian and I filled out lengthy forms that had to be copied and stamped. I paid the fees with pleasure and gave Guvuru a generous tip. I loved these rickety, eccentric, underfunded African museums with their reciting guides, improvised displays, and snoozing assistants. The museums never let me down in Africa, and neither did the dive bars or nightclubs.

THERE WAS A young man working in my hotel who took it upon himself to arrange the next stage of my journey. His name was Juma Shabani, he was well-educated and ambitious, spoke very good English, and followed global news and policy debates in great detail on the Internet. He took me out drinking on the eve of my departure in a place called the Nkilaha Social Club, an open-roofed place by the bus station where working men devoured skewers of grilled meat and warm beer, grandmothers took their infant grandchildren, and moochers, prostitutes, and hawkers of colognes and perfumes went from table to table.

Juma had worked in the refugee camps around Kigoma, and he made some more entries in my file of African prejudices and stereotypes. "The Congolese are obsessed with clothes," he said. "You would see them in the camps wearing designer suits, with high-waisted trousers, but no shoes. Or they have a silk tie from Paris, but their shirt has a big hole in the back. They love to drink and dance, and they are terrible, shameless liars. They would train the children in the camps to say that they saw their mothers raped and their fathers killed, so they can get sent to Europe or Canada. The Congolese, they don't want to work. They prefer to hustle and steal."

"What about the Burundians?" I asked.

"They are hardworking," he said. "But they have too many guns and grenades and terrible politicians. If they get ten years of peace, they can get past this and do what we all want to do."

"And what is that?"

"Develop. Live more like the West."

Juma wanted to be a lawyer. He had a place waiting for him at Dodoma University, but he couldn't get a student loan sufficient to cover his tuition costs. I waited for him to ask me for help, but it never came. He seemed satisfied to have my respect and friendship, and he earned my deep gratitude for his help and advice.

Burton had traveled by boat to the northern end of Lake Tanganyika, where Bujumbura is today, and I wanted to do the same. Juma insisted it was too dangerous: "The rains and storms are here, the boats are overcrowded, people are capsizing and drowning all the time. Also, when the boatmen see you, they see a rich man, so they call on their phone to the robber boat, and they come and rob you. They will say they don't know these robbers, but nothing happens without a plan."

"Do they kill also? Or just rob?"

"They want your money and belongings. Very rarely do they kill. If someone kills here, we think they are crazy. Or from Burundi. But Richard, you must not take a lake taxi. Please. The way to Bujumbura is on the bus."

That night he took me to a muddy yard full of stones, chickens, trash, loiterers, and Toyota Hiace minivans. He made inquiries about going to Bujumbura, asking prices, giving the impression it was for him not me, and this was an easy impression to give, because white people did not go to Burundi on the bus. Then he said, "OK. You meet me here at six a.m. and don't be late. They say crossing the border is no problem. It is quiet there. You have to catch another bus on the other side."

"Another bus?"

"Be here at six. I will arrange everything."

I arrived at quarter to six with my backpack, and Juma was already there. He bought the ticket so I wouldn't get a special price. He made sure my backpack was stowed in a place where it was hard to steal. He said I would have to walk across the border and then catch a taxi to the nearest town, and get a bus to Bujumbura from there. I gave him ten dollars as we shook hands good-bye in a sudden rainstorm, and then I sat down inside the Hiace and waited for it to fill up. "Max. capacity 13," said the writing on the back of the vehicle. The driver and his assistant managed to get in twenty, but that wasn't good enough. We sat there squeezed in for forty-five minutes until two more passengers arrived and then two more.

Then the driver roared out into the muddy streets, skidded, lost control, fishtailed, and almost flipped. The passengers were angry, especially the women, and they gave the young man at the wheel a barrage of scolding. He responded by turning up the radio to its maximum distorted volume and roaring off again at the same idiotic speed. Whenever the Hiace went over a large bump, which was every few minutes, I cracked skulls with the young man to my left and learned to appreciate the fact that his hair was long enough to cushion the blow slightly. But his body odor made my eyes water.

To my right, I was jammed up against a serene-looking Muslim with a white beard, a white prayer cap, and a kind smile. He spoke some English, and over the racket of the music I determined that his name was Sudi, and he had been visiting his wife in Kigoma, where she was pregnant with his fifth child and staying with her family. Now he was returning home to Bujumbura, and when I said I was going there too, he said we should travel together. I trusted him immediately and completely, and I felt greatly relieved to have an ally in negotiating the border crossing and the Burundian bus system.

Alongside our muddy, potholed road, the Chinese were building a paved highway. It seemed odd to see Chinese faces under the hardhats on that rainy African morning and Chinese drivers in the cabs of muddy Chinese earthmovers, but it's a normal sight in Africa these days. China is the biggest foreign player on the continent now, with a presence in all fifty-three countries. Unlike the West, which feels a moral obligation to reduce suffering and improve African lives, China looks at Africa purely as an economic opportunity. Its basic strategy is twofold: strip out the natural resources and sell Chinese-made goods to Africans, everything from fighter jets and tanks down to flip-flops and combs.

Starting with the missionaries, the West has always had this idea that Africans need to change their ways and live more like us, but the Chinese, who started trading here in the seventh century, do not feel this impulse. Chinese officials, for obvious reasons, don't upbraid African leaders about human rights or democratic governance. Nor do they have any objection to bribery and corruption, if it helps business get done. While the West concentrates on partnering with Africans in the areas of education, health, environmental issues, gender issues, community development projects, and bends over backward to be culturally sensitive and politically correct, China comes in with Chinese workers, hiring Africans only for the most menial tasks, and builds roads, factories, ports, dams, airports, and presidential palaces, all with the aim of boosting its trade. In 1996, China's trade in Africa was $5.6 billion. In 2010, it was over $100 billion, with more than a million Chinese living in Africa.

I had talked about this with Juma Shabani in the bar last night. He wanted Africa to develop, to become more like the West, but he didn't think it was going to happen. The naive, altruistic approach of the West had been ineffectual, hamstrung by post-colonial guilt. The Chinese knew how to get things done in Africa, primarily by appealing to the greed of African leaders and elites, and it was the Chinese who would now prevail. He wasn't happy about it, because he didn't think this Chinese economic imperialism would lead to development, democracy, or more just and fair African societies. But it was a force of history now, and there was no point pretending it wasn't happening.

THE HIACE STOPPED in a small village in forested highlands with mist drifting through the trees. It was immediately surrounded by shouting young men, getting off their bicycles, shoving and shouldering each other aside to wrench the back door open and start grabbing at our bags. I must have looked alarmed because Sudi said, "It's okay. I will talk to them."

He stood there gentle and beatific as five men began yelling and gesturing in his face, then he spoke some words, more yelling, more soft words from Sudi. "These are bicycle taxi men," he explained. "They will take us to the border. They want ten thousand for the two of us, and another five for your bag. It is a fair price."

I didn't understand why the bus didn't go to the border, but it was a pleasant relief to ride on the back of a bicycle in the cool, fresh highland air. Sudi was on the bicycle next to me, smiling happily, and my backpack was on a third bicycle. The road curved along a high saddle separating the two countries, and we caught glimpses below of misty valleys with small patchwork fields. We were close to the headwaters of the Malagarasi River, although exactly how close depended on which map you believed. The two maps I carried had a twenty-mile discrepancy.

At the border itself, there was none of the usual commotion and opportunism that you find when crossing from one poor country into another. This was a remote area with no town either side. There were two small buildings in a quiet forest, a handful of people crossing, and no one else around. A friendly Tanzanian official stamped our passports and wished us well, and then we walked across a patch of no-man's-land to his Burundian counterpart.

He was a big, sullen, muscular man turning to fat, and when my turn came to stand in front of his desk, he glowered at me for a good twenty seconds without saying anything, full of sneering contempt and pig-eyed menace. Then he gave a dismissive grunt and looked down at his papers.

I stood there for a while. Sudi was waiting outside. Several minutes passed. "My passport," I said, holding it toward him.

"Hmmpf. *Parlez-vous français?*"

"No," I said, wanting the linguistic advantage.

He took my passport, examined it, and said, "Where is exit visa?"

I pointed to the stamp in my passport.

"You can buy Burundi visa for twenty dollar."

"I have Tanzanian shillings," I said. I also had a hundred-dollar bill in my wallet, and cursed myself for not breaking it down in Kigoma.

"Dollar only. No shilling."

"Excuse me, I must talk to my friend."

I went outside and told Sudi that I had 50,000 Tanzanian shillings ($50 approx), or a $100 bill. "Don't show him the hundred dollars," said Sudi. "There will be no change. Give me twenty-five thousand shillings."

I gave him the money and he went off to the taxi drivers waiting by the side of the road on the Burundian side. I went back inside and said my friend was bringing the money. The official studied my passport with small, avaricious eyes. "How much is Tanzania visa?"

"A hundred dollars," I said. "For ninety days."

"Hundred dollar," he said, nodding slowly. "You give me hundred dollar."

Sudi came back with a $20 bill, and I gave that to him, saying I didn't need ninety days in Burundi. He inspected it on both sides, gave me a filthy look, and stamped my passport for three days. I wasn't angry or offended, just relieved to get out of there.

Seven of us got into a taxi, an old Toyota Corolla with a spiderweb crack across the windshield, upholstery spilling out of the seats, loose muffler rattling on the ground. We drove down through the quiet forest into Mabanda, a highland town heaving with people and strewn with trash. Hard challenging glances and mad-dog stares came at me from out of the crowd, then jeering catcalls and sharp whistles, "Eh, *muzungu*!" A dog was shaking on the ground with malaria or some other fever. There were soldiers and police with machine guns, teenage boys with thousand-yard stares, presumably from their years as child soldiers in the war, malnourished children with muddy rags and white hair like little old men.

Women were selling cassava and tomatoes, bananas and flip-flops, cans of USAID cooking oil and donated Louisiana rice, various medicines marked "NOT FOR SALE" and "Donated by . . ." The earth was a dark brick red, almost a wine-stained color, where it wasn't black with charcoal dust. Raw and edgy, says my notebook. Heavy vibes in Mabanda. No other white faces.

Sudi had lived in Mabanda for two years, working as a driver. Watching him move through the crowd with such calm, easy grace, stopping to say hello to his friends and exchange greetings, I realized how tense and jumpy I looked by comparison. I told myself to cool out, look bored, at ease, seen it all before, come through here all the time. Then Sudi asked for my backpack and stowed it on the front seat of a Hiace. "Come," he said. "We will eat now. We leave the bag here. There is no problem. The driver is my friend."

We walked through the market and ducked into a four-table restaurant that served only rice and beans. Stacked against the back wall were sacks of uncooked rice and beans stamped with the logos of UNICEF and other aid agencies. The donated food had found its way into the local economy, and now it was being consumed by people who could afford to pay for it and not the hungry malnourished children begging outside. The tired-looking women cooking this food and running this little restaurant were using their tiny profits to feed and clothe their own children and buy them donated medicine. The morality of the situation was messy and complicated, but one thing was certain. None of this would be mentioned in the NGO press releases or fund-raising literature. There would be a glowing report, listing an impressive quantity of food and medicine successfully delivered to a needy area, and that would be it.

Maybe that was all that could be hoped for. Or maybe it was teaching people that food arrived on aid trucks, and they didn't need to grow it. Maybe if Medecins Sans Frontieres and other medical charities were to pull out of Burundi, the government health department would be under more pressure to actually do something with its budget. But it was so hard to say. In a region where hungry people watched their cattle starve to death without selling or eating them, where people took donated food away from starving children and sold it instead, how could I trust my *muzungu* thought patterns?

I could never know what it was like to stand in rags and Chinese flip-flops, having lived through thirteen years of ethnic warfare, with all the chopping, hacking, raping, and mutilating that went out of European warfare a long time ago, and watch squeaky-clean, super-polite white people step out of their $60,000 Land Cruisers with a plan to make poverty history, to enroll you in a gender sensitivity workshop, to reconsider the environmental implications of your hunting and farming practices, to change the way you have sex, take a crap in the morning, gather water, plant crops, graze livestock, raise your children, treat your wife, manage your anger issues. Would I feel intruded upon, grateful, puzzled, angry, shy, resentful, disinterested? Would it encourage me to fix problems or depend on others to fix problems? Would I think: they have so much, I have nothing, so give me, give me, give me? I had no idea.

Driving out of Mabanda, in the front seat of an otherwise horrendously overcrowded Hiace, hurtling at a lunatic speed through the descending mountain curves on the way to Bujumbura, every town and village was preceded by a big white sign proclaiming an NGO project underway or completed and listing its funders and partners. Water projects were popular, at least among NGOs and their donors. It was easy to get funding for a water project, because in the West access to clean running water from a tap is considered an inalienable human right, and a universal human desire.

On an earlier visit to Tanzania, I went to a village by Lake Eyasi where a Spanish NGO had built a water project. The villagers had tried to stop it, but this made no sense to the NGO. Why would anyone willingly gather water by hand when they could have a tap? Also, it was an oppressive system to the young women and the girls who did most of the water gathering, and since the NGO had already raised the funding, its engineers went ahead and built the project. Now the villagers had taps outside their huts, and they were not happy about it. Why? Because for as long as anyone could remember, walking through the village to fetch water was how the marriageable girls had caught the eyes of marriageable boys. The NGO had wrecked their courtship system.

In Kigoma, I heard another water project story from a nearby village. NGOs are always trying to learn from their mistakes, and they know all too well that development projects tend to fall into disrepair after they leave. So the NGO in question was careful to involve the villagers at every stage of the water project, so their labor and ideas would be "invested" in the project and they would think of it as their own, rather than something that foreigners came and built for them. The NGO trained up villagers as maintenance engineers and set up a fund and delivery system to pay for future spare parts. All this was time-consuming, and the project took nearly three years to complete. A week later, the villagers tore the whole thing apart. Why? Because they wanted to sell the pipes, it was easy money.

Stories like these are a dime a dozen when NGO people get together and drink, but they don't like them getting into the media, because they think it damages their fund-raising abilities. I have my doubts about this. Most people give money to NGOs because it makes them feel better. It's a kind of tithe, or guilt tax, and people show remarkably little interest in finding out how effectively their money is spent. Good intentions are good enough for both donor and NGO. The many well-documented failures of the aid industry and its overall ineffectiveness—the more aid a country has received, the more likely it is to be getting poorer—hasn't hurt its fund-raising abilities in the slightest.

IT WAS A four-hour drive to Bujumbura and the driver drove like he was in a video game, passing every car on the road, using the horn to clear the road in front of him of bicyclists, goats, scurrying pedestrians, hitting eighty miles an hour on the straightaways, honking his way impatiently through the crowded villages and towns, which came one after the other as we descended into the foothills and flatlands. Burundi is the size of Maryland or Belgium. It's a green and well-watered country, but with 8 million people, an agricultural economy, and over 90 percent of the population living in rural areas, there was serious pressure on the available land. In some provinces there were six hundred and seven hundred people per square mile, and

Burundian women were averaging six children apiece. Burundi and Rwanda, the two Hutu-Tutsi countries, are the most over-populated in Africa, and this fact cannot be separated out from either the chronic poverty or the ethnic violence.

As we entered the villages and towns, the driver made frequent stops to haggle with fruit vendors, flirt with young women who caught his eye by the side of the road, and exchange greetings, and sometimes loud angry words, with various young men of his acquaintance. He got out several times to inspect barrels of palm oil for sale, and when he found one that met with his satisfaction, the passengers in the back had to squeeze up further to make room for it. Then this wild young knight of the road took off at top speed again, scattering the goats, bicyclists, and pedestrians in his path, coming within a few inches of hitting them.

"Sudi," I asked. "Do you drive like your friend here?"

"No, no," he laughed. "He likes to go very fast. I am a careful driver."

"Thank you again for helping me. You are a good man."

"Welcome to my country," he said. "I see from your face that you are my friend. Why are you traveling in Africa?"

"To learn. And to write about what I learn. Writing is my job."

"When we arrive at Bujumbura, you no go hotel. You stay at my house. You see African house, stay with African family, learn more."

"Thank you again. I am happy to stay with you. What is your job in Bujumbura?"

"I have a taxi with my brother and uncle."

"Ah, this is good. I will need a driver, and someone to show me around the city. Is it dangerous for me?"

"You must be careful in some areas. Where I live, if you are with me, you have no problem."

Lake Tanganyika came into view, rippling with white-capped waves in the wind. The road ran along the lakeshore, past fishing boats, the occasional lone hippo that had somehow managed to survive amid all this hunger, and many roadside kilns where people were baking mud into bricks. A policeman stopped us on some pretext and extorted a bribe. A mile further, another policeman, another bribe. The driver pounded his wheel in frustration.

Then we entered the outlying sprawl of Bujumbura—brick buildings with tin roofs, crankshaft repair shops, brightly painted storefronts, bustling roadside stalls, a traffic jam of motorbikes, taxis, and Hiaces mixing their vapors with charcoal smoke from grilled meat vendors in the heat, noise, commotion, and humidity.

There were electricity poles, cables, and transformers but no electricity. Bujumbura was currently getting its power from Congo, but it had been delinquent in paying its bills, and the Congolese were restricting the supply to teach them a lesson. Normally Bujumbura got its electricity from a big, donor-built hydro project, but the reservoirs were dry. The managers had run all the water through the turbines already, or the main dam had sprung a leak and no one had done anything about it. No one was quite sure. Later, I would meet a World Bank water expert who attended a meeting of the Burundian government to address this situation. The officials began the meeting by asking him to join them in a prayer for rain to fill the reservoirs back up. He turned them down politely, saying, "I'm with the World Bank. We don't believe in that sort of thing. If my bosses find out I've been praying for rain, I'll get fired."

Central Bujumbura, the old Belgian colonial city on the lakeshore, with its sandy beaches, hillside villas, art deco buildings, elegant Francophone restaurants, and lively nightclubs, had been a haven of cosmopolitan sophistication in the middle

of Africa, a choice posting for diplomats and NGO workers in
the 1980s and early 1990s. Now, having endured wave after
wave of ethnic cleansing and gangsterized ethnic war, conducted with phenomenal cruelty by all the groups involved,
the city was pockmarked, grimy, and traumatized, with packs
of half-feral children roaming the streets, but the aid money
was flowing again, the NGO people were back in greater numbers than ever, and there was a vibrant illegal economy in
smuggled gemstones and minerals from Congo. Cafés, restaurants, and nightclubs were open again, and Sudi said there was
a good spirit in the city these days, a feeling that despite all
the problems—the terrible poverty, lack of jobs, and the worst
corruption in the world, according to Transparency International—things were now getting better and maybe this time
the violence was gone for good.

We got off the bus in the crowded streets near the central
market. People were speaking French, Swahili, and Kirundi, the
subtle, allusive language of Burundi, switching back and forth
fluently between the languages, and many of them also spoke
some English. I had grown so accustomed to women in *kangas*
that it was a surprise to see so many wearing Western clothes
and small-framed glasses and sunglasses in the Whoopi Gold-
berg style. Sudi told me to be careful of pickpockets, and there
were plenty of beggars, including glue-sniffing children with
one hand outstretched and the other holding a bag of glue, but
the streets felt less dangerous and threatening than Mabanda,
or Bagamoyo, or a bad neighborhood in an American city.

Sudi's house was in the Nyakabiga quarter, a majority Tutsi
area. During the war, the city had been strictly divided on ethnic lines, and anyone trying to cross from one area to another
ran a high risk of being killed. Soldiers, militias, and ethnic
street gangs would all enforce these boundaries by dragging
people out of vehicles and beating, stabbing, or necklacing

them with a burning tire by the side of the road. Sudi, being of mixed Hutu-Tutsi parentage, was able to cross these lines in his taxi, because both Hutus and Tutsis thought that despite his mixed blood he was really one of them.

It's important to understand that Hutus and Tutsis are not separate tribes, although many Hutus believe they are. They are more like ethnic castes. They both speak the same language, and for many centuries, in Burundi and Rwanda, they lived together as part of a unified society ruled over by kings and princes. Tutsis, the higher caste, tend to be taller, thinner, lighter-skinned, and longer-nosed, and traditionally they lived by herding cattle. Hutus are typically shorter, heavier, more muscular and darker-skinned, and traditionally they lived as farmers. But there has been so much intermarriage between the two groups that physical type is not an accurate guideline, and sometimes Hutus and Tutsis have a difficult time telling each other apart.

For the Belgian colonial authorities, however, this was too untidy. They classified the Hutu and Tutsi as two separate races, and anyone who had a long nose or lighter skin was marked down as Tutsi. Colonial patronage went to the Tutsis, and the grievances of the Hutu majority sharpened and intensified. By the time the Belgians left in 1962, both Hutus and Tutsis were thinking of themselves as separate races, and violence followed swiftly in both countries, culminating in the Rwandan genocide and the ethnic civil war in Burundi. In both countries, the ethnic tensions were whipped up by politicians seeking power and wealth, and the violence was fueled by an atmosphere of swirling rumors, deep paranoia, escalating hatred, and vengefulness.

In Sudi's neighborhood, there were now some Hutus living peaceably among the Tutsis, although I couldn't tell the two groups apart. All I could see was lots of Africans in a wide variety of shapes, sizes, and skin tones, and all they could see was *"Muzungu! Muzungu! Muzungu!"* The children were wildly excited to have a real live white man on their block, the adults were gently amused on the whole, and only the drunks harassed me for money. One of Sudi's neighbors shook her head and laughed and laughed when she saw me. "Oh Sudi," she said. "Did he get lost from his safari? Is he looking for elephants?"

He led me down a narrow alleyway that was also an open drain and into a small, shabby courtyard shared by three houses. There were laundry lines strung across it and a communal bathroom consisting of a bucket of water and a hole in the ground. "Welcome welcome," said Sudi, leading me through the doorway of his small house and proud to show it to me. "You see we have built it *muzungu*," he said. "When we build something well, something to last many years, we say we have built it *muzungu*."

The floors and walls were concrete. The walls were painted royal blue and growing mold, and the ceiling was a woven-reed matting. Sudi knew that *muzungus* had delicate stomachs and could not drink the lakewater like normal people, so he sent out one of his head-scarved teenage daughters to buy bottled water. When she returned, he sat me down in his best armchair with a big glass of water and turned on the television. "I must go to the mosque and pray," he said. "You stay here. Relax."

There was a gold-threaded velvet painting of Mecca on one wall, plastic flowers on a plastic tablecloth on the coffee table, a large plastic thermos on a sideboard with a glass tea set. On the small color television, President Nkurunziza, wearing a blue Adidas tracksuit and a white bush hat with the sides pinned up like a taco shell, was passing bricks along a line of people volunteering to build a new hospital. He was making a dance out of it, dipping his knees and twisting his hips to a rhythm and exhorting the others in the line to do the same. There was a kind of blank, glowing, happy spaciness in the president's eyes that I couldn't quite pin down. Was he just bugged out on Jesus? Was there some war trauma mixed in? Did he seriously believe, as he kept stating in public, that physical exercise and born-again Christianity were the keys to rebuilding the world's poorest and most corrupt country?

When Sudi returned from the mosque, we ate rice and beans with his sister, aunt, and two teenage daughters and then settled down to watch *bongo flava* videos on television. One of his daughters tried out a few flirting moves on me, much to the amusement of her sister, and in general the women were more confident, outgoing, and generally in charge than one might expect in a Muslim household. Sudi was a gentle, yielding patriarch. With all the fearful angry barking about Muslims in America and Europe these days, it's easy to lose track of the fundamental decency of Islam, its emphasis on compassion, humility, and hospitality to strangers. During the war in Burundi and the genocide in Rwanda, Muslims had generally stayed neutral and pacifist, while the majority Catholic population hacked away at each other.

When the time came to sleep, Sudi offered me half his sagging marital bed, but I elected for my sleeping pad rolled out on the floor and plenty of insect repellent against the house mosquitoes. Sudi rolled himself up like a sarcophagus in an embroidered white cotton sheet, pulling it over his head, tucking it in around the sides. That was his protection against the mosquitoes and the malaria and other diseases they carried. His brother slept outside in the taxi every night to make sure no one stole it.

THE NEXT MORNING, I bought Sudi a phone at the Obama Shop. It sold mobile phones and computers; posters of Obama hung on the walls, the employees wore T-shirts with Obama's picture on the back, and all the different models of phone had been renamed and repackaged on the Obama theme. While a reggae song called "Barack Obama" played on the stereo, Sudi looked at the Yes We Can phone, the I Love Obama phone, and settled on the Living the Dream model. "This will be good for my business," Sudi said as he thanked me for buying it. "Many times customers want to call me, and they ask why I don't have a phone. It is because I have many people to feed in my house and no money left over."

I bought myself a Burundian SIM card, and loaded up both our phones with credit. I was starting to like this city, with its crumbling art deco buildings, its sense of fragile peace, a spirit that seemed traumatized but vigorous and undefeated. I wanted to know more about this beleaguered, corrupt little country and its efforts to heal and repair itself after so many years of war and hatred. Was this the beginning of a lasting peace or an interlude in the cycle of violence? What could be done about ethnic hatred? Who were these people and how did their society fit together? Were they doomed or was there hope? By comparison, the geographical details of the Malagarasi River, which had consumed my thoughts for so long, seemed an irrelevance, and I felt no urgency to race up to the source of the Nile in Rwanda.

Sudi drove me down to the immigration office to extend my visa and warned me that things happened slowly in this place. It was like walking back in time to 1971. People were clacking away on typewriters behind grimy perspex windows. Stacks of dog-eared green files were heaped up in slumping disarray on battered formica desks and tables. There were no computers or air-conditioning, no apparent filing system, and no system of queuing. The supplicants displayed great skill at cutting in line while maintaining a cool surface politeness with each other and restricting body contact to the faintest of grazes. Unfortunately I was too English to do well in such a system, and it took a long,

long time to reach the window, whereupon the official told me to come back with a passport-sized photograph and copies of two different completed application forms.

There was a shop for passport photographs just down the street and a copy shop just a little further. It would have been a straightforward task but for one detail: there was no electricity in the city. It took us two hours in the sapping heat to find a shop that contained both a working photocopy machine and a working generator. Then we began the long search for someone with a Polaroid camera and film. When eventually we got our photograph, it depicted a sweaty, pink-faced white man looking mean, angry, gaunt, and half-crazy. We took these hard-won items back to the immigration office and then waited three hours until they closed up and told us to come back tomorrow. Examining the photograph, I realized how much Africa had ground away at my sanity and well-being. It was an alarming thing to see. I looked like a dangerous convict or a mercenary just released from jail. No wonder the beggars and hustlers had been keeping their distance.

We went back the next day and the office was closed for no apparent reason. The following day I waited there for five hours, watching my file and passport move from stack to stack, then get lost, then found again, then forgotten. I knew I should have inserted an extra twenty-dollar bill into my application, but it was too late now. At the close of the day, one of the clerks took pity on me, retrieved my languishing file, gave me a two-week visa, and—here was the detail Burundians couldn't believe— did not require a bribe.

ONE MORNING, Sudi drove me to Buterere, a poor area near the airport. He wanted to show me what happened to the garbage collected from the embassies, the UN buildings, and the rich neighborhood on the hill where the foreign NGO people lived. They all paid to have their trash collected by a private company, whose trucks came around once a week and dumped the foreigners' garbage by the side of a long dirt road paralleling a filthy stream in Buterere.

Naked boys were swimming and fishing in the stream. On the other side of the road, amid thick buzzing clouds of flies, skeletal men in rags were scavenging through the broken glass and filth for scraps of food. They were Twa pygmies, displaced from the forest and now living in a small shantytown. Sudi gave one some money to talk. He took the money and ran away. Sudi held up another banknote, called him, and he came running back.

The man said the Twa wanted to be left alone and hunt in the forest, but the forest was gone now, cut down for charcoal, and all the animals had disappeared. He was holding a plastic bag, and Sudi asked him to show us its contents. He had some rotting fruit covered in black filth, some fishheads, a plastic water bottle, and a sooty gray object that I thought was a chunk of dried mud. He wiped away the dirt on the object to show us it was a packet of American instant mashed potatoes. "Today is the best day," he said. "This is when we get the good things to eat." He held up his instant mashed potatoes like a prize and smiled.

"Oh God, I wish you hadn't told me that," said T that evening over glasses of wine at a large open-air bar with manicured lawns and the tables set fifteen feet apart so no one could eavesdrop. She was a lively intelligent American woman, very fit, clean, trim, and healthy-looking, and she had been in Burundi for two years working on women's issues with an American NGO. She had no authorization to talk on the record to journalists, hence the initial T. She lived in a four-bedroom gated villa on the hill with four servants, two vehicles, and a swimming pool, and like so many of her tribe, she felt guilty and awkward about having these luxuries in such a poor country. She justified it by saying the house was bequeathed to her by her predecessor at the NGO, that she was in Burundi for the long haul, and to be at her most effective she needed a quiet, safe, comfortable refuge. I found her argument faultless. Sleeping on Sudi's floor with the whining mosquitoes and 4 a.m. muezzin calls from the mosque at the end of the street was wearing me out.

Why, I asked, with all the aid flowing into Burundi and the dozens of NGOs headquartered in Bujumbura, were people excited about eating her garbage? Couldn't someone go down to Buterere with some food aid? "I know, I know," she said. "The trouble is that no one is doing projects for the urban poor in Bujumbura. The funding isn't there. We're all so focused on truth, reconciliation, and justice. Underdevelopment in the rural areas. Democratic governance. Human rights."

"What about the government?" I asked. "What is it doing?"

"Well, the international community supplies more than sixty percent of the government's budget, and supposedly there are strings attached. They're supposed to show evidence of democratization and improved human rights before getting the money. In reality they got another thirty-five million dollars, with no strings attached, because they threatened to resume the civil war if we didn't give them the money. And of course most of that money ends up in private bank accounts."

I told her I was going to interview President Kagame in Rwanda, and asked what she thought of him. "I think he's fantastic," she said. "I wish Burundi had one like him. Kagame is a dictator, but he has a vision, and he's dragging that country toward it by the scruff of its neck, and development is actually happening. It's the only way. Here we're trying to have a democracy, and we have a shambles."

I asked, "If Burundi was a horse, would you bet on it?"

She said, "All it takes is one leader with vision and power. Unfortunately I don't see anyone here like that at the moment. The only ones with vision have no power. And the ones with power are only interested in getting rich, and strengthening their hold on power. They really are a bunch of thugs, Neanderthals. Oh god, did I just say that?"

Meanwhile, Kenny Rogers was playing through the speakers, as Kenny so often does in Bujumbura. It's a minor curiosity of Burundian life that I feel compelled to record. There are a surprising number of country and western fans in this part of Africa, and Kenny Rogers is their stone favorite. As we sat there discussing Burundian politics and the dilemmas of aid, Kenny was crooning, "Know when to hold 'em/Know when to fold 'em . . ."

9

Maneater

Patrice and Gustave—Rusizi Delta—Sudi's mothers—Hope and cynicism—Orphans—Congolese nightclub—Hutu gangster—Burundian politics—La Troupe Pili-Pili

IN TIME, SUDI'S floor lost its charms, and I moved into a cheap place with cold showers called the Hotel Agasaro, where the desk clerks kept coming up with excellent reasons why I should give them money, sponsor them for U.S. citizenship, find them American or European girlfriends to marry ("not too ugly"), buy them laptop computers, and finance their higher education. I had to keep explaining that I wasn't the solution to their problems and also that I didn't bring prostitutes to my room because I was being faithful to a distant girlfriend. They were thoughtful, intelligent men who spoke many languages, but these were difficult concepts to understand.

"In the clubs you can find a woman for a dollar," said one of the clerks. "She will do it for cassava."

"That's sad."

"Yes," he said. "But that's life. A man needs a woman. A woman doesn't need a man, but she needs money."

Living next door to the Hotel Agasaro, among warping wooden cages of deadly African snakes and squawking parrots, with a pool full of crocodiles and a front yard always busy with pygmies, orphans, dogs, actors, theatrical equipment, crates of honey and frogs, was the most famous *muzungu* in all Burundi, and the only *muzungu* who had been able to move freely around the country during the long, bloody mayhem of the war. He was a gruff, red-faced, straw-haired Frenchman with a magnificent humpbacked nose, and his name was Patrice Faye. I would go over there and drink coffee with him, and he soon infected me with his obsession: a twenty-foot, one-ton Nile crocodile called Gustave, who was rumored to have killed and eaten more than three hundred people, including the Russian ambassador's wife.

When I asked Patrice about the rumored three hundred, he exploded with Gallic indignation and flew to Gustave's defense, "No, no, no, *non!* This is what they write but it's not true, *unh!* I have records. I have investigated every case for eleven years, and Gustave, he has killed only sixty people, maybe even less."

"And the Russian ambassador's wife?"

"This is a lie they keep repeating!"

"How did it get started?"

"Yes there was *un accident* with a lady from the Russian Embassy, and yes Gustave he eat her, but she was not married to the *ambassadeur!* She was just a diplomat. Not even high ranking! She was walking along the lakeshore and she start wading in the water, and Gustave he take her."

Patrice shrugged, smiled, turned up his palms, as if to say what does anyone expect if they go wading in Gustave's territory? How can anyone blame Gustave for being Gustave? Even with sixty victims, he still probably qualified as the most voracious man-eating crocodile in the world.

One Saturday we drove down to the lakeshore in Patrice's bush-worn Land Cruiser to look for Gustave and ask the locals if anyone had seen him lately. We passed Le Gustave snack bar, signs warning of dangerous crocodiles, and there in the water behind the signs, dozens of people were wading, swimming, and frolicking. Smiling parents called their hesitant children into the shallows where Gustave had taken a dozen victims or more. Patrice said, "I don't like this, I have tried to stop it, but what can I do? This is Africa. When there is *un accident* with Gustave, no one goes in the water for three weeks, then they start swimming again. Why? Because they forget. Because the weather is hot and it is very nice to swim here. Because they think it will not happen to them."

It certainly wasn't ignorance of the danger. Gustave was nearly as well-known in Burundi as Patrice Faye, who couldn't drive anywhere in the country without hearing his name or one of his nicknames called out by pedestrians and bystanders. Gustave had been the subject of a television documentary, a bad Hollywood film (*Primeval*, 2007), and the former president of Burundi, Pierre Buyoya, was nicknamed Gustave because of his alleged ruthlessness toward his enemies. Here on the lake-shore and over in the delta of the Rusizi River, where Gustave had taken even more victims, local witch doctors were selling amulets, potions, and bundles of roots that tied around the leg or foot to keep him away. Some claimed to have Gustave under their power and for a fee they could send him to devour your enemy or rival. A male witch in Bujumbura was claiming that he could shift form and actually change into Gustave.

"Oh, there are so many myths about him," said Patrice. "Some say he has grass on his back or growing out of his head, because people see clumps of marsh grass floating in the lake and they feel afraid. A few years ago some soldiers fired their Kalash-nikovs at him and they say he swallowed the bullets. Probably Gustave was opening his mouth from the pain. Now we have people who see him wearing jewelry around his neck—this is wonderful, no? And there are many who say he doesn't exist, that Gustave himself is a myth, even though all the fishermen know him by sight, even though he has been filmed and photographed many times."

Patrice assured me there was no mistaking Gustave if you got a good look at him. He was so much bigger and fatter than any other crocodile in Burundi, perhaps the biggest Nile crocodile left in Africa, and the top of his enormous head was covered in scars from old bullet wounds. It's entirely possible that Patrice Faye made some of those scars, because his relationship with Gustave, best described as a one-sided love affair, began as a determined attempt to kill him in 1998.

Patrice, a self-taught reptile expert, naturalist, and hunter, was often called on to dispatch troublesome crocodiles around Bujumbura, and this time it was personal. He was building a collection for a small natural history museum, and one of his field assistants had been eaten by a huge crocodile well known to the local fishermen.

"The first time I see him, I shoot at him, I shoot again, I didn't kill him," said Patrice. "I keep hunting him, and then one day I get a really good look at him. I see this magnificent prehistoric creature, the last of the really big crocodiles. I put the rifle down. I cannot kill him. I must save him. For the next two years, I follow him, I study him—oh, it was *fantastique*, just me and him before the journalists arrived. I give him the name Gustave because . . . I don't know why. It's a good name for him, no?"

ASIDE FROM THE occasional hangover and one flare-up of my feverish malaise, I woke up feeling good at the Hotel Agasaro, eager to get to grips with another day in Burundi, to deepen the friendships I was making, and learn more about this ruined, shambolic, and strangely inspiring country. Sudi took me all over the city in his uncle's taxi, up to the hilltops where diplomats, ministers, big businessmen, and NGO honchos lived with their servants behind high walls draped with bougainvillea and down into the poorest, dustiest ghettos where packs of white-haired children in rags hunted for garbage to eat.

One day we left the city to visit the rock where Burundi-ans claim that Stanley found Livingstone, even though both explorers' journals make it absolutely clear that the meeting happened at Ujiji. Beggars and children came after me there with such hungry insistence that we cut the visit short, handed out some money, and scrambled back into the taxi. Five minutes up the road, a policeman stopped us and extorted a five-dollar "fine" because one of the five licenses that a Bujumbura taxi driver must renew every year had expired. Driving on toward the Rusizi delta by the border with Congo, a group of drunken soldiers stepped out in front of the taxi. Their approach was more honest and direct: "We want money for beer. Give us ten dollars."

"That is too much," said Sudi, and he gently bargained them down to three dollars.

Near the fishing village of Gatumba, where Gustave had eaten at least thirty-five people, and fishermen were wading around unconcerned in the shallows, the Rusizi River emptied its sluggish brown waters into clear blue Lake Tanganyika. This is the river that crushed Burton's hopes. He came up here from Ujiji in a war canoe paddled by stoned, chanting boatmen, looking to confirm the Arab reports of a big river flowing north out of the lake toward Sudan and Egypt. Instead he found fear-some crocodiles, mosquitoes, malaria, a surprisingly timid tribe of cannibals, and the Rusizi flowing south into the lake, not the Nile flowing out of it.

This marked the furthest extent of Burton's penetration into central Africa. Feeling "sick at heart," he decided to turn around and start making preparations for the long return journey. The expedition made it back to Kazeh on the plains with the usual desertions, thefts, extortions, squabbles, punishing weather, and near-fatal attacks of disease. Burton arrived there very weak and sick. Speke was a little stronger. He had regained his sight and was now fully obsessed with the idea that the Nile source was up at that northern lake. Partly because Speke was being so rude to their Arab hosts, treating "all skins a shade darker than his own as 'niggers,'" Burton sent him off with a small party and stayed behind in Kazeh to recruit his strength, repair equipment, and compile vocabularies of Swahili dialects and more ethnographic notes.

Six weeks later, gunshots announced the return of a triumphant Speke. He had reached the southern shore of the great inland sea that he would rename Lake Victoria, and there was no doubt in his mind that it was the source of the Nile. The moment Speke first saw the lake, he felt absolutely certain that the great river flowed out of its northern extremity, some two hundred miles from where he stood, but he hadn't been up there to check and had conducted only one ambiguous interview with a local traveler for evidence. It was, in fact, a preposterous claim, an insult to the scientific principles of geography, but Speke was convinced that he had solved the riddle of four millennia and won the grand prize of African exploration.

When Burton began pointing out some of the enormous holes in his reasoning, Speke became angry and hostile, and for the sake of the expedition, Burton thought it best to let the matter rest and concentrate on getting back to the coast. Along the way, Speke fell victim to a trifecta of pleurisy, pneumonia, and a particularly agonizing type of fever that the Africans called "the little irons." Staggering around the camp in delirium, pursued by hallucinations of "devils, giants, lion-headed demons . . . stripping the sinews and tendons off his legs," Speke began pouring out all the grievances and resentments he had been storing up against Burton, going all the way back to Somaliland and crowned by Burton's refusal to accept his discovery of the Nile source.

Burton was stunned. He had no idea that his companion harbored such bitter hatred for him, but he nursed Speke back to health, never mentioned his ravings and accusations, and kept up the pretense of camaraderie all the way back to Zanzibar. Burton then collapsed with exhaustion and fell into a deep depression, as he did after nearly all his major expeditions and long journeys. On the voyage back to England, Burton stopped to recuperate in Aden, and Speke went on ahead, promising that they would appear together at the Royal Geographical Society to give the report of the expedition.

Instead, when Speke reached London, he went straight to RGS headquarters and announced his discovery of the source of the Nile. Poor old Burton, he told the RGS and let it be known to the press, had been too sick and weak in Africa to do much of anything except make mistakes, and he, Speke, had been the real leader of the expedition. "My companion now stood forth in his true colours, an angry rival," as Burton wrote later.

Speke claimed that the whole expedition had been his idea in the first place, that Burton had tried to poison him, engaged in "blackguard conduct" with the native women, cheated the porters out of their salaries, and committed various other unmentionable horrors that he could only hint at. Except for the part about the African women, it was all untrue, but it succeeded in damaging Burton's reputation, undercutting Burton's discovery of Lake Tanganyika, and winning Speke the command of his own expedition to go back to Africa and confirm his discovery of the Nile source.

By the time Burton sat down in his London club to write *The Lake Regions of Central Africa*, working for long hours on a single cup of coffee, no food, and copious amounts of tobacco, the very word Speke had become an abomination to him. Considering what Speke had done to him, how he had done it, and the habitual satisfaction that Burton took in skewering his enemies in print, he is remarkably restrained in his tone and judgments, but throughout the two volumes, Speke is referred to as "my companion" or "the other European," and his filthy name is not allowed to despoil the pages.

AS WE DROVE around the city, Sudi would sometimes point out the invisible demarcation lines between the Hutu and Tutsi *quartiers*, but he didn't like talking about the things he had seen and escaped so narrowly at these crossings. All that was over, he kept saying. Things were better now. He was happy to be alive, and looking forward to a better future. He prayed five times a day in the big new mosque at the end of his street. His fifth child was in his wife's belly. Life went on, and it required hope, faith, and a strong measure of denial and forgetting.

In addition to the taxi, his extended family ran a small, cheap, busy restaurant in Buyenzi, a majority Hutu neighborhood of rubble, trash fires, hubbub, clattering mechanics' shops, raucous banana beer joints, and two-room houses of mud brick and concrete that often slept seventeen or eighteen people. In a room off the restaurant, Sudi introduced me to his mother, and his other mothers, as he called them, the second and third wives of his late father. The Belgians had left Burundi as a nominally Catholic country, and his father had been one of the early Muslim converts.

The three mothers, smiling, unveiled, wrapped in fabrics, sat on rugs in a room with fabrics hung on the walls, with various fabric-wrapped aunts, nieces, cousins, and babies. They were amused to have a *muzungu* man in the warm female fug of their coterie, and they went straight into questions about my marriage, divorce, progeny, and future prospects. Sudi's mothers had produced seventeen children, and they counted themselves as fortunate to have lost only two in *la crise*, the crisis, as Burundians often called it, even though it had gone on for thirteen years, and then another two while the last rebel group, the FNL, was coaxed out of the bush and persuaded to form a political party instead.

The women of the family ran a kind of informal travel agency for arranging trips from Bujumbura to Mecca. This brought in some more money, and they were also getting remittances from relatives who had made it to the promised lands of Europe and Canada. All the money was shared out among the extended family and swallowed up by the expense of feeding so many mouths. Sudi's mothers didn't even know how many grandchildren they had, "too many to count." They lived on rice, beans, a little dried fish, cabbage, and sweet milky chai, with an occasional piece of beef or goat meat and chicken at New Year. They felt fortunate to eat twice a day, instead of once a day like most of their neighbors, and some of the ladies who worked at the restaurant had managed to gain some heft and bulk.

In the evenings I would dine with foreign or Burundian NGO people, eating good European food with French wine or Belgian beer and spending by Sudi's standards a staggering amount of money. Or I would sit in cafés with the sharp, energetic young journalists I had befriended. Or I would be escorted into dive bars and ghetto nightclubs by the youth organizers I had met. In all of these places, conversation was lively, profound, and fully engaged with big important questions. How do we build a country from this? How do we make the most of our individual lives under these circumstances? What is the best way to cope with our trauma: by the traditional method of denial or the Western methods of talking and group therapy? Why did we spend so long killing each other, and how do we stop it from happening again?

In the West, when you hear about yet another bloodthirsty ethnic conflict in some obscure country in the middle of Africa, there is a tendency to think of it as normal weather in that part of the world, as something that keeps happening over there and is therefore to be expected. The Burundians I was meeting didn't think of it in that way at all. They looked back at the civil war as a kind of madness, an aberration, a descent into evil, and at some level they couldn't quite believe that it happened.

Yes, there were historical causes and precedents. In 1972–73 the Tutsi military regime administered the slaughter of some 100,000 Hutus.* When the civil war began in 1993, sparked by a Tutsi coup and the murder of the democratically elected Hutu president, 1972 was very much on the minds of the fearful, vengeful Hutus, who conducted a mass slaughter of Tutsis in the countryside. Then came brutal reprisals by the Tutsi army and a kind of chaotic degeneration in which Hutu rebel groups fought Tutsis and each other. But none of this was inevitable, my Burundian dinner companions kept insisting. It was not an ancient, implacable, tribal hatred as it was often portrayed in the Western media, but a modern, cynical form of African politics, orchestrated from above by politicians and rebel leaders with an eye on the spoils and enabled by poverty and anger at the country's mismanagement, broader regional instability, and the ease with which propaganda works on fearful, uneducated people.

It soon became apparent that nothing was more useless here

---

* Burundian Hutus were so subservient to Tutsi authority at that time that they waited in line at the prisons and police stations to be killed. When the executioners had filled their daily quota, they told the waiting Hutus to come back tomorrow. And they did.

than the sort of depressive cynicism that came over me so easily when considering the problems of Africa. Cynicism was an outsider's luxury that Burundians couldn't afford. Yes, the problems were daunting: by some measures the worst poverty, hunger, and corruption in Africa, 50 percent adult illiteracy, only one in two children going to school, an economy dependent on foreign aid, no exports except coffee and tea, a traumatized population with a disastrous history of ethnic violence, and a superabundance of guns and grenades. Half the population was under eighteen, and already the overpopulation was an extreme as anywhere in Africa. The odds were stacked against Burundi, but this wasn't a horse race. It was their lives and the lives of their children.

So they told themselves that no condition is permanent, that they had reached bottom and were now on the way up, that God or Allah was watching over them, that they had been led astray by their leaders, and they looked across their northern border at Rwanda, a sibling country of Hutu, Tutsi, and Twa that had also been traumatized and destroyed by horrific ethnic violence. Since the 1994 genocide, under the ruthless, authoritarian leadership of Paul Kagame, Rwanda had achieved peace within its borders, vast improvements in education and health, and truly remarkable progress against corruption. It was now the safest, cleanest country in Africa, with no slums, almost no street crime, 99 percent of its children in school, and one of the highest sustained rates of economic growth on the continent.

Burundians looked at Rwanda with a mixture of hope, envy, unease, and distaste. By and large, they respected Kagame's toughness, his vision, his ability to get things done, but they were glad they didn't have to live under his dictatorship. In Rwanda, there was no free press, no real political opposition, and it was illegal to talk about the Hutu-Tutsi question. On balance, the Burundians I met preferred the corrupt, dissolute, more democratic shambles of Burundi where Hutus and Tutsis could air their differences in the media or in open conversation, the music and nightclubs were better, and a sense of joie de vivre had survived the war. In Rwanda, they said, it was too hard to breathe.

PATRICE FAYE'S front room was a dusty bachelor clutter of tribal masks, spears, rifles, slumping piles of moldering natural history books, animal skulls, aquariums, overflowing ashtrays, paintings of snakes and birds, pots, gourds, drums, padlocks, rope, knives. His marriage to a Rwandan refugee had ended twenty years ago, and their two children were living in France. His beautiful young Burundian girlfriend came padding through sleepily on her way to the bathroom. From the kitchen a silent manservant in a dirty white coat brought coffee. Patrice cleared some space on the coffee table and put down a photograph of Gustave on a grassy riverbank.

It was a poor-quality print from a cheap digital camera, but you could see his individual scales clearly and derive a very immediate sense of his enormity, fatness, and prehistoric menace. His tail was in the foreground, and from the downward angle you could tell that the photographer had been standing just behind him.

"Two meters," Patrice said. "That was the closest I ever got to him. Yes, I was afraid, but it's good to conquer fear. Adrenaline is coming. Fascination is coming. Oh, it was *fantastique*."

As he followed Gustave and studied the records of crocodile attacks, reinterviewing witnesses and lucky survivors who had lost arms and legs, Patrice determined that he had an unusually large territory for a bull crocodile, extending from the lake some twenty miles up the Rusizi River into a roadless area inside Rusizi National Park. Sometimes Gustave stayed up there for a year or more, and people wondered if a poacher or a soldier had finally managed to kill him. Then he would swim down again to the delta and the lake, driven not by hunger but by the desire to mate with as many females as possible. Lust initiated his migrations, but there was invariably a rash of attacks, or "accidents" as Patrice preferred to call them, once he encountered so much easy meat in the form of fishermen and swimmers. The worst was in 2004, when Gustave killed and ate seventeen people in thirty days.

"He also eats fish and cows but he really eats a lot of people, sometimes the whole body, sometimes just the arms and legs," Patrice said. "You must understand that many bodies were thrown in the river and the lake during the wars in Congo and Burundi. Every day when I was following him I would see dead bodies in the water. Four, five, some ten every day, with hands tied behind their back. This is how he get the taste for eating people."

I asked Patrice how he felt when Gustave killed people. He shrugged, turned up his palms: "It's the law of nature. People say Gustave is evil but this is absurd. He has no moral choices to make. He can only follow his instincts. He eat, he fuck, he sleep. It's a good life. I wish I could live like him, but it's not possible for me. Even when I am sick with malaria, typhoid, sleeping sickness, I must get up and do something, make something, create something."

Patrice arrived in Burundi by bicycle in 1978, a bearded, long-haired wanderer who had cycled from France to South Africa and was now on his way back north again. "Bujumbura was small then, very attractive, and everybody knew everybody," he said. "It was the best city in Africa for me, but I am not really a man for the cities."

First and foremost, he was an outdoorsman, and it was the forests and abundant wildlife in Burundi that persuaded him to stay. Now those forests are nearly gone, cleared for farmland and charcoal, and so are the gorillas, chimpanzees, elephants, and hundreds of other species that used to live in them.

"In 1978, there were 1.5 million people in Burundi," Patrice said with a shrug. "Now we have eight million. The thing I came here for is over. It's finished. I remember very well the last elephant. I spent two weeks following him. Now there is only Gustave. He is a survivor like me, a soul mate, but he is the last one. So I ask myself, what can I do here now? And the answer is that I can help people. I can help the little children who have nothing and nobody."

Every day he visited his orphans' school in the filthy slum behind the high-walled, razor-wired UN headquarters. A hundred children sat on rough-hewn benches under a tin roof. They ranged from toddlers to teenagers, orphaned by war and AIDS in equal measure, and there was always a great outpouring of joy and excitement when Patrice arrived. The little ones would rush forward to grab onto him, and he would stride through picking them up, swinging them around, laughing, joking, teasing, asking for kisses from the little girls, spreading around compliments and rough good cheer, and exhortations to study hard and learn well. Then, when it was time to leave, five or six of the bolder children would cling on the ledges and bumpers of his Land Cruiser. Patrice, grinning broadly, would give them a two- or three-minute ride before stopping and saying, "OK. Far enough. Back to school with you. See you tomorrow."

His orphans' home was on the lakeshore. He had built it with turrets and crenellated walls, and named it Castel Croc in honor of Gustave. It had a revolving cast of about twenty children, and on his daily visits Patrice would usually pick up one or two for a ride around the city as he visited his various construction projects, or a trip to his house with the scary snakes and crocodiles, or up into the hills to visit the pygmies.

He was always in a hurry, lighting another cigarette and peering through his glasses at the long daily list of things to do, "the program," as he called it, which was scrawled on the back of an envelope and kept in a many-pocketed blue canvas vest that he wore every day. He drove everywhere at top speed, always ready to overtake on the hard shoulder if the other lane was blocked, and frequently exploding into rages at the other drivers, "Ah, *c'est pas possible*! Look at this! These people are crazy!"

In between these outbursts, which he explained and excused by saying that he was French, Patrice would poke, tickle, and tease the orphans. They would squeal and giggle and sometimes hit him back, whereupon his big meaty hands would fly up off the steering wheel as he protested his innocence and then thump down again as he laughed his hoarse throaty laugh. The laughter would provoke a coughing spasm, followed by a finger-search through his vest pockets for cigarettes and lighter.

Patrice had given up the idea of capturing Gustave, but he lived with the constant anxiety that his old friend and soul mate would eat one of the Castel Croc orphans. He had warned them so many times, in so many different ways, but still the children ignored him and swam in the lake. Patrice's latest plan was to shoot a tranquilizer dart into Gustave, get a radio-collar around his neck, and release him back in the water. "Then he can have his freedom, and I can warn people that Gustave is coming, Gustave is here, don't go in the water until he is gone."

The scheme sounded far from infallible, and like so many in Burundi it was awaiting funding and equipment from abroad. But what else could he do, except the unthinkable.

"What if Gustave does eat one of your orphans? Two orphans?"

"Ah no, even if there is *un accident* with my own children, I cannot blame him, I cannot kill him. He is the last of the Mohicans. There will never be another like Gustave, and I am proud to call him my friend, even though I know very well he would eat me if he got the chance."

IT WAS A Saturday night in the ghetto, an outdoor bar with no lights, an atmosphere of uplifted spirits and scattered inhibitions, although people kept their revelry confined to their own tight circles, and the plastic tables were just far enough apart to discourage any interchange from one to another. Drinking and smoking next to me was Adrien Tuyaga, founder of a ghetto youth organization called JAMAA, a Swahili word that means "family" or, on the streets of Bujumbura, "very close friends." It specialized in the hard cases—ethnic gangsters, youth militia members, child soldiers—and its mission was to bring Hutus and Tutsis together, convince killers to stop killing, and counsel them through the trauma.

"You cannot underestimate the trauma in Burundi," he said, speaking fluent English with a slight French accent. "Some people cope with it by using drugs and alcohol. We also have a big rise in miracle churches and ecstatic religion. This is how the president copes. We have seen a shift also in the way men and women relate to each other. Women want strong, brave men for protection, and this leads to a lot of stancing to be tough and dangerous among the young men, who misunderstand a little bit what the women want. For the men, the main thing they want from a woman is help in the struggle against poverty."

"And love?" I asked.

"Sure. Everyone wants love, but love is hard to do when you've been through what we have been through. Not for a mother and her children, but for men and women."

During the war, Adrien's work with JAMAA had won international acclaim. He had been flown to NGO conferences and award ceremonies in Europe, Canada, and the United States, but now the foreign donors had changed their focus and JAMAA's funding stream had dried up. Adrien was forty-three, living with his mother again and flat broke. He had no phone, and he was thin and drawn, with a gaunt face under a Yankees baseball cap, and warm, intense, charismatic eyes with flecks of discoloration on the left iris. We were joined at the table by a bright young journalist called Eric Nsengiyumva, who had just been elected the new president of JAMAA, a Rasta musician called Richard, and then an old friend of theirs from the neighborhood called Suzy. She was a stunningly beautiful young woman who had just been jilted by her boyfriend, a government minister's son, and she arrived with a half-empty bottle of vodka in her hand and was now smoking the joint going around the table, looking wild and distraught.

"Suzy, there will be another one," said Eric.

"You don't understand," she said. "He hurt me. He got to me."

"Suzy, you are beautiful," said Adrien. "You can have anyone you want."

"Say that in the morning when I have no makeup on."

"Come on," I said, a little tipsy and high. "You're beautiful now. Forget tomorrow morning. It doesn't exist yet."

The guys liked this, which meant there was a round of bottle-clinks and knuckle-bumps. Suzy gave me a quizzical look. "Do you want to be with me?" she said.

"No, no," I said. "I'm just stating a fact. I already have a girlfriend."

Then I became a challenge to her. As we left the bar and walked up the dark cratered streets looking for a taxi to a nightclub, she hooked her arm in mine. Then she changed her mind, said, "Fuck this shit!," took off her heels, and ran off down the street. Now the guys became alarmed, because she was drunk and high and beautiful, and it took a lot less than that for a woman to get raped on these streets at night.

Eric caught up to her and settled her down. We got her in a taxi with us. We were going to Cinq Sur Cinq, the Congolese nightclub, and she said she would come with us. Then she changed her mind and said to drop her at Havana, a flashier, more expensive place where the men had more money. As we watched her walk inside, Adrien and Eric stressed that Suzy was not a prostitute. She was a beautiful girl from the ghetto in a poverty-stricken city with massive unemployment, and it went without saying that she lived off her boyfriends.

There was a line outside Cinq Sur Cinq, but Adrien knew the bouncers and we went straight inside and were shown to a banquette by a waiter with dreadlocks swept up into a mound. He wore a white shirt and a tuxedo vest with fluorescent numbers on the back. The clientele was a mixture of Burundians and Congolese, and at the sight of me, the lone white face, the whores were up and prowling, and my companions sat down on either side of me to form a barrier. Maybe because I was slightly stoned and drunk, I thought it was the most fantastic nightclub in the world.

There were Congolese dandies in zoot suits, in pleated mustard-colored pants with green shoes, in cummerbunds and Armani, one wearing a suit that looked as if it was made out of white chicken feathers, and women in red dresses, yellow dresses, tiny skirts and outrageous coiffures, bumping and grinding as the dandies spun and whirled. The DJ was playing some kind of raw, stripped-down, galloping Congolese music I had never heard before, just a drummer pounding out polyrhythms and a cheap, fuzzed-out electric guitar playing scorching licks over the top of it. It was like a Congolese version of the White Stripes or the Black Keys, and it raised the hairs on my arms, and I couldn't get enough of it. To my companions, it sounded too rough and ready. They wanted more studio gloss.

Later, when the DJ started playing reggae and *bongo flava*, they got up to dance, leaving me exposed, and the night took a darker turn. A whore slipped in beside me and set up a furious shrieking when I caught her hand slipping into my pocket. Then I was pinned back against the banquette by an enormous drunk Hutu whose eyes were blazing with madness and violence and glowing red in the black light of the nightclub. His name was Richard and this meant we were brothers, this meant I would understand, and he leaned into me, pronounced the names of various Tutsi leaders and politicians, and then erased them in the air with his big forefinger. "Genocide," he kept saying. "This is the reality."

When I told him I was going to Rwanda, he snarled "Kagame is a rebel!" and then moved his forefinger across his throat. I concentrated on not trembling, not shaking or quaking, trying to maintain my cool.

"I like you," he said. "I like journalists. I have done many things. These Tutsis want genocide. No! I pray to God. You pray with me. Yes! God will save us. I have done many things. You are my friend."

His crazy bulging eyes bored into mine, his words came in blasts of sour alcohol breath, his huge muscles were taut with anger, and every time I tried to get up, he would loom over me and the big forefinger would appear in front of my eyes, and he would shake his head, draw his finger across his throat, tell me to pray with him and buy him another beer.

Finally, I managed to wriggle free, find Adrien, and insist that we had to go right now. In the taxi back to the Hotel Agasaro, unable to stop trembling now, I said, "Who was that guy?"

"A Hutu gangster, a very dangerous man," said Adrien. "The police are afraid of him, because when he smashes a bottle, or grabs a gun, he doesn't think. He just does. We've been working with him, and he's really trying to reconcile his issues, you know."

"He still has a long way to go."

"For sure. But the miracle is that he's trying, no?"

THERE WERE FORTY-THREE political parties registered in Burundi for the upcoming election. Most were tiny and inconsequential, "little clubs of people looking for an income," in the words of a Burundian NGO worker. They gathered in a few contributions, discharged a few blasts of rhetoric, and were now often hard to reach on the telephone. Of the six or seven real parties, most knew more about bush warfare than balancing a budget or governing a country in the way that aid donors thought countries should be governed. Only one of these parties, the center-left Movement for Democratic Solidarity (MSD), led by Alexis Sinduhije, a crusading journalist–turned-politician and one of *Time* magazine's men of the year, had a Western-style political ideology with a platform of policy proposals. The others hoped to practice African politics as usual. The purpose of elections was to get power. Once in office, the priorities were to get money, distribute patronage to cronies and supporters, intimidate enemies, live well, drive an expensive car, spout the right jargon to keep the donor money flowing, and bank the surplus in Europe.

The ruling party called itself the National Council for the Defense of Democracy–Forces for the Defense of Democracy (CNDD–FDD). It had formed out of the rebel Hutu army that was winning the war when the UN and the African Union finally managed to end it with peace talks, and in some respects it had done better than expected. On the crucial ethnic issue, it had dialed down the tensions and integrated Hutus into the formerly all-Tutsi national army without too many problems. President Nkurunziza, by making a lot of unrealistic promises and by washing the feet of the poor—an astounding gesture in such a top-down hierarchical society—had achieved a genuine popularity in the impoverished, overcrowded, 85 percent Hutu countryside where most Burundians lived.

My journalist friends in Bujumbura described their singing, dancing, testifying president as a kind of George Bush figure, a born-again sports nut with a folksy charm who was set out in front of the cameras by ruthless, sinister Cheney figures behind the scenes. And I wasn't the only one who thought there was something strange about the look in the president's eyes. "How can I put it?" said a journalist from Alexis Sinduhije's radio station one night over beers. "The president is not normal. He spends nearly all his time praying, playing soccer, training, and watching sports. We think this is his way of coping with his trauma and guilt about the things he saw, and the things he did, during the war."

His administration had been plagued from the get-go by corruption scandals, and a leading anticorruption investigator had turned up murdered. The presidential airplane, a luxurious Falcon 50 donated as a gift to Burundi by President Mitterand of France, had been quietly sold off for cash, and later the government announced that the president needed a new plane to fly to the Olympics in China in the proper style. When a journalist asked how the expense could be justified, given that Burundian hospitals lacked the most basic medical supplies, a spokesman cut him down to size with a line from precolonial Burundi: "You do not look in the king's plate."

According to the UN, Burundian officials were heavily involved in running guns to the rebel armies in Eastern Congo and smuggling out gold, diamonds, and other minerals in return. They were also siphoning off aid money by various methods, and bribery, swindling, sham contracts, and what the West calls nepotism were so bound up in the way the country worked that it almost didn't make sense to identify them as separate problems. It was explained to me like this: in the West we think of corruption as a tick fastened on to a dog; in Africa the tick is often bigger than the dog.

Alexis Sinduhije was out of the country for his own safety, following a series of arbitrary arrests, attempts to close down his radio station, and the beatings and torture of some of his supporters. After I left Burundi, two of them were killed by grenades lobbed into their houses, and an opposition figure from another party had his penis severed in a police station. Burundi was often a confusing, contradictory place to a newcomer like me. I wasn't expecting to find such a vibrant intelligentsia, or so much hope and enthusiasm for the future, and these things coexisted with extraordinary squalor and brutality, and a deep sense of unease about the latest political developments.

Running in formation past the Hotel Agasaro one Sunday morning came a squadron of sixty tough-looking young men in matching athletic clothes, chanting slogans and carrying wooden staves. This, I found out later, was a squadron of the so-called "youth wing" of the CNDD-FDD. Ostensibly, they were keeping fit and participating in group sporting activities. In reality, they were demobilized fighters paid by the party to demonstrate its muscle on the streets and intimidate the main opposition parties, who all had youth wings of their own. You couldn't get anywhere in Burundian politics unless you could turn out a menacing youth wing, because your party would be perceived as weak and ineffectual. As the election drew closer, the youth wings started acting like youth militias, breaking up political rallies, beating up rival supporters, and throwing grenades into each other's political meetings.

"We'll tie you up and shoot you," was one of the chants from the CNDD-FDD youth in the countryside. "Do you really think we have given up our guns?" chanted a rival group. I worried for Burundi. Originally I had looked at it on the map as a small but dangerous obstacle on the way to Rwanda, but I had friends here now and hopes invested in their future.

PATRICE HAD WRITTEN and produced more than fifty plays in Burundi, and his latest was a comedy about ethnic hatred and civil war called *Kamenge '94*. Kamenge, a poor Hutu neighborhood in Bujumbura, had experienced terrible violence during the war, and the worst of it was in 1994. When I asked him for more details about the play, he invited me to its second performance in the hill town of Mwaro, an hour and a half southeast of Bujumbura.

We assembled in his front yard on a cool, overcast morning: five actors, three young European volunteers who were going to film the production, Patrice's everyday crew of *askaris* and assistants, all of us helping to load up two vehicles with sound equipment, props, and a long, rolled backdrop. Patrice barked angrily into his telephone while emptying a box of live frogs into his stone-walled crocodile enclosure. Various cobras, vipers, pythons, and boomslangs lay inert in their warping wooden cages. Patrice's congenital lack of caution extended also to his snakes. He liked picking them up, and he had been bitten three times on the hands by snakes considered deadly, including a Gaboon viper and a boomslang. He survived because the snakes hadn't delivered a full load of venom.

With the vehicles loaded, the *askaris* pulled back the gates and we convoyed out across the city and up the first steep switchbacks into the mountains. Young men on bicycles grabbed onto the back bumpers of produce trucks to get pulled up the road and paid a few cents to the drivers for the service, and we gained immense views behind us over Lake Tanganyika into the green folds of Congo. After the initial ascent, the road dipped and rolled through misty green hills and patchwork fields. We passed loitering soldiers, children in yellowish-brown rags, presumably the same color as the muddy stream nearest their hut, a woman standing by the side of the road with an enormous cabbage on her head, a boy holding up a live rabbit by the ears, and then a teeming roadside market. A wave of excitement passed through the crowd as people spotted Patrice and a chorus rang out of, "Patri-ce! Patri-ce!" and "Pili-Pili!" The name of his theatrical company was La Troupe Pili-Pili, after the Swahili word for chili pepper, and it had become one of his nicknames.

We drove on through fields of tea. Shafts of sunshine angled down through the low clouds, and fresh rain glistened on the leaves of the tea bushes. Over the next pass, we saw Tutsi cattle, conical huts dotted around the hills, a woman walking down the road with a hand-woven conical basket on her head. "Oh, it's so beautiful," said one of the volunteers, a young Frenchwoman leaning out of the window with her camera. "I love this country so much. It's amazing there are so few tourists and travelers here."

I said, "There are still serious travel warnings. The war hasn't been over for long."

She said, "There was a war? Congo, yes, but here too?"

As we came into a small Tutsi town, Patrice said, "You see that school? The Hutu rebels took out all the Tutsi children, put them over here at the petrol station, and burned them all alive. Then the army come and kill a lot of rebels."

"Oh, that is terrible," she said. "But everything is all right now."

Patrice said, "Yes, yes, no more war for now."

Women toiled with hoes in the fields. Women carried heavy baskets of sweet potatoes and bananas on steep foot trails, often with a baby slung on their backs. Women sold the produce at the roadside markets. Aside from the occasional teenage boy pushing a bicycle loaded with charcoal, there were no men to be seen.

"Where are the men?" I asked. "What are they doing?"

"The men are thinking," deadpanned Patrice.

Arriving in Mwaro, we found a large, cavernous restaurant on the main square and ate the classic Burundian meal of grilled meat on skewers (brochettes), fries, and Primus beer. The actors felt an actorly need to keep us all entertained, and this led to extravagant comic storytelling, bursts of singing and clowning, laughter and flirtation. One of the actors was an educated, urbanized Twa, and he taught us all some bar tricks with beer bottles and banknotes. After lunch we looked around the town a little, then set up the stage gear, sound system, and backdrop in a large hall at the local high school.

The three young Europeans had a wonderfully carefree, confident, naive enthusiasm. One of the girls sprained her ankle and she wasn't fazed in the slightest. She took the scarf off her neck, tied it around her ankle, and continued having a fantastic time in this marvelous country. She wanted to meet as many of the local people as possible, and if some of them seemed shy and awkward with downcast eyes as she limped toward them with her camera, she had no doubts that her smile would soon set them at ease. It gave me a pang of nostalgia. I remembered traveling at her age, reveling in my freedom for the first time, unburdened by knowledge about the countries I was moving through, fully immersed in the joys of the present moment and convinced I could live this way forever. Then came writing, reading, journalism, a deeper level of curiosity, the attraction to difficult questions rather than easy answers, the habit of observing, analyzing, comparing, and contrasting. The simple joy of travel was more elusive now.

The hall began to fill with people. Most of them were teen-age boys who held hands and draped arms over each other, which signified nothing more than friendship. We gave them all a questionnaire to fill out after the show. One question was, "Do you think the Twa are capable of reason?" Another asked, "In your opinion, which were responsible for the war in Burundi: history, cultural differences, colonization, human nature, politicians, overpopulation?"

The lights went dark, and the sound of aerial bombardment and machine-gun fire filled the hall. The lights came on to reveal a terrified Hutu hiding in a scruffy front room, and a terrified Tutsi hiding in a different part of the same house. The audience was instantly rapt. The Hutu and Tutsi discovered each other with a start, then started arguing, each blaming the other for starting the war and telling the other that he had no right to be in the house. Then the Twa entered the house and raised the first nervous laughter from the audience with some jokes and puns, *"Non! Je ne suis pas toi. Je suis moi. Et je suis Twa."*

The fourth actor was a man in drag with huge breasts, lipstick, and a club, which reduced the audience, and the proud playwright sitting on the sidelines, to helpless, uproarious laughter. The main joke and conceit of the play was that this woman's Congolese husband had been cheating on her, she had gone after him with a gun, Hutus and Tutsis alike had completely misinterpreted the gunshot, and this was how the war got started. The audience loved it. They laughed, they cheered, and afterward they all filled out their questionnaires avidly.

We had to make a speedy exit because soldiers closed the road back to Bujumbura at dusk because of bandits. As we drove back, I looked through the completed questionnaires. An overwhelming majority of respondents thought the Twa were capable of reason, which gave a certain wry satisfaction to our

Twa actor. And all except three people had singled out "politicians" as the one sole cause of the war.

"For me, this is not true," said Patrice. "For me the war happened for all these reasons: history, cultural differences, colonization, human nature, and overpopulation, as well as politicians. It was a mélange of reasons."

I agreed with Patrice, but I was glad these young Burundians thought it was all the fault of their politicians. It was the explanation that afforded the best hope of change, and without hope Burundi was doomed. It was entirely possible that it was doomed anyway, but when hope failed and people stopped trying in a place like this, the human spirit would be extinguished entirely, and that was the worst of all possible outcomes.

10

Monstrous Shadow

Farewells—Journey interrupted—The end of Speke—
Border crossing—Kagera River—Nile duel—Kigali—
Genocide tourism—Dr. Kandt—Shopping for clothes

I DIDN'T WANT to leave Bujumbura, but my visa was running out and my interview looming with the president in Rwanda. It was time to say good-bye to friends I might not see again. Patrice Faye had just returned from one of the Twa communities he worked with upcountry. They had torn up the water project he had built for them, sold the pipes, and got drunk for a week on the proceeds. I told him the similar story I had heard in Kigoma, and he said, "Yes, short-term thinking. For the Twa, they live today, tomorrow doesn't matter, and next week doesn't exist."

Adrien and Eric didn't want me to leave Burundi without seeing the JAMAA youth center, the flagship and headquarters of their organization. As we arrived, a ripple of excitement went around the outdoor benches, and the game stopped on the basketball court. Seeing their leaders escort a *muzungu* onto the property, people naturally assumed I was a donor, or a prospective donor, and the place was in bad need of fresh funds. The original grant had run out before the construction was completed. There were no computers and the rooms to house them were still raw and half built. The planned barbershop and youth radio station hadn't materialized, and there were more intractable problems. The property was on the edge of an eroding bluff, losing ground every time it rained, and there were no jobs in the city for the bored, rehabilitating killers eking out their days and cigarettes on the benches.

If I had come here on my first day in Burundi, I would have dismissed it as yet another failing NGO project, another waste of donor money that was falling apart before it was completed. Now my cynicism didn't come so easily. I had more understanding of context—what these young men might be doing without it, what a herculean task it was to get anything done in Africa, and how much it mattered that it had got this far. Three-quarters built and slowly crumbling away over a cliff, it was still an inspiring monument to the human spirit, and I wished it all the luck and funding it needed.

Adrien was hunting for new grants and donors, convinced both that JAMAA would rise stronger than ever and Burundi would find a better future with God's help. I didn't share his faith and optimism, but I was beginning to realize that the most accurate analysis is not necessarily the most useful analysis. My habit of reading history books and twenty years as a journalist had led me to Raymond Aron's conclusion, that optimism is usually the effect of an intellectual error. Now I saw that in a place like Burundi optimism was a basic necessity of survival and moral behavior. I understood the surveys that consistently rated sub-Saharan Africans as the world's most optimistic people, with the lowest rates of suicide and no word for clinical depression in most African languages. The alternative to optimism here wasn't pessimism, but succumbing to hopelessness and despair, and that wouldn't feed you or your children.

Sudi, wearing a wild multicolored robe instead of his usual gray slacks and long beige shirt, drove me to the bus station and made sure I wasn't overcharged for a ticket on the first-class bus going to Kigali, Rwanda's capital city. Crossing the border was no problem, he said, but once inside Rwanda, I should be extremely careful when I opened my mouth. "Please, Richard, you cannot ask anybody about war and politics. You must not ask people if they are Hutu or Tutsi. It is dangerous for them to answer. The Rwandese are good people but Rwanda is not a free country like Burundi or Tanzania."

Sudi also needed funding, for that license renewal and some running repairs on the taxi, and I gave him enough to cover it. Then I gave him a hundred dollars more from my dwindling money belts, out of gratitude, because he had so many mouths to feed, and so he would know for sure that my friendship was real.

THE FIRST-CLASS BUS was clean, white, fairly new, and made in Korea, and I luxuriated in the comfort and spaciousness of my allocated seat, the wondrous absence of bumping skulls and bodily pains. The other passengers were mostly Rwandan men in suits and black shoes with elongated toes, and churchy looking Rwandan women with coiffures, clutching their handbags primly on their laps and looking disapprovingly at the scruffy Burundians and scruffy Burundi.

Forty minutes out of Bujumbura, the bus broke down in the hills. We all milled around and fiddled with our possessions and phones for a while and eventually sat down to wait on the grassy roadside. I talked to a Rwandan man who spoke good English and said it would likely be a couple of hours, but the bus company was sending up a replacement bus. We could see no villages or homesteads, but commerce soon arrived. Its first representative was a teenage boy with a speech impediment, a face slightly twisted by a birth defect, and a keen sense of business. We all grumbled about the prices he was charging for his cigarettes, bananas, and strawberries, but we bought everything he had. Then two women appeared with charcoal-grilled corn and brochettes of goat meat, followed by an old man with bottles of beer in a hand-woven basket.

Waiting for the rescue bus, I lounged back with a full belly in the thick green grass, watching these neat, formal, polite, self-assured Rwandans and asking myself the forbidden questions: who was Hutu and who was Tutsi, and what had they done during the genocide? I found it impossible to imagine any of them hacking into human flesh with a machete, or fleeing in terror for their lives, but then the whole Rwandan genocide, no matter how many books I read about it, seemed to defy my understanding. Visitors to pre-genocide Rwanda often described it as the Switzerland of Africa, clean, tidy, orderly, churchgoing, hardworking, and while there had been earlier pogroms and purges against the Tutsis, none of the experts saw the genocide coming. It had its frenzied paranoid bloodthirsty aspects, but it was also carefully organized and structured. The killers assembled in the morning for "work," as they called it, and put in a hard day of hacking, raping, torturing, and looting, with shirkers upbraided, before retiring to the nearest saloon for some well-earned beers. Already I could feel the long, cold shadow of that monstrous event creeping over me.

The replacement bus was there within two hours, and all the passengers but me were soon dozing or asleep. On the outskirts of Kayanza, we passed through a multitude of wood-fired kilns and bricks stacked up like buildings without interiors, then rolled slowly past a busy market, ranks of men sitting at outdoor sewing machines, hungry listless children. We went on through brick-colored hills and green terraced valleys, vaguely reminiscent of Tuscany with banana groves instead of olives. Storm clouds opened and the rain came down in ropes. Terra-cotta floodwaters surged through the town of Ngozi, and people took refuge under cheap Chinese golf umbrellas.

In Kirundo near the border, with the bus stuck in traffic, I saw skeletal men trembling with hunger not fifty yards from a German NGO office with a sign reading WELT HUNGER. One of them came tottering over to the bus. He banged on the window and woke everyone up, and then he spotted me. He pointed to his concave stomach and mimed the action of eating with his fingers. He was trembling uncontrollably and looked utterly distraught. I got some money out of my pocket, but the window by my seat didn't open, and other passengers refused to open theirs, and the driver drove on when the traffic started moving. None of the other passengers showed the least desire to help the starving man. They looked at him with annoyance and at me with patient disdain. Typical soft-hearted *muzungu*.

A heated argument broke out on the bus between a middle-aged woman and a sheepish young man, and it lasted all the way to the Rwandan border. When we got off the bus to cross the border, I asked the woman what they had been talking about. Was it about the starving man? She explained in English that she was Rwandan, and the young man was Burundian, and she was telling him that his country was dirty, that the roads and houses were filthy, that there was garbage everywhere. What was wrong with Burundians, she wanted to know, that they couldn't keep their country clean like Rwandans did?

The young man had said, "We don't have leadership."

She had said, "This is what you Burundians always say."

"But it's true."

"You don't need a president to clean up in front of your house."

"I clean up my house, but what can I do about my neighbor?"

"You can ask him. You can tell him. You can shame him."

The border was astonishingly clean, efficient, and straightforward, with no beggars, hawkers, or hustlers. I stood in line for five minutes. No one cut in front of me or called in a special favor with their friend the official. There was no charge for a Rwandan visa. The official simply stamped my passport, welcomed me to Rwanda, and directed me back to the same bus.

We entered Rwanda on an immaculately smooth paved road, and I couldn't get over the complete absence of garbage on the roadside. It was absolutely spotless, cleaner than any roadside in America or Britain. "You see," said the woman proudly. "People are afraid to throw anything, even a banana peel or a cigarette butt. The police will catch you, and here you cannot bribe them."

This was leadership. Kagame had gone after corruption in the police and the other branches of government with an energy and determination that Africa had never seen before. Some corruption still persisted, but if the perpetrators got caught, they went to prison after a very swift trial. His government had also passed antilittering laws, enforced them strictly, and banned plastic bags from Rwanda for environmental reasons.

We were crossing a plateau with scattered lakes and marshes, hills stacked up in the distance, high mountains on the western horizon, sunflowers in bloom, and a beautiful golden light spreading out under the stormclouds. The huts by the side of the road had no electricity or running water, but they were in good repair. The ground around them had been swept clean, and there were no scattered possessions or falling-down chicken coops. It was poverty without squalor, without the usual rags and garbage, filth and wretchedness, and there were none of the mangy, rib-showing, yellowish dogs that I had almost stopped noticing after two and a half months in Africa. Having stopped the 1994 genocide and seized power, Kagame's soldiers shot all the dogs in Rwanda. With 800,000 bodies lying around, the dogs had gone feral and were gorging themselves on human flesh.

The woman drew my attention to some peasants hoeing in a neat rectangular field, "You see that lady? She is cultivating in a white shirt. She knows to present herself. You see that even the children have shoes. You will not see barefoot people in Rwanda. It is against the law. You must wear shoes."

The man sitting behind me, perfectly groomed in a dapper gray suit, was a born-again Christian tax-collector named Geoffrey Rusagara. "I came back here in ninety-four," he said, and by this I knew he was a Tutsi, one of the exiles that returned to Rwanda when Kagame took power. "Everything was destroyed. Everything! The treasury was looted. The national archives were gone. We started with nothing. Now we are becoming exemplary in Africa for economic progress and lack of corruption. The conflict we had is behind us now. This is all leadership. Leadership! When I go to Tanzania, Burundi, Uganda, it's the only thing people want to know. Is Kagame a normal man? How can he do this? Is it true what's happening in Rwanda?"

"What do you mean, a normal man?" I asked.

"He is not an angel. He is not a witch doctor. Work, work, work! This is what he believes in. He wants everyone to work so very hard, to work as hard as he works. Yes! I love him because he loves his people, and loves his country. No one thought it was possible that we could come this far, and it is all Kagame."

Other passengers chimed in their approval. They were so proud to be part of the new, reborn Rwanda, the improbable African success story. At the end of the long golden afternoon we reached the deep, broad Akagera River meandering through a lush valley. The landscape looked so serene and pastoral until the setting sun glinted on the machete blade of a farmer walking home along the road, and I recalled that tens of thousands of butchered corpses had been dumped into the Akagera River, whereupon they floated down into Lake Victoria, creating a serious health hazard.

SPEKE WAS THE first European to see this river, also known as the Kagera. Having successfully slandered Burton's reputation and won command of his own expedition, Speke returned to Africa in 1860 with a solid, obedient underling called James Grant and now came genuinely into his own as an African explorer. He led his expedition with skill, discipline, and fortitude to Kazeh, and then up the western shores of Lake Victoria into present-day Uganda, where he found cruel despotic kings with elaborate courts and intricate hierarchies of nobles and officials, but without any method of writing, counting large numbers, or marking the passage of time, and no wheels or ploughs. Here the Kagera River entered from the west and poured its muddy waters into the lake.

As they neared the northern end of the newly christened Lake Victoria, and all the locals confirmed that a large river flowed out of it, Speke sent Grant away on a contrived errand so that he, Speke, would have the sole glory of discovering it. At a place he named Ripon Falls, the lake poured out over a majestic waterfall to form a powerful river, and Speke and Grant followed it intermittently all the way through Sudan and Egypt to the Mediterranean. "The Nile is settled," Speke cabled back to London ahead of his return, but it wasn't.

One doubt was raised by the Kagera River, which poured so much reddish brown water into Lake Victoria that it formed a long plume going northward through the lake. British geographers, studying Speke and Grant's reports, wondered if Lake Victoria was better described as a reservoir, a place where inflowing waters spread out and slowed down for a while, before flowing out again at Ripon Falls. Burton pointed out that rivers usually have their sources in mountains. And since Speke had once again failed to circumnavigate Lake Victoria, how did he know that other even larger rivers didn't feed into it from the south? How did he know there weren't two lakes?

To debate these questions, Speke, Burton, and Livingstone were invited in 1864 to a scientific and geographical conference in the English town of Bath. Burton was now married, but Isabel hadn't seen much of him since the wedding. His "migratory instinct" had led him across North America in a stagecoach, and then he had spent two years as British consul in the pestilential hellhole of Fernando Po in West Africa. Isabel had stayed in England because nearly all the white women who had gone to Fernando Po had died swiftly of disease. Now Burton was back in England, and relishing the chance to destroy Speke in learned geographical debate.

Livingstone had been chosen as the moderator, although he was far from impartial. He was plotting his own journey to discover the source of the Nile, so hardly likely to agree with Speke that the question was settled, and he also detested Burton for his immorality, his agnosticism, and the rude remarks he had made about Christian missionaries in Africa. The conference drew 2,500 people (almost half of them women) and the full press corps, all eager for the big duel between Burton and Speke. The two men hadn't seen each other for nearly five years, and while they made eye contact—Burton was struck by how much Speke had aged—they refused to greet each other or acknowledge each other's presence. The first day was taken up with preliminary speeches by other people. Speke became bored and impatient and left early.

The next morning, with the duel set to begin at 11 a.m., and the hot crowded room growing impatient as the minutes slipped past the hour, and everyone muttering and murmuring about the fact that Speke was late, a note was delivered to the speaker and passed around the presiding dignitaries. When the note reached Burton, he slumped back in his chair with an expression of extreme shock. Sir Roderick Murchison, the president of the Royal Geographical Society, got to his feet and explained to the crowd what had happened. Speke had met with a fatal accident while hunting on his family's nearby estate the previous afternoon. He had been climbing over a stone wall, and his shotgun had discharged into his chest.

Burton suspected suicide; Speke had always been so instinctively conscious of where his gun barrel was pointing, even when their canoe was being upturned by a hippopotamus. As for a motive, he speculated that Speke was intimidated by the prospect of defending his geographical hunches at such a high-profile conference. But as Mary Lovell points out in her biography of Burton, it's not easy to deliberately shoot yourself in the chest with a long-barreled shotgun. Speke was apparently holding the muzzle of the gun and using it as a stick to support himself on the wall. The trigger must have knocked against some protruding stone, and whether this happened accidentally, or was contrived deliberately, is impossible to say.

TWO HOURS after crossing the border of this small, exquisitely beautiful country, all terra-cotta reds and banana-leaf greens, and known as the Land of a Thousand Hills, we reached Rwanda's capital. Kigali came as a revelation. Here was an African city of nearly a million people with no outlying slums, no yawning potholes, traffic chaos, or beggar swarms, and reportedly very little crime. There were no roadside vendors or street kiosks, because they offended Kagame's sense of order, and no vagrants or street children because the police arrested them and took them away to "rehabilitation camps," where they learned work skills and patriotic songs.

The city spread over four hills with skycrapers rising at its center, and it had some hustle and bustle to it, some fast-talking shopkeepers and taxi men, but the streets were swept clean every day by women in blue aprons, men trimmed the grass verges and maintained the gardens planted in the traffic islands, and the police enforced the traffic laws, right down to the seat-belts and playing the radio too loud, without extracting bribes. After a couple of months in Tanzania and Burundi, it was like walking on the moon.

"Oh, if you could have seen it in ninety-four," said Geoffrey. "Kigali was not even a city. It was just rubble, bodies, destruction. There was nothing. For months we worked without pay, all of us in the government, because there was literally no money. No banknotes in circulation! No legal tender! For eight months, we were paid with beans, rice, and maize."

On Geoffrey's recommendation, I stayed that night in an overpriced hotel catering to businessmen, NGO people, and tourists, most of whom were in Rwanda to see the habituated gorillas in the Virunga Mountains and willing to pay a thousand dollars each for the privilege, plus three hundred dollars or so for transportation. I badly wanted to see the gorillas myself, but my money belts were thin now, and everything was expensive in Kigali.

The prostitutes in the hotel bar were not permitted to approach the customers directly. Instead, they used their eyes, and one of them slipped me a bundled-up note on her way to the bathroom, "Hello! We think you are very handsome. I am Felicia (brown dress) and my friend is Katie (grey skirt). Please join us. I like you very much! Fxxx."

I had been so long without a woman. They both looked so warm, poised, welcoming, and lovely. Felicia had the most extraordinary skin, although I was to see it on other well-groomed Rwandan women—extraordinary in its fine, smooth, flawless perfection and the way it seemed to glow from within, rather than reflect the light. It didn't seem fair. Why couldn't they be hard-bitten, cold-eyed, and acne-scarred? Why couldn't they have running sores and crack jitters? I was severely tempted but I ended up drinking Scotch that night with an Indian-Ugandan businessman, going to bed alone, missing my girlfriend, missing my dog.

AFTER THE MOUNTAIN GORILLAS, Rwanda's number two tourist attraction is the Genocide Memorial in Kigali. Housed in a large white modern building on the site of a mass grave, it was largely designed by the UK Holocaust Centre and its NGO partner Aegis. The exhibits inside were presented with dignity, discretion, almost unbearable poignancy and power, and the same Tutsi revisionist version of Rwandan history that Kagame's government was teaching in the schools. Namely, that there was harmony in Rwanda before the Belgians arrived, and the conflict between Hutu and Tutsi was all the creation of colonialism. "We had lived in peace for many centuries," read one noticeboard referencing the arrival of the Belgians, "but now the divide between us had begun . . ."

There is no question that the Belgians sowed the seeds for the genocide by making a racial classification with Tutsis superior and Hutus inferior, by measuring skulls, noses, darkness of skin tones, and issuing racial identity cards based on the results, but there were serious tensions and conflicts between Hutus and Tutsis in precolonial Rwanda and an escalating cruelty and despotism on the part of the Tutsi monarchs. Perhaps the worst thing the Belgians did was to use the "superior" Tutsis to administer their rule over the Hutu majority, and then switch sides when Tutsis began organizing a movement for Rwandan independence. Shortly before they left, the Belgians transferred power to the Hutus, and the first massacres of Tutsis began directly after independence in 1959.

As I moved deeper into the memorial, and a wailing Tutsi woman was led past me by her sons, these analytical concerns fell away and were replaced by a feeling of stunned, peeled shock. The corridors were walled with black fabric, the horror steadily mounted around each bend, and again I felt unable to understand the depth of the cruelty and hatred. Looking at the one smudgy video recording of men hacking at living, shrinking victims with their machetes in the streets of Kigali, I realized how much physical effort is required to kill another human being with a machete, and yet at least 800,000 were hacked and clubbed to death in 100 days—a much faster kill rate than the Nazis had managed in their death camps, perhaps three or five times faster. With their simple farm tools, ordered in bulk shipments from China by the Hutu regime as it planned the final solution, the Rwandan Hutus had carried out the fastest genocide in history, and yet they still found the time and energy to linger over torture, to rape women so many times that the women lost count. I was shocked all over again by the complicity of the Catholic Church in one diocese after another. Two thousand Tutsis had fled for sanctuary into the church at Nyange when their Hutu priest, Father Seromba, gave orders to bulldoze the church building in order to kill his congregation.

My tears came soon enough. It wasn't the accounts of women being forced under threat of rape to kill their own children because the children had Tutsi fathers. Nor was it the accounts of overworked executioners cutting the Achilles tendons of the waiting victims, so they couldn't run away, or the extraordinary efforts made to ensure that the deaths were as agonizing, terrifying, and humiliating as possible.

I came through all this into the hall of children. Mounted on the walls are photographs of young children, blown up from snapshots taken by their parents and accompanied by a brief summary of facts.

> Ariane Umatoni. Age 4.
> Favorite food: cake.
> Favorite drink: milk.
> Enjoyed: singing and dancing.
> Behavior: A neat little girl.
> Cause of death: Stabbed in her eyes and head.

I walked on past five-year-old Patrick, who liked riding his bicycle, eating fried potatoes and eggs, a quiet well-behaved boy whose best friend was his sister. Hacked by machete. Two year old Aurore Kirenzi, smiling in her white dress and white shoes, liked cow's milk and playing hide and seek with her brother. She was a talkative little girl who was burned alive with many others at the Gikondo chapel.

At the end of the exhibit, in order to place the Rwandan genocide in context, there was a display showing some, but not all, of the other genocides undertaken by humanity over the last hundred years or so—the Holocaust, Cambodia, Armenia, the Hereros exterminated by the Germans in Namibia, Bosnia, Darfur. The conviction settled on me that committing genocide is normal behavior for our species, as normal as waging war, an urge or a tendency that waits in our gene pool for an opportunity. Maybe the distractions of shopping, sports, gadgets, and entertainment were the best possible defense against war and genocide. Maybe consumerism really was progress, and our last best hope.

I came out of the memorial and sat down in the garden with its PLEASE DON'T WALK ON THE MASS GRAVES signs. Two hundred and fifty-eight thousand bodies had been gathered up from the city and the surrounding countryside and buried here in underground catacombs. I felt so hollowed out and shattered, and I was just a tourist here. What was it like to have lived through it, as a survivor or a killer? And how on earth were these people living together now?

Having fled from Kagame's advancing army into the neighboring countries, and Congo in particular, hundreds of thousands of Hutu killers were now back in Rwanda and living again in their home villages. The government had abolished the death penalty, because to administer it to all the Rwandans who had committed murder would amount to an even larger genocide. The leaders of the genocide, except for those still at large in Congo, in France and Belgium, and elsewhere, were being tried at international courts in Arusha, Tanzania. At the village level, the government had instituted a traditional form of justice called *gacaca,* where villagers gathered and testimony was given and discussed. Judges picked from the local community determined guilt and gave lighter sentences to those who expressed guilt, showed remorse, and asked forgiveness from the surviving relatives of those they had killed.

There was an economic incentive for the survivors to forgive the killers. The government and the foreign NGOs who specialized in reconciliation work would give them cows, goats, houses, wells, and money if they made the effort, or pretended to make the effort, to put the past behind them and reconcile their differences. It was an imperfect system, and *gacaca* judges were perhaps the easiest people to bribe in Rwanda, but it was also an impossible situation, and like so much of post-genocide Rwanda, it was working out much better than anyone would have predicted.

It wouldn't happen in Texas, that was for sure. Here's the man who hacked up your father and brothers, raped and butchered your mother and sisters while you hid in the bushes, ran and hid for weeks eating insects and roots. He's going to be living next door to you now. He says he's sorry. He was following the orders of bad leaders. You're going to see him with a machete in his hand every day because he needs to farm the land so Rwanda can have food. He will ask for your forgiveness, and you must try to give it to him. We know how difficult this is, but if we Rwandans are to have any kind of future, it has to be done. We can give you a cow to make it a little bit easier. And if you take the law into your own hands, things will go very badly for you indeed.

It seemed so unjust that it was the traumatized survivors who had to make such mighty efforts, while the ex-killers could merely say "I'm sorry" and then get on with their lives. But what else could be done when such a huge percentage of the population had participated in genocide? Most killers had served some years in prison, but you couldn't give them all life sentences without turning Rwanda into a huge prison unable to feed itself.

In such a situation, it seemed an enormous advantage that Rwandans were inclined to obey the dictates of their government, and that nearly all of them believed fervently in a god who could work miracles and whose only son preached forgiveness. It was the churches that had the most success with reconciliation out in the hills—Protestant churches because the Catholics were so tainted with the blood of genocide.

LEAVING THE GENOCIDE MEMORIAL, I told my taxi driver to go directly to Nyamata, thirty kilometers south of Kigali. His name was Peter. He was always late and unreliable, but there was something likable and easygoing about him. He was a survivor of the genocide, although he refused to talk about it, or anything political, putting up his smile like a wall. As we drove away, he turned up *Between the Sheets* by the Isley Brothers on the radio, and I wanted to weep with happiness and relief at the happy, tender, horny soulfulness of the music, which sounded like the exact opposite of genocide by machete. I felt a weird desperation for me and Peter to be friends, to transcend the gulf between our cultures and prove something about human brotherhood. I didn't care that he was flagrantly overcharging me. I wanted to give him a stupid, shocking amount of money. "Who gathers knowledge gathers pain," says the Book of Ecclesiastes. Normally I try to resist this bleak conclusion when I'm traveling, but there's really no alternative for a genocide tourist.

When we reached the brick church in Nyamata, he stayed in the car, listening to music. Eleven thousand people were killed here in the church and its gardens. Their clothes were piled on the pews, and their bones stacked up in a basement mausoleum. The bodies of 40,000 more were collected from the surrounding area and buried in a mass grave. I walked up to the church entrance and was welcomed by a tall, broad-shouldered young man in white jeans, black square-toed shoes, black shirt, and silver tie. I was the only visitor.

The young man's name was Mukandori Anonciatha. He wrote it down carefully in my notebook, and said I could call him Charles. There was a sad, troubled, distracted air about him as he told the story of what had happened here. He showed me a coffin near the nave: "She was a Tutsi married to a Hutu. She was raped, then they put a spear from her private parts into her skull, and impaled the three-year-old baby on her back. The ones who found her in the pit were traumatized. Yes. So now she is in her coffin." Then he had stop and compose himself again.

When the killing began in this part of Rwanda, orchestrated by the radio, the army, and the government-trained paramilitary squads called the *interahamwe*, "those who work/attack/ kill together," the local Tutis fled their houses and congregated here in the sanctuary of the church. The *interahamwe* surrounded them, singing and chanting "We're going to kill the cockroaches, kill the snakes." Then two big trucks of soldiers arrived and began to kill the people outside the church with their bayonets. If you had money, you could pay to be killed by a bullet instead of a bayonet. This killing went on for more than six hours. The Tutsis inside the church locked the doors, but with guns, axes, and grenades, the Hutus outside broke in.

"You see the bloodstains on the wall here? This is where they picked up young kids below four and smashed their heads. This is the altar. Here is where they cut open three pregnant women and took out the fetuses to kill. When the *interahamwe* got tired of cutting people, the soldiers threw grenades. You see the stains on the ceiling? This is how high the meat fly. The killing inside the church went on for three days. Then they came back."

He walked over to a nondescript spot on the floor toward the far wall of the church. "This was my place," he said. "I hid under the bodies and pretended to be dead. There was a lot of blood, so much blood. It was hard to breathe. I was one of seven people that survived from the six thousand eight hundred killed inside the church."

"How old were you?" I asked.

"I was eight years old."

The man who killed his father denied it at *gacaca*, perhaps bribed a judge, and was now back living here. "It is very difficult," said Charles. "I see him every day. How can I forgive him when he will not admit it?"

I asked him how things were now in Nyamata. "Many Tutsis are angry and want revenge, and many Hutus are angry because they have spent time in jail. There are good Hutus who are my friends and we share food. Others are bad. It could happen again. On the surface we pretend. Maybe you don't know rural Africa but we do not tell you how we feel. We show a smiling face. But in the heart there is still a lot of anger and hatred. They came like animals, and there is still a lot of genocide ideology in the air, people who want to finish it."

I asked him how he saw his future.

"If I get the chance, I must get as far away from here as possible, to a different country."

THE PRESIDENT'S communications director informed me that His Excellency had decided to go ahead with the interview, but it would be a week until he could spare the time in his busy schedule. I spent most of it sick in a cheap hotel. It seemed to be a recurrence of the same feverish malaise that had come down the river with me and flared up once in Burundi. I had the same headaches, aching joints, sweats, and chills, but they came now with a new sense of misery and mental unraveling in that grim noisy hotel with its echoing elevator shafts and mosquitoes that whined all night and came through the holes in the netting. The waking hours went past like days, and machete horrors found their way into my fever dreams. I felt increasingly desperate to get out of Africa and never return.

All the suffering and harshness I had seen on my journey paraded through my anguished head, beggars trembling with hunger, war orphans, AIDS orphans, white-haired children like little old men, the incessant toil of the exhausted-looking women in the fields, whipped forward by the scourge of their six hungry children, the dust bowls, the teeming slums, the fat laughing politicians, sunset glinting on a machete blade. For the sake of emotional self-preservation, I had been trying to keep it all sealed away in hard-shelled compartments, but now my head was raw and fevered, and it was all starting to spill out and bleed together, and I felt overwhelmed with despair and melancholy.

Then the fever lifted, and things started to settle back down into their compartments. I ate four boiled eggs with toast. I slept for a long time without nightmares. My spirits started to revive, my curiosity returned, and I ventured out into Rwanda again, with occasional tingling numbness in the limbs and descents of blurry fog into the brain. The communications director called to say the interview had been delayed further and I bided my time by exploring the city.

There was a good bookshop in Kigali and I spent a lot of time reading in cafés about Rwanda past and present. Scholars and historians found plenty to argue about, as they must to stay in business, but they could all agree that a defining characteristic of Rwandan culture was obedience to authority. It went back to the precolonial monarchy when the king was considered a god on earth. It was reinforced by Belgian colonialism, and it fed right into the genocide. When their leaders told them to exterminate the Tutsi snakes and cockroaches, the great mass of Rwandan Hutus did not question their orders or their duty. And those that did—the moderate Hutus—were killed as traitors.

I was struck by the seriousness of Rwandans. They didn't paint their buses in bright colors or give them names. They didn't wear wild or colorful outfits, and they listened to a lot of bland, schmaltzy, twinkling pop and gospel music. The way they greeted each other was cool and restrained, without the big smiles I was used to, and the men didn't knuckle-bump and low-five. I went to some dive bars where people were getting unsteadily drunk on banana beer and warm Primus, but I failed to make any friends or see anyone laughing or joking or entertaining each other with improbable stories. There was a reserve here, a wariness, a serious and solemn correctness.

I wondered if it stemmed from the experience of living through genocide, but then I came across some books by and about an early German explorer called Dr. Richard Kandt, whose last name sounds so unfortunate in English. A small, meticulous, partially repressed homosexual who was prone to fits of melancholy, he stood in the Vatican staring at the sculpture of Ancient Father Nile and decided that his destiny was to go to Africa and find the true source of the river.

Ripon Falls had fallen out of fashion, and from reading Stanley, who felt certain that the Nile source lay at the headwaters of the Kagera river, he decided to go to the mysterious highland kingdom of Rwanda, which only two Europeans had visited. Dr. Kandt started out from Bagamoyo, reached the Malagarasi River on Christmas Day 1897, came up through Urundi, as Burundi was known at the time, and then crossed into Rwanda: "There were no more noisy welcomes, no laughter, no dances, but neither was there plebeian obtrusiveness; instead I observed calm, reserved, serious, almost sullen forms of behavior."

Kandt went on to found the settlement of Kigali, compile the first dictionary of Kinyarwanda, the rich, allusive Rwandan language, draw the first maps, and make the first ethnographic studies of the kingdom, which he noted was seriously overgrazed by a million Tutsi cattle and ruinously expensive, with everything paid in cloth. He described Tutsi rule as tyrannical and cruel over the Hutus, with hands regularly severed for minor and even imaginary infractions. "All over the country," he wrote, "a deep bitterness on the part of the Wahutu (Hutu) against the rule of the Watussi (Tutsi) can be felt."

Something else that kept cropping up in the literature was the Rwandan attitude toward dissimulation. The ability to conceal your true motives, and lie without being discovered, has been traditionally regarded as a sign of superior intelligence, and it used to be singled out and praised by teachers in Rwan-

dan schools. It occurred to me that in a culture where dissimulation and concealment are admired to this extent, suspicion and
paranoia are bound to flourish, and these are key elements in
any genocide: we must destroy them because otherwise they
will destroy us.

The Rwandans I was meeting said there were government
spies and informants everywhere. I couldn't determine if it was
true or not, because Kagame's government was so tightly secretive, but the perception certainly contributed to the general
atmosphere of wariness. So, of course, did the shadow of the
genocide, and the worry that it might happen again.

I made a point of telling everyone I met that I was interviewing the president. Then I would say, "If you could ask him one
question, what would it be? I will ask it for you." Most Rwandans looked alarmed, then smiled and shook their heads with
great determination. Among those that did respond, no one
wanted their names used, and the most common questions were
about the tension between Hutus and Tutsis: "How can we live
with the division in our hearts?" "What is your strategy for the
division in our minds?" "How can we live with the ones who
killed our families?" Another common response was, "What if
Kagame dies tomorrow? Will there be another genocide?"

I got very different responses, betraying very different
assumptions, from the expatriate foreigners living and working
in Rwanda. They wanted to know when Kagame was going to
relax his dictatorship, improve the human rights situation, stop
clamping down so hard on free speech, and allow a real political opposition. In other words, when was Paul Kagame going to
start behaving like a Western democratic leader?

I talked at length with a Belgian military attaché who had
been in Rwanda as a soldier in 1994 and seen the outbreak of
genocide; it had killed his commanding officer and a number of
men in his unit. "One question for Kagame?" he mused. "OK,

how is it possible for the ten percent to rule the ninety percent without problems in the future?"

He was referring to one of the main criticisms of the Kagame regime, that it rigidly enforced the idea that Hutus and Tutsis were all Rwandans now, but in reality Kagame and his inner circle were all Tutsis, and as far as most Hutus were concerned, it was very much a Tutsi regime.

"Rwanda is really a big misunderstanding," he continued. "The Tutsis feel like they have to keep the Hutus under strict control or else they will finish the genocide. And the Hutus think they are poor because of the Tutsis. For me, neither one of these ideas is true, but the truth doesn't matter. This is Africa. Everything is perception. The ninety percent feel oppressed. Sooner or later, they will try to get power. This is the problem. Power does not change hands without violence in this part of the world, and the violence can easily turn genocidal."

"What about the economic growth and development that's happening?" I asked. "If the ninety percent start seeing real benefits from it, maybe the dynamic will change."

"I think this is Kagame's plan, and I think it's the only hope. Nearly all Rwandan children are in school now, and soon all these schools will have Internet. This will make a big difference, but will it happen fast enough? Can he keep the growth and development going? This is the question."

"So what's your opinion of Kagame?"

"The best choice in a very dangerous situation."

FOR MY LAST WEEK in Rwanda, I stayed in the back room of a Thai-French-African restaurant called Comme Chez Moi. After three months of African travel, it was the pleasant, inexpensive, welcoming sanctuary that I badly needed. The tables were set out on the verandah with red tablecloths, white napkins, flowers and candles, and there were imported wines and whiskeys, a fire kindled every night in the garden, good conversation at the bar in French and English, and a litter of puppies that gamboled across the lawn and skidded into the shrubbery—African plants with big, shiny leaves that resonated when the rain hit them.

I had plans to cross the border into Congo and visit Goma, where a volcanic eruption had partially drowned the town in lava. It had filled the ground storey of many buildings and then cooled into rock, but no problem, the town had just moved upstairs and built on top of the lava. I had good contacts there, including musicians and nightclub owners, but somehow my will and desire just faded away on me. Increasingly all I wanted to do was stay behind the gates of Comme Chez Moi and read, eat, drink, talk in English, and sleep. My head was slightly blurry, and I couldn't shed my fatigue. Some nights I still woke up drenched in sweat with my heart pounding, and my dreams were all bad.

The proprietor was a strange and wonderful man called Djamil Kaputula. He looked like Bela Lugosi with a suggestion of Alfred Hitchcock and Sydney Greenstreet, a beautiful ogre with yellowish brown skin and completely hairless from head to toe with alopecia. His mother was Indian, his father was half-Indian and half-Congolese, and he'd grown up in Congo and then spent twenty-three years in Brussels before returning to Africa. He loved good food and drink, fine clothes, and witty conversation, and several times a day he exploded in volcanic rages at his staff for their incompetence, laziness, disobedience, and stupidity.

The fact that I was about to interview the president became a matter of grave sartorial importance to Djamil, and his young maître d'hôtel Abel. I had my good shirt, but how could I present myself to His Excellency in such worn and stained gray chinos and scuffed brown boots? Djamil was happy to lend me anything from his fine Parisian wardrobe, but we were shaped completely differently. What I needed was a suit and a pair of shoes, but I didn't have enough money left to buy them. Abel came up with what sounded like a brilliant solution. He would take me down to the Nyabugogo market, where all the best clothes from Europe and America could be found secondhand in great condition at bargain prices or expertly copied by the Chinese.

So we went there with Abel's taxi-driver friend who overcharged me and became thoroughly belligerent and unpleasant when I protested. Abel took me by the arm into a more familiar Africa, loud, packed, heaving, insistent, and chaotic. We barged, slipped, and shouldered our way through narrow avenues of sportswear and dresses, ignoring the pleas and demands and grasping hands of the vendors, and entered a vast covered warren of menswear. The excitement of a white man in the market, and the promise of the fantastic wealth in my pockets, stirred up the suit vendors into a kind of tense expectant panic. There were hands tugging on my sleeves, grabbing my arms to steer me one way or another, suits snatched down and presented with a flourish, jackets helped onto my shoulders. How about this very fine black Versace suit knocked off for next to nothing in a Chinese factory with a shiny finish, a red pin-striped lining, and loose threads sprouting from the seams?

And all the time Abel was pushing me in the small of the back, moving me forward, jabbing at me with his finger, losing patience with me, wanting to know what my problem was with this suit, or that one, and why wasn't I buying? "Yes, yes, yes! This man give very good price! This very good clothes! Yes, yes, how much you want to pay? You give this man two hundred dollars."

The suits looked like they were all made in the same Chinese factory and then given different labels: Boss, Armani, Cerruti. They were all shiny, and this was presented as a virtue. "Look! This one! Very good shiny!" Tape measures were unfurled, and desperate vendors measured my legs. I tried on some suits and said no to all of them. They were too shiny and poorly made. The vendors thought it was a bargaining ploy and kept lowering their prices. It was hot and sweaty in there, and I became claustrophobic. I wrenched myself loose, charged away from all of them, with Abel barking annoyance behind me as he tried to catch up. I found myself in a warren of shoes, and similar scenes repeated. All the shoes had elongated toes, some pointed, some squared-off, all extending three or four inches further than I wanted. "This is African style," I said. "I want *muzungu* style." I pointed down to my round-toed boots.

The suit vendors tracked me down there. Abel had told them to bring their very best because I was interviewing the president tomorrow. Everyone was frustrated with my dithering, my fussiness, my failure to pull out my wallet. They began crowding in closer again, taking my hand, slipping inside the sleeve of a suit jacket. I pulled it back. Then I was saved by the trill of my phone. It was Kagame's communications director. The interview was confirmed for tomorrow morning, she said, but I told the mortified suit and shoe vendors, and a bitterly disappointed Abel, that I had to leave right this moment and meet the president.

11

Please Rise for His Excellency

Presidential compound—Lessons in dignity—Shade tree classroom—The rise to power—Matters of Congo—No strategy manual—Umaganda drunkards—Lake Kivu—The source

ON THE OTHER SIDE of the second metal detector, floppy-haired Englishmen were pacing up and down in well-tailored suits, talking intently on their phones. "'Blair's Boys,' we call them," said the communications director as she led me through the presidential compound toward its inner sanctum. Tony Blair, the former British prime minister, was a great admirer and supporter of Kagame, and he was here with a team to do some unpaid advising on financial and economic matters, while the economy he had bequeathed to Britain lay crushed by debt and recession. "Are you sure you want free economic advice from Tony Blair?" I asked. "You're not the first one to ask that question," she said with a professional smile.

The compound was built in a neutral corporate style with pleasant lawns and gardens, and it resembled an upscale office park or hotel conference center. Bill Clinton and Bill Gates were also frequent visitors here. So too was Pastor Rick Warren, the evangelical leader who spoke at Obama's inauguration, Andrew Young the former U.S. ambassador to the United Nations, and the respective CEOs of Starbucks and Google. All of them were spilling over with praise for Kagame and the miracles of reconciliation and economic growth happening in the new Rwanda. All of them had come here to help by consulting, investing or bringing investors, or arranging for aid and NGO projects. And none of them, to judge by their public statements, were unduly troubled by the dark side of Kagame's regime, the arrests, imprisonments, flights into exile, murders, and disappearances that kept befalling his critics and political opponents, or the fact that Rwanda was ranked 183 out of 195 countries in the world for freedom of the press.

Kagame presented himself on the surface level as the democratically elected leader of a free country, implied between the lines that he was really a benevolent dictator transitioning his country through a very tense, difficult time toward Western-style democracy, and denied or counterattacked with venom and skill when it became apparent that his dictatorship wasn't that benevolent after all. This was really the crux of things with Kagame. Every dictator pleads necessity and raises the specter of the bloody chaos that will ensue if he should relax his grip on power. But in Kagame's case, it might actually be true.

There didn't seem any point in challenging or accusing him in the interview. I didn't want him reaching for his stock responses and counterattacks or losing his brittle temper and cutting the interview short. I had been promised an hour, and the communications director said that it would probably last longer if he felt interested and engaged, perhaps less if he was displeased. That was fine by me. I wasn't here to score points off him, and I seriously doubted my ability to trick or cajole him into admitting any war crimes or acts of tyranny. I wanted to see how his mind worked and find out where he got his ideas from, and how he became so astute, disciplined, and ambitious growing up in a refugee camp. With my traveler's faith in firsthand experience, I wanted to be in the room with him and see what my senses and intuition made of this extraordinary man.

The communications director led me through the tiered conference chamber where he got his briefings, issued his directives, and delivered his famous tongue-lashings to anyone who fell short of his high standards. In some ways, Kagame was typical of a rebel general who had come out of the bush and made the switch to civilian leadership. He placed a high premium on loyalty and discipline, and he tended to equate criticism with treason. On the other hand, and this was highly unusual in any African leader, he didn't seem motivated by wealth or luxury for himself or his relatives. He had no ostentatious palace or dazzling motorcade. His wife didn't glitter with jewels or wear the latest Parisian fashions. One of his sisters ran a small dairy. Another operated a souvenir stand at the airport.

The presidential chair, lean and straight-backed, awaited its occupant in a big, hushed room with glass-topped tables and long beige curtains drawn against the sun. I sat there fiddling with a tape recorder, feeling a little nervous, a little feverish around the gills, wishing my trousers and boots were in better shape. I had never interviewed a head of state before. The nearest I had come were movie stars whose publicists mistook them for heads of state. I had never interviewed anyone who knew so many secrets about how Africa really worked, who had seen so much horror, or had so much blood on his hands.

The communications director spied Kagame's approach and said "Please rise for His Excellency." He entered the room at a brisk loping stride, a tall thin gangly man with steel-rimmed spectacles, a narrow moustache, a long nose, a reddish brown complexion with random black freckles, and a blue suit hanging off his bony shoulders. His eyes had a look of keen, piercing intelligence, and his presence was both impressive and intimidating. He folded his long frame into the presidential chair, and the interview began with Kagame asking the questions. "So tell me your impressions of Rwanda," he said, "(a) before you came here, and (b) now that you are here."

"The progress and achievements are extraordinary," I said, "but they also seem fragile. The country still feels so traumatized and volatile. I have been asking Rwandans what they would like to ask you and two questions keep coming up: How can we heal the division in our hearts? And what happens if Kagame drops dead tomorrow? Many think there would be another genocide."

He stiffened slightly. My remarks hung in the air for a few moments, sounding more impertinent than I had intended. Had I really used the phrase "drops dead tomorrow"? Then he nodded slowly, placed his long spidery fingers on his kneecaps, and composed his reply.

"For me, this fragility is to be expected. The trauma runs much deeper than people from outside, however well meaning, will ever understand. Sometimes our partners from other countries ask us why we have not got further with our reconciliation, as if we possess a magic to just get rid of this tragic history of ours. No, we have to find a way to live with it, and also to build a new nation. The first phase was to achieve peace and stability, and now we are moving forward with development. And if Kagame, for one reason or another, is no longer there, people can look back at everything that has been done, and they can feel a part of it, and be reassured that this stability will continue."

He carried on in this vein for another fifteen minutes. He was restless in the chair, he spoke with increasing drive and passion, his long fingers rising up to shape and clarify and stress his remarks. When I tried to raise objections or ask for concrete examples, he was extremely skillful in beginning to answer my questions, then veering around them and continuing with great unstoppable force until the original question was left far behind and irretrievable. Sometimes his eyes would get wide and animated, and I would see the beginnings of his anger. Occasionally he discharged bitter, sibilant little chuckles to suggest that while he and I understood these obvious things, some of his critics and partners from abroad did not share such a clear view of reality.

"They expect Rwanda to be a normal country, like the ones where they grew up. Yes! Even in ninety-four, they would come, and they would want to help, and they would ask questions that would just put you off, but you would have to swallow it. They would say, 'But there is no justice, no security, no reconciliation, no this, no that.' And you would look at them and say, 'How do you expect it to be there? It has all been destroyed.' We are now fifteen years from the genocide, and we have come a long way in some areas, but for people's grief, and for people's trauma, fifteen years is a very short time, so yes, fragile is to be expected."

The communications director cut in, "There were still thousands of unburied bodies when they started calling for free and fair elections."

"It's a question of context," said Kagame. "Some of our partners have very clear ideas on what we should do. And we believe in the same things that they do—good governance, democratic government, strong institutions of civil society, and so on—but please, let us bury our dead first. Understand what we have been through. Make the effort to understand our context."

When Kagame spoke to the Rwandan people, he stressed two things over and over again: the need for hard work and the vital importance of dignity. One reason he had so much support in America is that he preached the gospel of self-reliance, entrepreneurship, and free market capitalism as the way forward for Rwanda, rather than continuing to look to the wealthy nations of the world for handouts and solutions. Kagame was the first African leader to describe aid as an indignity.

"To live off other people's money, paid by the taxpayers of other countries? This is a shameful thing. When we began in ninety-four, we had no choice, because we began with nothing—no infrastructure, no food, no economic activity—but now we must take responsibility for our own challenges. If we allow ourselves always to be helped out, and do very little for ourselves, which is without question what other African countries have done, we will develop a mentality to depend on this aid forever. And this goodwill, this support, this aid, will come with control. Somebody who feeds you will dictate to you, based on his interests. No question about it."

Rwanda's dependency on aid was declining, down from 100 percent to 42 percent of the government's budget, but it was aid that had rebuilt the infrastructure, funded the big advances in education and health, and fueled much of the economic growth. Donors loved Rwanda. Here at last was an African country where their money wasn't embezzled or squandered but used promptly and efficiently to get the promised results.

One way that Rwanda planned to wean itself from aid was by getting many more of its citizens to open bank accounts, make themselves available for microcredit loans, and start paying taxes. This would help, but the real challenge was that Rwanda was a small, poor, landlocked, overpopulated country with long trade routes, few natural resources, and nine out of ten citizens living as subsistence farmers. They considered every child a gift from God, they raised a large proportion of their crops solely for the purpose of making beer for their own consumption, and they were in the habit of blaming the other ethnic group for all their problems.

Kagame wanted to turn their children into computer literate entrepreneurs, bankers, technologists, communications experts.

Rural Rwanda already had faster Internet connections than rural Britain or America, and fiber-optic cables were going into every school in the country, with laptops provided by NGOs for every child. Rwanda, the most populous country in Africa, was also the first African country to recognize the crippling effect of population growth on its ability to feed itself and provide health, education, and economic opportunities to its people. There were contraception and education campaigns underway, led in part by Rwanda's First Lady, Jeanette Kagame, and the government was promoting a three-child-only policy. Kagame wanted fewer children in his country, and he wanted a whole new type of Rwandan.

"The most important thing is to tackle the whole mentality in my country. I know how difficult it is, and I know how right it is to do. I open every discussion in this way: Don't expect that somebody will bring respect to you. It starts with you making a choice. You either find nothing wrong with the way you are living, with others having responsibility over your life. Or you can say, 'What is wrong with me? Why am I living in this way? What can I do to create a situation where I can give myself what I am asking from others?' Again, it comes back to dignity."

I asked him if his attitude toward dignity was related to the indignities of his childhood and he said, "Oh, absolutely no question about it. The lining-up for food every day, the rationing, the lack of this and that. It had a tremendous impact on me."

HE WAS BORN in 1957 into an aristocratic Tutsi family that fled Rwanda when he was a small boy. His earliest memories were of houses burning on a hill, shouting, commotion, his desperate mother, the family scrambling into a car as a Hutu death squad came running down the hill toward them. This was after independence in 1959 and again in 1960, during the first pogroms against the Tutsi by the newly empowered Hutus. The Kagames were among tens of thousands of Rwandan Tutsis who fled across the border into Uganda and raised their children in refugee camps.

"When we started primary school, we used to study under a tree because there was no classroom. There were no pens or paper. There was nothing! We used to write on our thighs with a piece of hard, dry grass and the teacher would come over and look at your thigh, and write his mark there with another piece of dry grass. In a situation like this, you develop some sense of questioning, some sense of justice, saying, 'Why do I live like this? Why should anyone live like this?' There was also a hardening that is still there in the way I approach many things. You can't shock me, because what can be worse that what I have seen and experienced all my life?"

As a young man he joined the leftist Ugandan rebel army led by Yoweri Museveni and spent five years as a guerrilla fighter in the bush. Intelligence was Kagame's specialty, gathering information about the terrain, the enemy, the villagers. It suited his observant, analytical, conspiratorial mind. Then, when Museveni took power in 1986 (disturbing the Ugandan Open golf tournament that year), Kagame and other Rwandan Tutsi exiles started building a secret army inside the Ugandan military, with the aim of invading Rwanda and overthrowing the Hutu regime. It has been described as one of the most audacious covert operations in military history, involving thousands of people with secret loyalty—this was the beginning of the Rwandan Patriotic Front (RPF), now the ruling party of Rwanda.

They crossed into Rwanda in 1990, ripping the Ugandan insignias off their uniforms, and began a four-year guerrilla war against the Hutu government headed by President Juvénal Habyarimana and backed by the French. When the genocide began in 1994, Kagame was waiting in the wings, expecting the UN or the Clinton administration to stop it. When they did nothing, he marched on Kigali, and the Hutu death squads and killers fled. In the conventional telling of this story by Western journalists, the RPF arrived as saviors and heroes to stop the genocide, but it's now clear that they committed several large-scale revenge massacres of unarmed Hutus, rounding them up, killing them systematically, and burying the evidence in mass graves.

At the time Kagame denied these massacres. Now he offered a defense, saying that it was extremely difficult to restrain his troops, especially the new Rwandan Tutsi recruits, who had seen their family members raped and butchered. "You can imagine trying to stand between people who are so seriously aggrieved, and having the desire to settle it because there was no justice infrastructure at that time. Then you have the ones being accused, and some felt justified and thought they did right in killing, and others said no, we weren't a part of it, even if they were involved, and trying to sort all this out was probably the most difficult thing of all."

But the great mass of Hutus, carrying what they had looted, fled into Congo, or Zaire as it was then, and a massive international aid campaign was launched to feed them, shelter them in refugee camps, and bring them medical supplies. Neither the television coverage, nor the televised appeals for money by the aid organizations, made it clear that the people in these camps were the perpetrators of a genocide. In accordance with the principles of humanitarian neutrality, they were described as "refugees from the genocide in Rwanda," and most viewers, myself included, assumed they were innocent, traumatized survivors fleeing the horror.

Kagame's blood starts to boil when he remembers this time. "They had armored personnel carriers, antiaircraft, with armories and ammunition in the camps, and every other day they were crossing the border back into Rwanda and shooting at us. And the human rights people, and the humanitarian people, were feeding them, and telling us and the world that they were feeding refugees. And, as they very well knew, these so-called refugees were selling what they were given to Congolese to get money so they could maintain their military machine."

"The same thing is now happening with the aid going into Darfur," I observed.

"Yes!" he cried. "At first you think these people must know what they are doing. Then you see what they do, and you say, 'How can they keep doing this? Why?'"

"So why do you think?" I asked.

"In our case, there was no innocence in it. They were growing their organizations with all the money they were raising. And with the French, there was the hope that this military machine would build itself up and come and overthrow us. They said we are agents of Anglo-Saxon culture taking Rwanda away from the French influence. According to them, this was our mission. It had nothing to do with our right to live in our own country! Not at all!"

There were two important long-term consequences here. One was that Paul Kagame developed a deep, abiding contempt for the international community and its claims to moral authority. The second was that his army invaded Zaire/Congo, scattered the genocidal Hutu war machine in the camps, committed a series of appalling massacres against civilians, and set in motion a horrific cycle of violence, upheaval, and pillage in Congo that has been dubbed Africa's World War. Depending on whose figures you believe, it has caused 3 million, 5 million, or 7 million deaths, mostly from war-related disease and privation.

I was expecting Kagame to dodge questions about his army's alleged war crimes and massacres in Congo, but I wasn't expecting him to look so awkward and sound so lame while doing it.

"Even if we were to take Rwanda away, and put it someplace else, Congo still has a lot of problems to contend with. We all have problems that we shouldn't attribute to neighbors. But at least for those problems related to us, we are gradually overcoming them, and are doing so by working very well with the Congolese."

I looked at him in slight disbelief to see if that was it. He looked back with a face of stone. I had the feeling that if I didn't change the subject, he would say, "Well, I must thank you very much for coming all this way to speak to me, and now . . ."

So I asked him about his political philosophy. Did he think of himself as an authoritarian? Right-wing, left-wing? A visionary? "My thinking is pragmatic," he said. "Doing what is doable. I can't find a better formula for dealing with our situation than what we are doing. If you show me one, I will try that. You know, fighting a war is much simpler. Even with all the hardships and hunger, it is clear cut. But building a nation from nothing? A nation that has just experienced genocide? There is no strategy manual for this. There is nothing that is not a priority, and the priorities are always conflicting. I try to look at problems very clearly and think, 'How do we get out of this? What will work? What will be the consequences for the different people involved?'"

He said that his thinking was mostly shaped by his experiences, but he was also a voracious reader. Having put in a twelve-hour day dealing with affairs of state, taken his exercise (gym or tennis), spent time with his wife and four children and said good-night to them, he would then stay up reading for three or four hours a night. "Mainly it is books about economics, business management, development issues, politics, international affairs," he said. "I get newspapers from Britain and other countries twice a week, and read them almost page to page. Sometimes I find I'm reading things I don't even need to read, because my mind is still hungry. I don't need much sleep. Four hours is enough."

Kagame's vision for Rwanda is derived from his reading about Singapore, South Korea, China, and the other "Asian Tigers" that managed to leap out of poverty in less than a generation, by means of disciplined authoritarian leadership and entrepreneurial capitalism. Lacking ports or natural resources, he identified technology, banking, and communications as the way forward for Rwanda. "By the year 2020, we can become the center for all these things in east and central Africa," he said.

The World Bank had just named Rwanda as the top business reformer in the world and Africa's most business-friendly country. The economy was growing at 9 percent a year. There was a majority of women in parliament, a national health system, a booming coffee industry, a tourism industry, unimaginable after the genocide, now bringing in $200 million a year. Foreign investment was pouring in, mainly from America and China.

Meanwhile Kagame had an election coming up. The government had closed down two critical newspapers, and arrested a journalist for defamation (he compared Kagame to Hitler). Two opposition parties were prevented from registering (the vice president of one turned up dead with his head almost severed by machete), political rallies were broken up violently by the police, and two Hutu opposition candidates had been arrested.

Kagame and I both knew he was going to win this election and stay in power for another seven years. But what then? Would he abide by the Rwandan constitution, which limits presidents to two terms of office? Or would he devise a reason to hold on to power as long as possible, in the normal way of dictators?

"If there is no peaceful democratic transfer of power in 2017, my presidency will have been a failure," he said. "We Rwandans believe in good governance, democratic governance, becoming an increasingly open society, not just because the West is asking or telling us, and not because we have to qualify for aid. No, we must do it because fundamentally we believe in these things, because these values are universal, and we share them, and because it is good for us."

We had been talking for nearly two hours. The communications director cleared her throat and reminded him of the time, and he said, "At twelve-thirty my kids come from school and have lunch with me. I have that slot, even if it is just five minutes. So. Thank you for coming all the way to Rwanda to learn about what we are doing here."

"And thank you for your time," I said.

"Where will you go now? Back to your country?" he asked.

"Actually, I'm going to the source of the Nile," I said.

"Ah yes. I have not been there. You understand that I have been quite busy. But we are glad to have it in Rwanda."

So he loped off down the corridor to meet his children, and I wondered about that last speech of his, almost but not quite guaranteeing a democratic transfer of power. Was it more deceitful rhetoric, or did he really intend to open up political space once development had got further, as the donors and many Rwandans wanted to believe? Was he ultimately a benevolent dictator, the strong hand needed to seize Rwanda by the scruff of the neck and drag it forward into a better future, or was he an incurable despot?

If you held him up to the light in the right way, you could see both facets glinting at once.

THE FOLLOWING MORNING, an hour before dawn, a horn sounded once outside the gates of Comme Chez Moi. I gulped down the last of my coffee, put on my rain jacket and hat, and walked down through the garden with raindrops drumming on the leaves. The driver was a crisp, efficient, go-getting young Rwandan, five minutes early in an ironed shirt and an impeccably maintained eleven-year-old Land Cruiser. His name was Aloys, he now owned the vehicle outright, and with a little more money saved and some credit from the bank, he was going to start up his own tourism company, having learned the ropes with a larger operator and taught himself fluent English.

"Do we have time to pick up some food and water?" I asked.

"Yes," he said. "They won't close the streets for another hour."

It was the last Saturday of the month, the day when Rwandans participate in the community work service known as *umaganda*. They clean the streets and buildings, repair roads and bridges, plant trees, clear storm drains, build schools and libraries and houses for the needy, and have communal meetings afterward to discuss any grievances or problems that need fixing. *Umaganda* is a precolonial institution, revived by the postgenocide government as a way to bring communities together and rebuild the ruined country. Participation is compulsory for all able-bodied Rwandans, and that includes the president and his ministers.

With forty minutes left until the police closed the streets, we stopped at a twenty-four-hour supermarket in the downtown shopping mall. I was surprised to encounter fifty drunken people in the food court, with their tables crammed with beer bottles and broken glass underfoot. Were they getting good and primed for a day of community service? Aloys, who stayed in his vehicle, thought they sounded like degenerate shirkers who would soon stumble off to bed, sleep through *umaganda,* and be fined for it by their neighborhood associations.

We left the city in darkness and rain. Dawn illuminated

drifting mists and a repeating landscape of maroon-colored hills and banana groves. Seeing how ubiquitous banana trees are in Rwanda, I had assumed that bananas were a staple food crop, but Aloys said that people very seldom ate or sold them. "It is all for banana beer. In the countryside, most people are drunk every day. Now the government has a program to take out a lot of the banana trees and plant coffee instead. With coffee, people can sell it, get money, buy things, pay taxes. With bananas, they can only get drunk and make more babies."

The rain stopped, the mist lifted and curled away, and in the distance there was a bright glare of sunlight on the orderly metal roofs of a government-built village. The Rwandan government had taken a lot of criticism from Western humanitarians for its program of forced villagization, uprooting families from their brick huts and farmhouses and moving them into these slightly sinister compounds. On the other hand, as Aloys pointed out, it was a sensible use of land and resources. With people living in one place, instead of scattered through the hills, it was much cheaper and easier to bring them electricity, education, health care, and Internet. "Also, they are safer this way," he added. "Less isolated."

Aloys, who had survived the genocide as a young teenager, had a high opinion of Kagame, and he didn't agree when people called the RPF government a repressive regime or a Tutsi dictatorship. "To me, Rwanda feels like a free country now," he said. "Before, you couldn't go to some parts of the country, because the other ones were there, and it was dangerous for you. Now we can all go anywhere, and there's no problem. We don't have this one, or that one [Hutu or Tutsi], on our identity cards, and the police are mixed, the army is mixed, the senators are mixed, the ministers are mixed. The economy is improving, development is happening. And people are no longer killing each other."

"What if Kagame dropped dead tomorrow?" I asked.

"Instant genocide," he responded without hesitation. "No question about it."

We drove over the swollen, swirling, ocher-colored waters of the Nyabarongo river, and I thought of Dr. Kandt struggling through the mud and undergrowth here in 1898. As he made his way up the Kagera River, he reached several places where two tributaries came together in a Y junction. Kandt's principle was to always choose the larger tributary and follow that upstream, and this is how he came to the Nyabarongo.

The 2006 Ascend the Nile expedition of Brits and Kiwis followed the same principle. By the time they reached the Nyabarongo, they had come nearly four thousand miles in various vessels and crafts, survived several crashes, three crocodile attacks, a broken leg, and an ambush and a man murdered in northern Uganda by the Lord's Resistance Army, perhaps the most evil and twisted group of rebels on the entire continent, and to my knowledge, the only ones who force their child captives to cannibalize other children. The worst of Africa was the cruelty of Africa, and it was nothing more or less than the cruelty of humanity given sufficient opportunity and rewards.

We were coming in sight now of the towering conical volcanoes that made up the Virunga Mountains, the majestic beauty of Lake Kivu with its forested islands, and the green hills and mountains of eastern Congo on the other side of the lake. Aloys gave me a brief tour of the serene and lovely lakeside resort of Kibuye, where vacation homes and hotels were going up on the waterfront. We went to a church where four thousand Tutsis had barricated themselves inside, while a horde of *interahamwe* and soldiers, drunk on banana beer and brandishing machetes and grenades, chanted their bloodthirsty slogans outside. In the end, it was the priest, Reverend Athanase Seromba, who showed the Hutus how to break into the church, and once they had thrown their grenades, he rushed about through the carnage pointing out the ones who were still alive and needed finishing off with bayonets and machetes.

Leaving Kibuye, we turned off the paved highway onto a rough dirt road that required four-wheel drive. As we bounced and squelched through the ocher mud, Aloys said, "We are seeing more and more tourists now who don't know there was a genocide in Rwanda."

I said, "What? Tourists from where?"

"Europe. Italy and Spain. Some from Japan. They come for the gorillas. They have an extra day before they fly home and they ask me if there is anything to see in Kigali. I say, 'Well, there's the Genocide Memorial.' They say, 'OK, let's go.' Then they come out the other side looking very shocked. They say, 'We had no idea. This is terrible.'"

"And how do you feel about that?" I asked.

"It's okay. Rwanda was the genocide place for so long. Now we are the gorilla place, and tourists are coming, so I don't mind."

WE DROVE THROUGH a large tea plantation that cloaked the gently rolling hills. Low gray clouds obscured the mountains behind them where we were going. There was a small village by the tea-processing factory and a park ranger was waiting for us there with his motorbike, as planned. He wore a grayish purple uniform with yellow stripes down the side, and he exuded good health, stocky strength, gentleness, and charm. His name was Sibomana Jean Aime. He had guided the Ascend the Nile team on the last three days of their expedition, and he was there at the historic moment when the source was finally discovered.

We followed his motorbike into Nyungwe Forest National Park and parked in a clearing where another park ranger was waiting with an AK-47 over his shoulder. "For poachers?" I asked. He nodded. In French, he added, "The poachers here are not bad these days, but Congo is also close."

Sibomana said, "Okay, are you ready to walk? It's not too far."

I said, "Let's go. I've come a long way to see this place. My people have wondered about it for four thousand years."

It was calm and cool in the forest, with a few small gray birds flitting through the trees. I was hoping to see the great blue turaco, which a Rwandan tourist pamphlet described as "an outlandish blue, red and green bird which streams from tree to tree like a procession of streamlined psychedelic monkeys." Sibomana said that unfortunately we were in the wrong part of the park for the turacos, and also for the chimpanzees and monkeys. Here the trees were introduced pines, not much use to the native wildlife, but they made a valuable buffer zone where people could cut their firewood and building poles without encroaching on the real wildlife habitat.

The trail wound gently down the flank of a mountain whose upper reaches were obscured by clouds. It was pleasant walking in pleasant company, with soft-toned conversation and gentle, husky laughter. Sibomana explained that 10 percent of the tourist fees at the park were now given to the surrounding villagers as part of an anti-poaching program. "Before, the villagers would see you, and say, 'Here comes another *muzungu* giving his money to the park service.' Now they see you, and they think, 'Ah, I get some of his money. This is very good. How can we get some more *muzungus* here?'"

The park service also compensated farmers if the baboons or other monkeys ate their crops, but on this side of the park it seldom happened because of the buffer zone. "We have the pine, then eucalyptus, then the tea, which is a very good buffer," said Sibomana. "The monkeys will not go in there, and the people can sell the tea."

In Tanzania and Burundi, the environmental destruction seemed unstoppable, and the plans to solve it so hamstrung by corruption and inefficiency. Rwanda still had a serious poaching problem in some areas, but the gorilla populations were increasing, and so many trees had been planted that deforestation was now in reverse. The forestry department was seven years ahead of schedule in its goal to restore the country from 10 to 30 percent forest cover. How much of this, I wondered, stemmed from simple fear among the department heads, and the expectation that they would be fired with a tongue-lashing if they had to report a disappointing performance to their president? How much had to do with Kagame's crusade against corruption? A game warden running a poaching operation in Rwanda, perhaps more so than anywhere else in Africa, would live in serious fear of going to prison.

The insect noise became louder and more insistent as we came down out of the pines into an area of big ferns and more tropical vegetation. "We are getting close now," said Sibomana. "It is just down from here."

I thought about all the brave and restless men who had tried to reach this place in vain. Herodotus, the world's first historian-journalist, tried to ascend the Nile in 460 B.C. to solve the mystery of where its waters came from. He was turned back by the cataracts at Aswan in Egypt, but he brought with him a story that the Nile arose in magnificent, upwelling fountains somewhere deep in the hidden heart of Africa. And since Egypt was the oldest civilization known to Herodotus and the ancient Greeks, the idea also took hold that the source of the Nile was the source of civilization itself.

Emperor Nero dispatched an expedition from ancient Rome. It got further than Herodotus but was foiled by the Suud, a vast swamp in what is now southern Sudan. Then came Persian, Egyptian, and later Greek explorers, all defeated by the Suud.

Artists in ancient Greece and Rome took to portraying Father Nile as a male god with its head obscured. In the first century after the birth of Christ, the Greek merchant Diogenes claimed to have traveled overland for twenty-five days from the eastern coast of Africa and arrived at two great lakes and a range of snow-capped mountains "whence the Nile draws its twin sources."

A century later, Ptolemy drew a map based on the testimony of Diogenes. It showed the Nile flowing out of two lakes in Central Africa and the lakes fed by rivers flowing out of mountains. And it was Ptolemy's map, seventeen hundred years later, that obsessed Richard Burton and convinced him that going overland was the best way to the Nile source. Then the mad questing torch had been snatched up by Speke, Livingstone, and Stanley, who had come sniffing up the Kagera in the right direction, and then by the diminutive, determined Dr. Kandt.

The main tributary of the Nyabarongo was the Rukawara, and as he waded, crawled, hacked, and scrambled his way up its banks, through cold mud, thick vegetation, and choking gorges, Dr. Kandt came at last to a shallow, swampy, overgrown valley basin, singularly lacking in magnificent fountains but containing a small spring that united with some others to form a stream that appeared to be the beginning of the Rukawara. This place is now known as the Cunt Source, excuse me, the *Kandt* Source, and it's about ten miles away from where the Ascend the Nile expedition, working with satellite GPS, finally established the true and furthest source of the Rukawara, and therefore of the White Nile.

When I saw it, there was nothing to do but laugh. *This* is what all the fuss had been about? This is what drew Livingstone to his death and caused Burton and Speke to drive themselves and their porters through such terrible hardships and loss of life? This was the source of civilization itself?

Picture a muddy, moss-fringed rabbit hole with a thin dribble of water leaking out of it. Behind it a hand-painted sign raised on wooden sticks: This Is the Furthest Source of Nile River.

I was delighted by the absurdity of it all. I've always used destinations as excuses and justifications for the desire to leave home and go off traveling again, and surely this muddy little hole was the most ridiculous excuse yet. I took a photograph, a souvenir of folly, and I asked Sibomana to describe the moment of discovery. "We had been going for three days, hacking with machetes, wading through a swamp with water up to our chests, and too cold!" he said. "The explorers were never tired. They got up very early every day and they never stopped. When they reached this place, they had newspapers and cameras and journalists waiting to meet them, and they were very very happy."

I was happy too, but in a different way. I felt the giddy happiness of self-mockery. Thwarted in five different ways on the Malagarasi, diverted and distracted in Zanzibar and Dar es Salaam, overwhelmed in Burundi and Rwanda, I had finally achieved one of my original objectives in going to Africa, and it was the biggest anticlimax of the entire journey.

It started to rain and Sibomana pointed up to a high ridge extending like a shoulder from the mountain. He explained that all the rain that fell on this side of the ridge would flow into the Rukawara, then the Nyabarongo, then the Kagera that ran its brown waters through Lake Victoria "like a snake," onward through the big whitewater rapids in northern Uganda, across the border into Sudan, and slowly through the vast and still undrained swamp of the Suud. When the water came out of the other side and formed itself into a river again, it flowed on magisterially across the desert to Khartoum, where it received its main tributary, the Blue Nile, flowing down from its source in the highlands of Ethiopia. From Khartoum, it crossed the border into Egypt and went all the way to the Mediterranean, more than four thousand miles from where we stood.

What a journey that would be. Or what about following a raindrop that fell on the other side of the ridge? That would take you down to the Congo River, and then you could ride the perilously overcrowded ferries, barges, and fishing boats all the way to the Atlantic, stopping in at nightclubs and recording studios on the way. I felt called in both those directions. But for now at least, there was a stronger desire for home, the woman I loved, the smell of her skin, the soft fur of a young dog who might remember me, a deep and profound glass of red wine, mesquite wood burning in the bedroom fireplace on a cold winter night.

I thought of Burton, who enjoyed these things as much as anyone but could never fully appreciate the comforts of home unless he was far away from them. He kept trying, but his restlessness would never let him settle down. Even as an old man in failing health, and inseparable from Isabel at that point, he insisted on shuffling doggedly from one French spa town to the next, up to London to see friends, back to their home in Trieste, where he would work on eight books at eight different tables, moving from one to another, until it became absolutely imperative that they pack their bags again, throw in the most pressing manuscript, and head to Zurich, Paris, Greece, or the next French spa town, where some ease and comfort might be found, at least for a while, until it was time to move on again.

Epilogue

RETURNING TO AMERICA, to the life we call normal, I felt at times underwater, with everything blurred and not quite real. At other times the mere sensation of being alive was almost unbearably vivid. I was still feverish and unwell, with a persistent ringing in my ears, although I never found out what was wrong with me. Arizona is not a conducive environment to sleuthing out tropical diseases, especially when you don't have health insurance, and over the next few months I simply and slowly recovered.

But those first few days. To see white people again in such numbers was strange and unsettling. I caught myself staring at their pale and blemished skin, the peculiar way they walked, the grown men dressed like big children in their shorts, college boys stepping out of expensive cars in expensively shabby clothing. Black Americans also looked and acted and carried themselves so differently to East Africans.

The things people complained about. The things that made them angry. I watched a woman lose her mind at the erroneous addition of full-fat milk to her coffee. Great dramas were taking place in the media about a flaw in the latest smartphone. There was so much anxiety and worry in the air about things that seemed fantastically trivial. I kept my mouth shut. My girlfriend said I seemed raw and wounded, and that's how it felt.

I spent my last two days in Rwanda with a gentle, serene, unstoppable man called Pastor Deo Gashagaza. He specialized in counseling killers and survivors in the matter of forgiveness and reconciliation. He took me to villages where killers and survivors were building houses for each other and living as neighbors again. We sat in crowded rooms sour with the smell of rural poverty, body odor, yesterday's banana beer on the breath, and one after another, people told their stories, and they cried and embraced, and sometimes the killers lied and stared at the floor, and sometimes the survivors' eyes went dead and blank as they spoke, and their words dried up.

They told me that reconciliation was very difficult but it was what God wanted, so it was going to happen, and it was happening already. For proof they pointed to the killers and survivors who were now married and having children together. A bigger problem was land, they said. How could they grow enough crops from this parcel of land to feed themselves and all the new children that were being born?

From there I went to the airport in Kigali, flew home to Tucson, Arizona, and went out the next morning to the local pet superstore to buy some dog food. I rolled my shopping cart through the aisles of dog toys and cat beds, pet medicines and health supplements, canine dental products, the in-store grooming salon where the stylists were hard at work with their brushes and clippers and nail trimmers. I picked up a forty-nine-dollar bag of premium dog food. It contained vitamins, minerals, and other supplements that were specially selected for the size, age, and breed of my dog. It guaranteed more shine and a softer coat. I felt dizzy and strange. On the banks of the Malagarasi River was a woman whose prized possession was an empty whiskey bottle. White-haired children in Burundi. Machetes leaning against the wall in that sour room full of tears in Rwanda.

I wheeled my cart up to the register. Next to the card-swipe machine was a stack of flyers for a local pet massage school. For an enrollment fee of $7,000, trained experts would teach you the correct massage techniques for your pet. I felt my equilibrium start to reel. I had come too far too soon. My brain struggled to span the distance between here and there, to find a line of connection, and then the entire pet superstore seemed to rise up slightly and start revolving in a big slow circle. I stood there queasily at its center, holding on to the cart for balance, and then wheeled my way unsteadily out into the bright blue morning.

Index

About the Author

Richard Grant is an award-winning travel writer who has published his work in *Men's Journal, Esquire,* and *Details*, among other publications. He is also the author of *American Nomads* and *God's Middle Finger.* Grant currenly lives in Tuscon, Arizona.